BROMLEY
Tireless Champion for Just Causes

Memoirs of
Bromley L. Armstrong

WRITTEN WITH SHELDON TAYLOR

Vitabu
Publishing
V

Bromley, Tireless Champion for Just Causes: Memoirs of Bromley L. Armstrong
Copyright © 2000 by Vitabu Publications

ALL RIGHTS RESERVED. No part of this book may be reproduced, stored in or introduced into a retrieval system, or transmitted in any form or by any means (electronic, mechanical, photocopying, recording or otherwise) without the prior written permission of the publisher, except in the case of brief excerpts in critical reviews and articles. All inquiries should be addressed to:
Vitabu Publications, 544 Rosebank Road, South, Pickering, Ontario, L1W 2N5
email vitabupub@yahoo.com

Canadian Cataloguing in Publication Data

Armstrong, Bromley L., 1926-
  Bromley, tireless champion for just causes : memoirs of Bromley L. Armstrong

Includes bibliographical references and index.
ISBN 0-9687798-0-8

1. Armstrong, Bromley L., 1926- . 2. Political activists – Ontario – Biography. 3. Civil rights workers – Ontario – Biography. 4. Labor union members – Ontario – Biography. 5. Black Canadians – Ontario – Biography. 6. Ontario – Social conditions. I. Taylor, Sheldon Eric Alister. II. Title.

FC3076.1.A76A3 2000   971.3,04,092   C00-932292-2
F1058.A76A3 2000

Design: McCalla Design Associates
Editing: Sheldon Taylor
Transcribing Services: Marlene Armstrong, Katherine Alicia Alleyne
Printed and Bound in Canada

Contents

	Foreword	7
	R. Roy McMurtry, Chief Justice of Ontario	
	Preface and Acknowledgements	9
CHAPTER 1	Leaving Jamaica	13
CHAPTER 2	Climbing New Stairs	32
CHAPTER 3	Solidarity Forever	53
CHAPTER 4	No Racism Here	71
CHAPTER 5	Banging on the Door	93
CHAPTER 6	A Fork in the Road	123
CHAPTER 7	Shedding the Old Coat	146
CHAPTER 8	Years of Tears and Turmoil	171
CHAPTER 9	Searching for a Brighter Tomorrow	205
CHAPTER 10	Legacy	228
	Afterword	245
	Index	251

The dapper Bromley in February 1948. On Yonge Street, following an evening at the movies.

Armstrong, Bromley Lloyd, C.M., O.Ont.; retired; b. Kingston, Jamaica 9 Feb.1926; s. Eric Vernon and Edith Miriam A.; e. Waltham Coll., Kingston, W.I.; immigrated to Canada 1947; m. Marlene d. Neville and Mae Schroeter 7 Oct.1972; child Lana Mae; Factory Worker, Massey Harris 1948-56; active leader in United Auto Workers (UAW) Local 439; mem., 1954 delegation to Ottawa urging the Fed. Gov't. to change restrictive immigration policy with respect to people of colour; Founder of numerous organizations incl. Jamaican Cdn. Assn. (Pres. 1970-72), Urban Alliance on Race Relations, Black Business and Profl. Assn. and Nat. Council of Jamaicans and Supportive Organizations (Founding Pres. 1986); Founder 1st Caribbean Soccer Club, Toronto; Vice-Pres., Toronto United Negro Credit Union 1950-54; former Comm., Ont. Human Rights Commission; Adv. Council, Multiculturalism Ont., mem., Ont. Labour Relations Bd. (Adjudicator); mem., Toronto Mayor's Ctte. on Race Relations; Chair of Bd. of Govs., Cdn. Centre for Police Relations 1993-98; Bd. of Dirs., Cdn. Centre for Ethics & Corp. Affairs 1997-; Bd. mem., Gleaner Company (NA) Inc. 1993-; recipient Order of Ontario 1992; mem., Order of Canada 1994; Stanley Knowles Humanitarian Award 1995; Toronto Onyx Lions Club Award for outstanding accomplishments 1995; Bahai Nat. Race Unity Award & Harmony Award 1998; Publisher, *The Islander* newspaper 1973-97; co-author *Bromley: Tireless Champion for Just Causes* (Memoirs) 2000; recreations; walking, swimming, reading, sports.

Taken from **Canadian Who's Who 2001 Edition**

Foreword

With the aid of his father's influence, Bromley Armstrong became in his words "a blood and guts" ally of the working poor. At an early age, he joined the Jamaican Trade Union Congress and this early experience shaped his career of dedication and, commitment to improving the lives of the disadvantaged.

In 1947, Bromley Armstrong, emigrated to Canada or as one of his teachers described Canada "our lady of snow". While he expected to return to live in Jamaica at some point, he decided to remain in Canada, which perhaps was unfortunate for Jamaica but was to be a great benefit to his adopted country.

As Bromley Armstrong made his way to Canada through the United States, he encountered for the first time the brutal reality of the segregation of Blacks. The experience became part of his "preparation for his life's work as a fighter against discrimination and intolerance". Another part of his preparation was the more subtle but overt racism he encountered in Canada. He came to realize that "a no Blacks wanted policy was part of the social economic and political fabric of its society."

The fact that the Canada of today is a more tolerant and civil society is in no small part as a result of Bromley's determination to fight racism in all of its manifestations. Indeed, Bromley Armstrong has had a considerable degree of influence in the development of public policy as it relates to the battle against racism. During my years as the Attorney General for Ontario from 1975 to 1985, I met frequently with Bromley and race relations became a priority for the government of Ontario. A Cabinet Committee on Race Relations was established and I became its Chair. A special race relations section of the Human Rights Commission was established. A new government race relations policy was posted in classrooms and public buildings throughout Ontario. A new independent citizen complaint process in relation to allegations of police misconduct was established. Almost every municipality in Ontario established a Mayor's Committee on Race Relations. In brief, the issue of race relations which had so often been "swept under the rug" became a part of public dialogue and debate.

As a trade unionist, community activist, member of the Ontario Human Rights Commission, member of the Ontario Labour Relations Board and the former Chair of the Board of Governors of the Canadian Centre for Police and Race Relations, Bromley Armstrong has made a truly remarkable and meaningful contribution to Ontario and Canada. His vital life's work has been recognized by countless awards including the Order of Ontario and the Order of Canada.

The autobiography of Bromley Armstrong represents a fascinating and important story of a great Canadian.

R. Roy McMurtry,
Chief Justice of Ontario

Preface and Acknowledgements

Bromley L. Armstrong has been a tireless fighter for disadvantaged people in their quest for justice and equal rights in Canada. A word that is used in this book to describe Bromley Armstrong is Tallawa. It is defined in the Jamaican dictionary as having a meaning that is associated with "being strong, sturdy and not to be underestimated." Tallawa is a derivative of the African word "Talala" taken from the Ewe language spoken in southern Togo and eastern Ghana. Talala means straightforward, thorough or basic. What comes to mind in Jamaica when someone is referred to as being "Tallawa" is a sense that he or she is strong willed and capable of withstanding life's challenges. In other words like Bromley L. Armstrong, Tallawa is analogous with the qualities of being a champion; one who has fought, struggled and survived among the masses at the grassroots in Jamaican and Canadian histories. In fact, the fight for justice and equality is a phenomenon that is universally understood by the disadvantaged. By fighting for more than fifty years for a more equitable society in Canada, Bromley Armstrong, the subject of these memoirs underscores a sturdy and single mindedness that meet both the spirit and the letter of the meaning of being a tireless champion.

Revealed on the pages of this book is that Bromley Armstrong's survival skills and his quest for justice were partially acquired as a consequence of his nurturing and educational development in Jamaica. When he settled in Canada in 1947, it was to these early lessons that he turned to ensure his survival in an alien environment. A unique individual has emerged from this crucible. One, whose survival is as a consequence of a willingness to adapt to the characteristics of his adopted country, Canada, while at the same time retaining aspects of his Jamaican identity.

In telling the Bromley Armstrong story (1947-1996) every attempt has been made to ensure that this book appeals to as wide an audience as possible. Furthermore, it is a story that is being told to encourage scholars and students to begin a process that will add depth to the various themes that are presented herein. This book is also meant to encourage others to write their stories. Not enough is being written about the Black experience in Canada. A dearth of material presently exists in this subject area. This circumstance has placed severe limitations on the scholarly development and teaching of African Canadian history beyond the rudiments of the usual contribution histories we hear and read about during Black History Month.

As is usually the case, such a literary undertaking comes to fruition with the help of far too many people to be mentioned here. We are however, indebted to Marlene Schroeter Armstrong for her tireless perseverance in transcribing the numerous hours of taped interviews, and for her support of this project through its many phases. The support of Dennis McDermott is appreciated not just in helping to get the story to print, but also for the time he has spent over the years with Bromley in the trenches. Financial support was received from Buzz Hargrove and the Canadian AutoWorkers (CAW); Gord Wilson and the Ontario Federation of Labour (OFL) and Bob White and the Canadian Labour Congress (CLC). Pam Lugonzo

Taylor's willingness to read, reread, edit, listen to the writers' rants and critique each page of the manuscript helped to validate the writing process. Mavis Burke offered her much-needed advice, criticisms and support in the form of reading and written comments of the manuscript and the loan of valuable secondary resources. With their help as readers, Maureen Murray, Anne Huggins, Jules Elder, Gail Scala, and Nick Harney gave fresh perspectives and eyes to a tiresome process.

In many instances, a lack of primary and secondary sources have usually made the task more difficult when a biography or historical account relating to the Black experience in Canada is undertaken. In this instance, this was not to be a serious stumbling block. Some work relating to this initiative had already been done. It was accomplished with the support of Bromley Armstrong through his provision of oral testimony when I completed my doctoral thesis, *"Darkening the Complexion of Canadian Society": Black Activism, Policy-making and Black Immigration from the Caribbean to Canada, 1940s-1960s*, (U of T, 1994). While at the University of Toronto, I completed some of the research and analysis appearing in various parts of this book in the history department under the initial supervision of the late Robert Harney. Ian Radforth later assumed the task, and additional scholarly support was received from Harold Troper, Carl Berger and Franca Iacovetta.

Daniel and Donna Hill were kind enough to give permission for access to their papers housed at the National Archives of Canada (NAC). Additionally, the papers of the Ontario Labour Committee for Human Rights and the Jewish Labour Committee of Canada housed at the National Archives of Canada were invaluable sources. Kalman Kaplansky helped shorten the research process by directing us to a number of useful sources including the aforementioned papers.

Researchers, Erica Phillips and Michelle Scott in Toronto and Adrian Harewood in Ottawa were unrelenting in their efforts to find related material and interview informants. At every stage of the book project we were fortunate to work with professionals who willingly supported our efforts above and beyond the call of duty. Darrell McCalla is one such person whose impeccable eye for detail enhanced the book's design. And his knowledge of book publishing in Canada was an invaluable resource for this project. The late Malcolm Streete and Al Mercury added their reminiscences to the tenor of the story that is being told. Doctor Odida T. Quamina provided much needed support throughout the various phases of this book. We would also like to thank the archivists at the National Archives of Canada for their guidance and support. Tom Eberlee was a valuable resource and he identified a number of locations where important resources were deposited. Our efforts in Jamaica to find appropriate research material were made easier with the assistance of the Honourable Oliver Clarke, Chairman of the Board, the Jamaica Gleaner Co. Ltd. The Gleaner Co NA and Ltd. supported our efforts in a variety of ways to ensure that this book became a reality. We would also like to thank Toronto entrepreneur Ronald King for his valuable support. Marguerietta St. Juste, Edward Baugh, professor of English and public orator at the University of the West Indies, and Maude Fuller, provided us with a clearer understanding of the word "Tallawa."

Sheldon Taylor

CHAPTER 1

Leaving Jamaica

Jamaica was a land filled with uncertainty in the 1940s, a condition that made going abroad even more attractive for many young Jamaican men and women of my generation. Most of my friends were convinced that leaving Jamaica, the "land of wood and water" was better for us. In part, this was due to the economic hardships of the Depression years that were later compounded by further human and economic sacrifices brought on by the Second World War. Those of us in Jamaica and elsewhere in the Caribbean who were too young to volunteer for duty in the British and Canadian armed services did our level best to contribute locally to the Allied war effort. Radio and newspaper reports of the German U-boat exploits against British ships on the high seas provoked a degree of anxiety among many West Indians. For we were dependent on the foreign ships to bring food and supplies regularly, to our respective ports of call. Blocked shipping lanes, and the possibility that the Nazis could operate in both the Caribbean Sea and Atlantic Ocean rallied many Jamaicans to add their contributions to the Allied war effort. Preceding the war, I was a member of the Boy Scouts, an experience that served me well when I volunteered for service in the early 1940s in the Jamaica Home Guard. When the war ended Jamaicans anxiously wanted to put their lives in order for we were tired of doing without. The fact that friends, family members and neighbours had left to fight in far off countries, some choosing by war's end to stay abroad, and make a life for themselves in foreign lands added to our curiosities about going elsewhere and starting afresh.

Many Jamaicans seemed to be always engaged in an uphill battle for the bare necessities of life. In the period after the abolition of slavery during the 1830s the newly emancipated slaves were involved in a struggle for genuine freedom against the landowners and political elites. Emancipation from British slavery did not bring about real change for most Black Jamaicans. Limited voting rights and taxation favouring the plantation owners for example, meant that the voices of the masses were being ignored. From the 1840s onward, many Black Jamaicans, namely former slaves were without significant landholdings. Even those who had been fortunate enough to purchase land and property sometimes lost their holdings if through their inexperience as property holders they were unable to provide proof of purchase and deeds. Without any access to sources of capital and political influence, the majority of Black Jamaicans were members of the much-exploited working class. The period between the late 1830s and mid-1860s was one in which they continued searching for solutions for their sorry situation. "As social conditions deteriorated, financial burdens piled up, living expenses increased and sporadic outbursts of anger and discontentment erupted across the island."[1]

The dreams of liberty that leaders like Paul Bogle and William Gordon inspired poor Jamaicans to aim for were trampled on in the 1860s. It was a period in which the British repressed the aims of ordinary Jamaicans to live in freedom and liberty, and acting therefore, on behalf of the planter class and its own interests, the imperial authority introduced

Crown Colony rule to Jamaica in 1866. "The governor was clad in all the panoply of imperial power, a helmet bedecked with plumes and feathers, a ceremonial sword that symbolized armed might. A nominated legislature dramatized the fact that the people had been stripped of the right to self-government."[2] Whitehall once again directly ran Jamaica's affairs and British rule manifest in its parliamentary decisions were executed by its representatives in Jamaica's capital, Kingston.[3] It would not be until 1962 that Jamaicans could really begin to refer to their country as "independent." The tenuous socioeconomic circumstances in the 1940s that we Jamaicans found ourselves in our leaders and politicians said, "were the consequences of persistent colonialism which only encouraged poverty and untold hardships."[4]

Jamaicans believed that because of the suffering and hardships they had endured from 1939-1945, the Allied victory against the Germans would give the British government cause to soften its heart, and, immediately following the war, sanction the idea of an autonomous Jamaica. This was not to immediately materialize. For as other British West Indians would soon discover, victory for the Allies, including the United States, did not automatically lead to a lessening of the colonial authorities' presence in the Caribbean. If anything, Britain's position, weakened by economic depression and war encouraged an increasing US presence in what heretofore had been primarily the playground of several European countries. Emancipation from slavery for the majority Black population in the Caribbean had not as yet been complete. After the war, the Caribbean increasingly became the United States of America's backyard. This development meant that British imperialism was replaced with a US brand. Attempts by Caribbean politicians to achieve genuine autonomy in the region, therefore, had to take US interests into consideration. My generation had a bitter pill to swallow, especially since, many Jamaicans and other West Indians had given their sons, their lives and their money during the Second World War, to help make Hitler's dream of enslaving Europe impossible. We watched the dream of determining our own destiny set aside by more powerful and earth crushing geopolitical considerations.

The choices that a young man like me faced were similar to those of the hundreds of thousands of Jamaicans who, since the nineteenth century, had migrated to different lands. Leaving home for strange lands had become part of the Jamaican psyche, and their lives were historically determined by an ability to find work, be it in places like Cuba, Panama, Costa Rica, Colombia, Britain, Europe, the US and occasionally Canada. With the war over, it was my turn to consider following a similar pathway. Jobs in Kingston where the Armstrong family lived were hard to come by. Family life in our household left us with the impression that there was a world that extended beyond the boundaries of our property, a fact underscored by the newspapers and books in our midst. Someone was always knocking at our door asking for advice or assistance. As I remember it, my mother had always given her children the idea that they were all special. She took pains to remind us that God's gifts to us required that we give back to our community by doing whatever we could to improve the society in which we lived. The attention that my parents paid me somehow signaled that I had leadership potential. On reflection, I am prone to believe that equally, the era in which I was born provided me with a particular kind of nurturing that has always been a part of who I am.

Unlike the American example, Jamaica in the 1920s was not in the middle of a thriving economic boom. It was a period in which the Jamaican-born Black Nationalist Marcus Garvey left an indelible impression on many Black people throughout the world. Before his death in 1940, Garvey responded to colonialism and White oppression by imploring us to move beyond the limitations that others had forged for people of African descent. We were to uplift ourselves, Garvey reminded us, and find a way to redefine and redeem ourselves. In Jamaica, a call for change for the better was the rallying cry of the working class, especially the wage labourers who attempted to fight back and rally in earnest against the planter class. I remember my father recounting the attempts of the banana workers to achieve better wages and improve their working conditions in the 1920s. Ordinary Jamaicans made many sacrifices when both the colonial office and the absentee Jamaican landlords left no stone unturned to ensure that their working-class aspirations amounted to naught. The banana workers' strikes in that period were part of the hallmark of twentieth century trade union history in Jamaica and the rest of the Caribbean. These workers responded to colonial hegemony in a similar fashion to their sugar plantation compatriots in the British Leeward Islands by putting themselves on the line. Ultimately, they summoned the attention of the British imperial authority, and in so doing, they ensured the legitimacy of trade union objectives in the region.[5] Postwar changes that grudgingly came to Jamaicans and other West Indians were the rewards of the toils and struggles that many members of the Black West Indian working classes willingly engaged in so that future generations could achieve the freedom they never experienced.

Born on February 9, 1926, I was the fourth of seven children in the Eric Vernon and Edith Miriam Armstrong (nee Heron) household. My other siblings are Esmine, Eric Jr.,

Everald, Olive, George and Monica. We were born at a time when the political atmosphere in Jamaica was rampant with the call for: "better must come". Later, this was to be the rallying cry of some of the 1960s Jamaican revolutionaries. However, credit must be given for this rallying cry to those leaders who fought and struggled against the few families controlling a disproportionate amount of Jamaica's wealth. In particular, the imperial authority in the early twentieth-century was fearful that, if the Caribbean jewel in its crown, Jamaica, broke free, the rest of the British West Indian colonies would see this as a signal and demand that the winds of change blow their way.

Alexander Bustamante[6] and Norman Manley[7], if they were still alive, would admit that their respective rise to prominence as twentieth-century Jamaican leaders occurred because of the sacrifices of the average person in the street. They endured the billy club, and when necessary, gunshots to provide more opportunities for all Jamaicans. It was Father A. G. S. Coombs that founded the Jamaica Workers and Tradesmen's Union in 1934. Coombs later invited Bustamante to become part of this pioneering trade union venture. In the 1930s Coombs rallied members of the working class protest against poor wages and living conditions. He cautioned them that their only salvation was to make the necessary sacrifices so that a new Jamaica could take its place in the modern world. I am indebted to the leadership in the period of my growing-up years. They made it possible that a son of the soil like myself could openly flaunt my ambition beyond the cane fields, fishing boats and rumshops of my beloved Jamaica. In the old days, the White Jamaicans who left home usually did so to attend some of the better British schools. Black Jamaicans on the other hand, quite often went overseas in search of backbreaking work in the metropolitan countries' factories and farms.

Following a similar pattern of those representing the interests of the working poor in Britain, our leaders called for socio-economic changes based on a political ideology that reflected on social democratic principles. But such options rather than uniting the populace against the landowners and colonial authorities oftentimes produced competing ideologies within the ranks. When I was twelve years old, I witnessed the upheaval caused by the first general strike in Jamaica. A development the newspapers of the day reported was filled with violent confrontation by the colonial authorities against men and women in the streets. Strikes and upheaval provoked the landowners to call for paramilitary force to be used as a means of discouraging the sugarcane workers from realizing their expectations of better wages. In Westmoreland, four strikers were shot dead; others were detained in prison. Alexander Bustamante was arrested as an agitator, and his cousin Norman Manley, soon to be his political rival, secured his release. It seemed to me that vying for power, based on the support of the Jamaican masses became the full-time ambitions of Manley, Bustamante and J.A.G. Smith in a period when Jamaica and I were coming of age. It was a process facilitated within the ranks of labour where the cane cutters and labourers engaged in road building and wharf workers rallied to the calls for change. I was greatly influenced by the voices calling for change in Jamaica in the 1930s. Change for the better was an aspiration I learned in my youth, to always hold dear. There was no shame in wanting to improve the world in which one lived. Wherever I went in life, it was this value that I seemed most wedded to.

My father Eric was a man steeped in the traditions of the nineteenth century. He was a no-nonsense Victorian disciplinarian, a characteristic his children acknowledged early enough in our youth. We adopted our father's ways, and in time his preference for discipline, a commitment to a strong work ethic and a love of athletics became our mainstay. We went with our father to a nearby park at five o'clock each morning, where he put both his sons and daughters through the paces of track and field and calisthenics. A commitment to nurturing a healthy body is another value that I carried with me into adulthood. Friends of mine know that my day begins with a workout.

Working as a boilermaker and welder for the Jamaican government, Desnoes and Geddes Brewery and the Jamaica Soap Factory in a period when workers had few rights was tough on my father. He believed, however, that hard work was a recipe for developing survival skills and he despised slackers. Our mother was a humanitarian. She grew up in Jamaica in an era when there was no social net. Welfare by any standard was nonexistent. Survival was based on one's ability to find his or her way in the world. The colonialists took out of Jamaica much more than they put in. Colonialism amounted to a form of neo-slavery, thus the poor, the orphans, the unemployed, and the elderly had as their constant companions, hunger, disease and an uncertain tomorrow.

After living for some time in Franklin Town we moved to another section of Kingston called Vineyard Town, where our mother continued her profession as a midwife, and operated her own Nursing Home. "Nurse" as her patients and people referred to her in her community, delivered hundreds of babies. Her midwifery practice was not always managed on a fee for service basis. The expectant mother giving birth to a healthy baby was given every priority. Only then was a method of payment discussed. There was always food in the Armstrong household, because when necessary, Nurse accepted chickens and other kinds of food as payment. Often she received no payment, for her patients had none to give.

With my father's influence, I too became a "blood and guts" sympathizer within the ranks of the labour movement. When I left school, I started working for R. Hanna and Sons, a dry goods merchant, and joined Jamaica's Trade Union Congress. Attending meetings, I often listened to the trials and tribulations of the Jamaican workers. As sympathetic as I was, the impatience of my youth countenanced that I needed less rhetoric and promises, and more action that would help me pay my way in an ever increasingly competitive world. My future in Jamaica seemed bleak. Turmoil was everywhere. The small farmers were being pushed off their lands on which many generations of their families had subsisted. Some of the traditional occupations associated with the artisan classes such as the blacksmiths, and coopers were being replaced with modern technology. Tailors and dressmakers were forced to compete with mass produced clothing made in factories in far off places. Getting a trade in Jamaica was becoming increasingly difficult at a time when the number of school graduates was on the rise. These conditions made it easier for me to consider going abroad as my only option.

Like many others my age, our decision to leave in no way indicated a lack of patriotism for our country. It was becoming impossible each day for us to be successful in Jamaica. Jamaica held opportunities, but not for us. Ironically, a Syrian or Lebanese would arrive one month with a suitcase of fabric, and make enough money several months later to open a store, hire and pay Jamaican citizens a mere pittance. Historic conditions and colonial subjugation had stayed the expectations of many ordinary Jamaicans of African descent. But we tried to demonstrate our commitment regardless of the odds against us.

A commitment to my community fostered by my parents' influence led me at age eighteen in 1944 to volunteer and help elect Florizel Glasspole in the Eastern Kingston constituency. Glasspole served for many years in a number of key government positions, including the Labour portfolio. Much later, after Jamaica became independent, he was knighted and appointed Governor General of Jamaica. Besides my volunteer work, I was involved in many extracurricular activities. I had already been very active in track and field, soccer, boxing and swimming. In 1946, I won the hundred metres in the Jamaica Junior Swimming Championship.

Two years after the end of the war, it was time for me to make a move. Some of my friends had gone overseas to train in the Royal Airforce. At war's-end, many of them did not return. Increasingly, the talk shifted from local struggles to the possibility of going abroad to England, and the US. That was difficult to do, especially because of the latter's colour bar. In this period Canada was seen by many West Indians as a difficult place to enter. To surmount this problem I even tried signing up for work as a seaman. The trade routes between the Caribbean and Canada were facilitated by a number of ships called "Ladyboats" and I thought that duty on any such vessel would eventually help me find a way of gaining permanent entrance there. Egged on by my elder brother Eric, I tried everything possible to go "foreign" as we called it back then. He and Everald left Jamaica in 1943, for service in the Canadian Armed Forces. After the war, their service made them eligible to de-enlist and obtain landed immigrant status; an option they took, when they decided to live in Toronto. I was impressed with Eric when he returned to Jamaica for a holiday. Arriving on a transport plane that brought supplies for a Canadian Regiment, the Brockville Rifles, stationed at Up

Park Camp, Eric seemed larger than life. He talked about the promise that Canada held for my younger Brother George and I. He said that after his week's holiday ended and he returned to Canada, he would get us there. Eric was true to his word.

Soon after returning to Canada, he tried everything possible to get us into the country. Of course, the possibility of leaving was silently upsetting, especially for our mother. West Indian mothers of African origin had forcibly given up their children during slavery. Girls and boys were oftentimes sent to other plantations, and in many cases they were never reunited. Leaving to find work in some other part of the region or going to a foreign country in search of work was a fact of life for many Caribbean nationals. With two of her children already in Canada, and my sister Olive having left in 1945 to live with our aunt in the US, my mother now faced the likelihood of losing two more of her boys to that cold country. It was emotionally upsetting to her as she realized that only two of seven children would be left in Jamaica.

Not having any success in his initial attempts to get us to Canada, Eric decided that we should enroll at the Toronto School of Business, and he set about applying for our student visas. This was a blessing in disguise since the idea of both of us studying abroad had great appeal with the rest of the family. Getting the news from Eric prompted us to obtain the required documentation, and we accelerated our efforts to make the necessary preparations to leave Jamaica. We traveled to Spanish Town in the parish of St. Catherine where we obtained our birth certificates and we also got clearance from the Department of Education. We applied for our passports, and with documents in hand, it was just a matter of time before George and I headed for the airport. By no stretch of the imagination did I think at the time that I was leaving home for good. In my mind, it was a matter of getting a suitable trade, one that allowed me to earn a lot of money, help my family, and return to Jamaica and enjoy a better livelihood.

Eric's efforts in trying to get us to Canada, we later learned, were in keeping with the practices of many Canadian residents with immigrant backgrounds, who wished to create a more stable future for their loved ones. After the war, hundreds of thousands of Europeans came to Canada as immigrants, including displaced persons living in European camps with nowhere to go. On being set free after the end of the war, even some captured German soldiers, housed in Canadian prisoner of war camps, applied for status, and were allowed to stay in Canada. Because of Ottawa's stern "no Blacks wanted policy", Eric's attempts to have his brothers come to Canada with permanent status were rebuffed by Canada's Immigration Branch. In those days, Ottawa did everything possible to prevent Black people, British subjects or otherwise, from gaining entrance to Canada.[8]

In 1947, all anyone spoke of in Jamaica was the existing or imminent hardships. It seemed more practical to go abroad and try one's luck. After all, the grass always looks greener on the other side. Some of us were well aware that economic conditions were not good anywhere else. Conservative leader Winston Churchill had warned Britons and indirectly citizens of the British Commonwealth that social and economic conditions were far from improved after the war's end. Jamaica was facing its second year of drought, which had caused severe food shortages. The Jamaica Agricultural Society and civic leaders organized food production drives.[9] With few opportunities and a cost of living that was continuously on the increase, it was a matter of our survival. Our economy was one that relied on significant numbers of imports. In 1947 for example, the rising costs of shoe production and textiles in the

US, Canada and Britain meant that Jamaicans would soon be forced to pay high prices for basic necessities.[10]

At age twenty-one I thought I had no other choice but to leave and my brother and I determined that we were definitely leaving Jamaica. My mind was filled with many conflicting thoughts. I had seen the promise of what a new Jamaica could be like. Three years before, in 1944, the never-ending struggle by many Jamaicans to help influence their country's political climate was finally achieved when Universal Suffrage was granted. Jamaicans who were not property owners could now vote. Yet, this still was not enough for me to stay within my country's borders. I wanted more. Ironically, the atmosphere induced by the union movement activities of Bustamante and Manley had fuelled my appetite and impatience. I could see that tough times lay ahead for the common working man and woman. I wanted to be a part of what the future might hold. However, I reminded myself that I needed to be equipped to take up such challenges, and I also remembered what I had been taught: with age comes responsibility. How could we be responsible for our own futures, especially when the Jamaican economy remained a pawn of the British and Jamaican economic interests. In effect, each succeeding generation of Jamaican Blacks remained the hewers, and the carriers, in the land of wood and water.

Before leaving, there were people to say goodbye to. After all, could you imagine what they would say if I up and left without acknowledging the roles they had played in my life? Sister Fidelis had been one of my mentors. Before retiring, she served as the Alpha Elementary Public School principal. In her retirement, she relocated to St. Catherine. Ever the teacher, Sister Fidelis lectured me about life and what I should expect during my travels. She warned me about leaving any glass that

I was drinking from unattended in a public place, since as she stated, "it was a common way for someone to harm you." I had similar discussions with a number of adults; it was all part of the process. Then the day came, and it was time for George and I to begin the journey. Determined as I was to go, and though happy to depart, a part of me was sad to leave. The time came when I had to face my mother who along with my sister came with us to the airport. At age twenty-one, I was leaving home for the first time. Standing in the Kingston airport I was overcome with emotions. I looked at my mother and silently wondered how she would fare in a changing Jamaica. I had been the one to whom she often looked to for assistance and direction for the rest of my siblings. Although she worried that I was going to cold Canada, I convinced myself that she understood my reason for leaving. In fact, she had been very supportive of our decision to go.

Staying would only add to her burdens. Even if I had married in Jamaica, an unstable income would have dictated that my wife and I live at home. In those days when you mentioned that you were going to Canada, everyone envisioned you as going to live at the North Pole. My mother was bent on making sure that since Canada was a chilled-to-the-bone-country, her boys were going to be protected from the perilous conditions of snow and ice. To this end, she ordered what were called "herringbone" winter coats equipped with padded shoulders. While we partied with our friends for what was to be the last time, our mother had a tailor make us two of these coats. Many of our local tailors and dressmakers attracted by the promise of a steady pay cheque would soon leave too, for the British and US garment factories.

In the two weeks leading up to our departure, we seized the moment and took every opportunity to celebrate our departure with friends and family. I was popular in my local community, especially because of my athletic abilities. Boxing, soccer and swimming had made it easier for me to command everyone's attention. George was also a popular athlete and a year earlier, he had won the lightweight and I the welterweight competition in amateur boxing. We were both selected to go to Colombia and represent Jamaica in the 1946 Pan American Games. Illness kept me away, but George attended the games. So although going to Canada was my first trip on an airplane, he had already experienced the vagaries of flight. Mother also bought us woolen underwear with the trademark, "Made in England", and she made us don felt hats, she thought, to keep out the cold. We were given thirty-five American dollars and all the money we had in the world was carefully sewn into the seam of my coat. We were fearful of being searched on arrival in Miami since Jamaicans at the time were only allowed a few American dollars for personal expenses when they left for foreign countries.[11]

As we took our first steps toward the Miami bound plane on the afternoon of December 11, 1947, I thought to myself, "Bromley you'll be back." We headed for Miami where we were to change planes and travel by another plane along what was called the "milkrun." Florida's capital seemed like a lifetime away. On board the plane, I had time to reflect on what I had left behind in Jamaica, and anticipate what lay ahead for me in a country that my schoolteacher had once referred to as "our lady of snow." Getting to this stage had not been easy. After a two and a half-hour plane ride, we arrived in the early evening in Miami. With time on our hands before continuing our journey, we decided to have something to eat. This decision bought us face to face with our first recognizable experience of culture shock. On entering a Miami airport restaurant, we were immediately ushered to a dingy section in the back of the room. I wanted to know what the hell was going on. What were we doing sitting in the back, while only people with White skin were seated up-front? I had not experienced anything like this in Jamaica, colonial authorities or no colonial authorities. Additionally, George and I recognized few items on the menu. Fortunately, ice cream was included, which I had along with some pears. I was already missing Jamaica, in particular, my mother's cooking. Anyway, we persevered. A few minutes later two Black women were seated at a table near ours. It must have been obvious that we were experiencing a great deal of discomfort, because the younger of the two, who was in her early forties, came over, and said, "excuse me." Well we were happy to speak to anyone. "Are you from Jamaica?" she said. "Yes!" I said. She went on to recount how she experienced a similar fate twenty years earlier when she left Jamaica for the US. She counseled us that we were in a new world, "don't despair, you will survive. Things will get better," she assured us. Her words did a lot to shore up our dampened spirits especially, at a time when she was on her way home to bury her recently deceased mother.

I came face to face with a brand of racism that I had not experienced before. Not being able to eat in certain places and this up-in-your-face outright refusal by some Whites to serve Blacks in public places were actions, I silently thought, I could not accept. Equally as bad was how a plane ride had somehow diminished my status. I went from being Jamaican to being the member of an endangered species; a Black person in America. Later on I came to realize that this and similar experiences were part of my preparation for my life's work as a fighter against discrimination and intolerance. My efforts in this regard had begun as a rank and file member in the Jamaican Trade Union Congress where I fought against Jamaica's classism.

The experiences garnered from such an apprenticeship, coupled with this brand of unapologetic North American racism influenced me to the point, where the road I traveled for the rest of my life, put me on a particular path. It has been one of searching for justice and fighting for equality for all downtrodden peoples. The few brief moments in that Miami restaurant embodied the words that I would later hear Mahatma Ghandi, Martin Luther King and Nelson Mandela repeat: "There is no justice until injustice is eradicated everywhere."

Continuing our journey, we boarded the plane and began what in earnest was a milkrun. Carrying passengers like us and US Military de-enlistees along with milk and newspapers meant that intermittently we touched down along the way at a number of airports. We had experienced nothing like what appeared in front of us in the Washington, D.C. and later Chicago airports. Thousands of army, navy and airforce personnel in transit, lying on the ground with their duffel bags, waiting to get home and restart their lives as civilians. The war for them was over, I soon discovered that mine was just getting started. Chicago had prepared us for what we would see in Toronto. As the airplane was about to land we saw a blanket of whiteness. Snow everywhere, just as my mother had imagined. The wait was eight hours in Chicago, and we did everything possible to contain our anxiety to get to Toronto. We discovered that if you opened your mouth and blew your breath in the cold, what appeared like steam was produced. We did so repeatedly. Waiting in Chicago's airport seemed like an eternity, and our experience in Miami made us hesitant to seek service in another American restaurant. We loaded up on chocolate bars and peanuts at a tuckshop and I remember buying a book entitled, *Body and Soul*. By the time we left Chicago and arrived in Buffalo, we had been travelling for many hours, a feat that is unimaginable to young people today since it takes less than four and a half hours by plane from Toronto to Kingston, Jamaica. In those days it took an eternity.

    During the first leg of our trip, we had seen the sunset as we journeyed to Miami. Somewhere along the way, the dark of the night had again been transfigured by the dawning of a new day. After boarding the Trans Canada Airlines flight that took us from Buffalo to Toronto, it was again nearing another sunset. The journey had been a long one. We had traveled for nearly two days and on December 13, 1947, as the plane touched down at Malton airport I could see the terminal, and surrounding areas. Later, it was renamed Pearson International. Back then, it was essentially a grey wooden, nondescript structure and the onslaught of the winter neither helped its appearance, or our nerves. After leaving the airplane, we walked briskly to the terminal. Finally, after all of the preparation, anticipation and roadblocks along the way, George and I had arrived at our destination. Soon I discovered however, that I had just begun a journey that would become part of an unprecedented chapter in the annals of Canadian history, in the second half of the twentieth century.

Chapter 1 – Notes

1. Philip Sherlock and Hazel Bennett, *The Story of the Jamaican People*. Kingston, Jamaica: IRP, 1998, chapter 21, pp. 246-262.

2. Ibid., p. 266.

3. For an in depth account of related developments see Philip D. Curtain, *Two Jamaicas* (Harvard University Press, 1955.

4. In *Persistent Poverty: Underdevelopment in plantation economies of the third world* (London: Oxford University Press, 1972, George Beckford makes a similar case.

5. Glen Richards, Friendly Societies and Labour organizations in the Leeward Islands, 1912-19." In: *Before & After 1865: Education, Politics and Regionalism in the Caribbean*, (eds.) Brian Moore and Swithin Wilmot, (Kingston: IRP, 1988), pp.136-149.

6. Born Alexander Clarke on February 24, 1884, and later his name was changed to to Alexander Bustamante. In 1943, he founded the Bustamante Industrial Trade Union (BITU).Norman Manley and Bustamante were the guiding lights of the People's National Party (PNP) established in 1938.

7. After Alexander Bustamante broke with the PNP in 1942, he set up the Jamaica Labour Party (JLP), and Manley continued to head the PNP. In effect, Jamaica now had a two party system, and by 1958, Jamaica had become responsible for its own internal affairs.

8. For an account of Canada's racial immigration bar, See Sheldon Taylor's unpublished doctoral thesis, *"Darkening the Complexion of Canadian Society": Black Activism, Policy-making and Black Immigration from the Caribbean to Canada, 1940s-1960s.*

9. JAS President Calls For 'Plant More' Drive. *Daily Gleaner*, September 11, 1947, p.1.

10. "Price Rise Seen Ahead For Shoes And Textiles." *Daily Gleaner*, September 12, 1947, p. 1.

11. There was a Jamaican government restriction on the amount of US currency its nationals could leave Jamaica with after the Second World War had ended. Additionally, the US government closely monitored US currency amounts that foreigners were bringing to American ports of call.

CHAPTER 2

Learning to Climb New Stairs

Touching Canadian soil was a happy occasion for me. After all, just getting here had been quite an ordeal. Given the nature of the struggle to enter Canada, I expected to see the streets lined with gold. Compared to the horror stories that some people had recounted to me about their experiences with immigration and customs officials at the airport ours was rather uneventful. After checking our passports and our bags, we were on our way to what we thought would be our home for a while. Brothers, Eric, and Everald were pleased that George and I were now with them. Being older, they relished the fact that they could show us around and that it would take some time before we would really be on our own. Sightseeing would have to wait until the next day, since it was dark, and cold outside.

Eric owned a Bungalow near Jane Street and Eglinton Avenue West, in an area that later became part of the City of Toronto's West-end. Returning from the war, he used the money given to him by the Armed Services to purchase his first home. We did not expect the reception that was waiting for us, when the car we were driving in pulled up in front of the house. Many of Eric's neighbours, from both sides of the street, all White people, were there to greet us, as if we were long lost family members. If only the workers in the Miami airport restaurant could see how decent people behaved. It was quite a happy feeling to see the fuss everyone was making over us. After surviving on peanuts and chocolates we were hungry and ready for a real meal. Needless to say, we ate heartily. Afterwards, we were taken to the back yard of one of our neighbours and his son showed us the basics of skating and hockey.

Later, we went to the neighbourhood outdoor ice rink where the youngsters would skate by at top speed. As we skated in a circle, little boys and girls would come up to me, and say "mister you don't skate well, do you"? I was not humiliated. Just pleased to see how experienced they were on the blades, and I hoped that one day I too, would be able to skate with such dexterity. My skating career came to an abrupt end after receiving a stick between my legs while attempting to play hockey next door. Falling on the ice and ending up with a big gash on my eyebrow was to be my final episode of trying to play Canada's favourite sport. Occasionally, I did enjoy going to the ice rink and trying to skate, but it really was not my cup of tea.

All new arrivals to Toronto are usually treated to the sights of the inner city. Downtown Toronto in 1947 was rather dreary by comparison with today's standards. There was not much to see, however, it seemed larger than life to us. We had gone from being in Jamaica where our images of Canadian winters were common representations on Christmas cards, hearing stories about the cold from visiting friends and family, and using our imagination to picture what Toronto was really like, to actually being here. We gladly went along with our brothers to see what they described as: "the great sights." After the usual trip to Eatons and Simpsons, and a jaunt through the downtown core, our day of fun abruptly came to an end. As we approached our home, we noticed the presence of fire engines outside our house and a broken down door where firemen had entered to put out a blaze. The fire chief told us that the fire began with a spark from the furnace, which then ignited a chesterfield in the living room. Unfortunately for George and I, we lost everything except for the suits on our backs. The items that were not destroyed by fire or water were damaged beyond repair by smoke.

Our misfortune summoned us to look for work. Finding a job I thought, especially with experience in the dry goods industry in Jamaica, would not be as challenging as it subsequently turned out to be. After all, though smaller in size, dry goods stores in Jamaica in the 1940s were modelled on similar standards to those in England and Canada. I developed a pattern of visiting department stores in search of work, applications were handed to me which I filled out and returned, but no one ever called. At times, I was told to apply at the railroad station, since they were hiring railroad porters. It was the Canadian way of saying: "Black people should not apply." My applications, like many of those filled out by other Blacks, years before I had tried, were politely ignored.

With the passage of time, I learned that the attitudes of Canada's Immigration Branch were mirrored elsewhere in Canada. A "no Blacks wanted policy" was part of the social, economic and political fabric of its society. A painful fact when there is no money in your pocket, and you need to urgently find work. It was clear to me from reading the newspapers that certain groups received preferential treatment in Canada. Soon after arriving from Jamaica, the talk of the town was about the attempts by Premier George Drew of Ontario to ensure that every preference was given to immigrants from the

Motherland, England. Drew set about ensuring that this was done and he even went as far as going to England to engage in the selection of immigrants on the basis of their Anglo Saxon stock. When Ottawa signalled only a lukewarm response to the Premier's idea, in 1947, he had 10,000 English men and women airlifted to Ontario.[1]

Fortunately for me, my brother Everald worked at Massey Harris, and the company was also hiring. After repeated efforts, he was able to persuade his foreman to use his influence to see if I could be employed in the factory. To this end, I would wait in line early each weekday morning from between 3.30 a.m. and 4.00 a.m. until the doors of the personnel office were opened at 9.00 a.m. With little money, only the clothes on my back and no overshoes, I stood shivering in the cold on King Street West at Strachan. This is how my foreign experience began in Canada. In the frigid weather each morning, all I could do was hope that my prayers would be answered. Years later, whenever I drove by that location, I would remember what it took for me to find a job in Canada. It was not easy.

In the second week of my vigil for a job, a rather strapping man approached the line of cold and tired men. "Armstrong!" he shouted. Answering "here!" led him to take me by the arm, into the personnel office. Before getting there, he said to me, "when they ask, if you can operate a bulldozer, tell them yes." If, nothing else, I was thankful to be inside, since it was a much warmer place to be. An application was put in my hand and it was promptly filled out. I was asked many questions. When the personnel manager queried about the bulldozer, I of course said "yes." My impression of a bulldozer was that it was supposed to be a big motorized vehicle. Anyway, in my desperation to find a job, when the question of when I could start work came up, I quickly said, "any time." The manager called the department foreman whose name was Len Shaw, and he escorted me immediately, to start working. Here I am, ready for work, all 137 pounds, in my black suit, white shirt and tie with my big hat and herringbone coat thinking that I am going to drive a bulldozer to earn my keep. We went into a room, walked over to the bulldozer that I was supposed to be able to operate. It was a machine that I had not seen before in my life. Standing near it was a man from Barbados named Baird. He was told my name and that I would be working with him. To which he responded with an expression of amazement. I was shown a box of material, bits of steel, and a tong that is used to pick up the steel, a long glove and an apron to cover my clothes. Baird told me to "pick up a bit of steel, and place it in the firebox." Inside the firebox were white flames that were shooting out all over the place on both sides. The steel was to be placed on the bed of the firebox and once the steel turns white from the heat, the tong is used to pick it up and carry it over to the bulldozer, a big machine with two dyes, one on each side. The hot steel is then fitted into each dye, a lever is pulled, which produces an awful crashing sound, and the steel is shaped accordingly. I could not get the steel into the firebox, and I repeatedly dropped the pieces of steel. Baird just stood there shaking his head and he then told the foreman "if nothing else the heat will probably kill him."

    The 62 cents an hour that I was promised seemed to hang in the balance when Mr. Baird gave thumbs down to the possibility that I was capable of working with him. I was very relieved when the foreman took me to another department, and introduced me to another Black man named Myers. He was the "straw boss", in essence the lead hand, and he too, was from Jamaica. He was a little man, around five feet tall, weighing not more than 120 pounds. Myers in turn handed me over to a big fellow, a Ukrainian named John, and asked him to take me under his wing and to ensure that I was able to do whatever tasks I was assigned. He gave me a little hammer weighing about three pounds along with a bin and some pieces of metal. I was shown how each piece was to be struck in order to bring it to the precise bend or shape required. I tried my best do as John had asked, but it was hard work, and certainly not the kind of work I was accustomed to.

The operation at Massey Harris was run out of what was a giant blacksmith's shop. Next, they tried me in the setting department where I went to work with my brother Everald. I was given a five-pound hammer for shaping steel for the combine. I remember missing the steel and hitting my brother in his stomach. It was pathetic, and I was getting worried, but they seemed determined to find me something to do. Finally, they found me a suitable job. My job was to ensure that steel bars were aligned on a machine and prepared for assembly line production. Looking for, and finding the right job, in addition to adjusting to a country in the midst of an inhospitable climate was stressful. I toiled from 7.30 a.m. until 4.30 p.m., and even with the help of my fellow workers, mainly Eastern Europeans, who took me under their wings, by days-end, I was exhausted. When I left work at the end of my shift, I visited the YMCA, where I became a member of the swimming club and continued my passion for swimming. To escape the drudgery of work and the feelings of being homesick, I sometimes swam for hours.

I was gradually making the necessary adjustments to Toronto, and since it is my nature to be active I started looking for more things to do. With Everald's encouragement, I began meeting some members of Toronto's relatively small Black community and I attended meetings at the Universal Negro

Improvement Association (UNIA).[2] The Jamaican-born Marcus Garvey had founded this organization in 1914, and the Toronto Chapter received its charter in 1920. At its zenith in the early 1920s, the UNIA had a worldwide membership of nearly 4,000,000 people. I also started to attend the meetings of the Toronto United Negro Association (TUNA)[3] in January 1948, E.A. Davis, a chemist by profession, was its president. Alfred Blackman was the president of the TUNA related, Toronto United Negro Credit Union. Meetings were held monthly on the last Friday and second Friday respectively. Other young people like myself were in attendance, and because of my union involvement before I left Jamaica, I had some knowledge of how an organization should function. I began asking questions about a number of things I observed in both the association and the credit union.

Since the TUNA was functioning at the behest of a small number of influential persons, questioning the status quo made me very unpopular in certain quarters of the organization. Paying my membership dues, however, gave me the right to speak up, and I was unwilling to accept business as usual. Containing no aims and objectives, the association's one page constitution was garbled. Although the credit union was a chartered corporation with proper documentation through the Credit Union League, I found some of its rules disturbing. My first task, therefore, was to become the association's auditor, and a member of one of the credit union's committees. This involvement brought me face to face with a group of older members of the community; many of them had immigrated in the pre-war years to Canada from the West Indies. They represented the backbone of Toronto's Black community, and through organizational development and a spirit of voluntarism, they had taken proactive roles in helping to build their community. Later when

I provoked the TUNA to discard the old ways of community organizational development, a majority of the membership elected me president in 1955. With Fitzroy Alexander as treasurer and Edna Braithwaite as secretary, we soon discovered the old guard's tenacity, when E. A. Davis refused to recognize what was a legitimately constituted succession. Business as usual prevailed.

The UNIA was one of the pivotal Black non-religious organizations in Toronto and B.J. Spencer Pitt, a lawyer was its president. Other such longstanding community organizations included the Home Service Association, the Eureka Friendly Club, established in the pre-World War I era was primarily an organization for middle-class Black women. There was also the Eureka Number 20 Masonic Lodge with a history dating to 1914 when it superceded an earlier Lodge that had been established for Black men. There were three historic Black Churches that were defining institutions for many Toronto Blacks. The First Baptist Church was then located at the corner of University Avenue and Edward Street; the African Methodist Episcopal Church (AME) was located on Soho Avenue, and the British Methodist Episcopal Church (BME) was housed on Chestnut Street. The Afro Community Church organized in the 1930s by the Jamaican-born Cecil Stewart, also had a newspaper called the *Afro Beacon*. Stewart was looked upon by many of the other leaders who were less willing to take risks as a maverick. He was too busy to really care about what others thought. Once there was some need to be met, and work to be done he set about tackling the problems. During the Depression era and into the 1940s Stewart found inventive ways to help community members survive. He convinced a number of bakeries to give him bread, and allowed some of it to get stale, which he then gave to out-of-town farmers as livestock feed. They gave him meat and vegetables as a trade-off, that he made available to the needy in his community.

With Stewart's tenacity the Afro Community Church was accepted as a member in the Red Feather Agency which was the forerunner to the United Way. With his urging, for a short while in the late 1940s and early 1950s, the City of Toronto declared one day each year, Black Tag Day. In exchange for a tag, we went around raising money, and surprisingly, many people willingly contributed. His Shaw Street building had a gymnasium and a donated printing press on which he had someone trained. A small print shop was established on the church premises and this enabled the church to have events' programs printed onsite. Other printing needs of the community and surrounding areas were met and in the process someone was gainfully employed. Stewart's philosophy of: "don't let others do for you the things that you can do for yourself" was repeated in a number of his endeavours. He did his work in the name of the Lord, and argued that accordingly, he would answer to Him. Stewart went to the taverns and ingratiated himself with entertainers who were playing their gigs for the downtown crowd. Some of them contributed their time and talent so that he could meet the church's financial commitments. I recall the Reverend holding a fundraiser on a Sunday evening when community members would not otherwise support his church in large enough numbers. This particular event had standing room only when he convinced the Ink Spots to do a benefit concert so that he could pay the building's mortgage.

His antics did not go uncriticized. Some people in the Black community said that moving the pulpit and erecting a stage in its place, albeit only temporarily, was blasphemous. Stewart ignoring the criticism on the night of the event reminded everyone that when the collection plate came their way, he did not want to hear the jingling of any coins, instead, he wanted to hear only the rustling of paper. By the time of my arrival, the Afro Community and BME Churches in Toronto were negotiating a union. Stewart and business-person Don Moore purchased an old synagogue on Shaw Street. When the unification of the BME and Afro Community Churches was finalized, both congregations united under the BME banner and operated from these premises.

Located in its own building at 355 College Street, the UNIA's survival was the product of a small number of men and women who laboured intensely to keep it solvent. Soon after I arrived in Toronto, I met the city's only Black lawyer, B. J. Spencer Pitt. After graduating from Dalhousie Law School and settling in Toronto in the late 1920s, he became a member of the association's leadership, and its president. Pitt and Samuel Michaels helped to keep the UNIA afloat. As Michaels was a carpenter and a member of the Carpenter's Union, his profession came in handy when the building was in need of repair.

The UNIA was not just a place for its members to hold their meetings, it was a community centre where Black adults and children went to socialize, attend debates, danced, and played music. In its edifice, leaders and members representing many different organizations gathered to plan the future direction of their community. When new arrivals and visitors to the city needed a place to go, they were referred to the UNIA. Jam sessions were regularly featured there, and musicians like Chiropodist, Dr. Oscar Brewton, and Esmond Rickets encouraged youth to develop an interest in music. All roads in the community led to the Saturday night dances at the UNIA. They had a reputation for turning into brawls when the passions of youth became uncontrollable. I paid my fifty cents and went there from 9.00 p.m. until midnight to socialize, and observe people. Fights took place when American men came to the UNIA in their Lincolns and Cadillacs, and tried to pick up some of the young women from the community. Their boyfriends' intervention usually caused an altercation that would be followed with the prompt appearance of the police. For a while these occurrences at the UNIA became part of the rhythm of the community.

Although some historians have described Toronto's Black community in the late 1940s as small, it should be added, that it was a vibrant place to be. On Sunday mornings, an observable number of Blacks, both men and women, went to church. Others went to the park at Bathurst and Dundas Streets. They played softball, women brought their children there for fresh air, and some of the men who liked to play three cards stud, gambled. It was in such an arena that I learned a lot about a community that I identified with, and too, it was here that I made myself familiar to others. Of course, the presence of so many Blacks in one place attracted the attention of the police, and they were on hand to, as they put it "protect the peace." After the morning church services, community youth met in the afternoons and evenings at the Home Service, located also on Bathurst Street. Young Black women came dressed in their fineries, and choirmaster, Bill White, who later headed the Workmen's Compensation Board, led a choral group, and gave lectures about social developments here and in the US.

Because many Blacks lived in proximity to the Bathurst and Dundas Street West area it served as a focus in their community activities. Many members of Toronto's Black community lived in or very near this area, and from my point of view, it was the centre of our universe. Downtown today takes in Bay Street, south of College Street to the waterfront. It stretches east to Church Street and with recent developments extends west to almost Bathurst Street. When I was new to Toronto, the downtown area was part of what was commonly referred to as the Ward area. It included Spadina Avenue over to Yonge Street and College Street to the Lakeshore. I have played a little bit with the geography since the Ward was in fact a municipal boundary, but those identifying with it, did so from a psychological perspective.

The settling patterns of many Black people placed them in most parts of the city and surrounding areas, but excluded the upscale bastions of Rosedale and Forrest Hills. The Black community's concentration was south of College Street to Front Street, and east of Bathurst Street over to Spadina Avenue. Yonge Street, as it still is today acted as the great divide for the city. Blacks east of it were called east-enders, and those west of the line were referred to as west-enders. Unlike in Nova Scotia and many American cities, historically there have been no distinctive Black communities in Toronto. The term Black community was an abstract concept. Blacks were in sectors of the city where other poor and immigrant people lived. It was evident to me that there was a growing number of young people in the community. Community residents were from the West Indies, Bermuda, the US, Southwestern Ontario, and after the war, a growing number of Nova Scotia Blacks were evident among the population.[4]

I have always found discussions about what amounts to the generation gap to be interesting. In my more than seventy years of living and over fifty years of surviving in Canada, I can attest to the fact that there always was, as I know it, a generation gap. Back then, those of us in our teens and early twenties thought that it was our time. No one was going to tell us how to groove! We made the best of our youth, but in retrospect, comparing ourselves to youth of today, we were novices.

Toronto and the rest of Ontario were very conservative. Going out for a beer with a young lady meant that once you got to what was called the parlour you entered through separate entrances. If a woman had an escort she could take him to the women's side, but she dared not venture to the men's side.

The restrictive culture of the era was manifest in many Toronto institutions. Buying liquor from the liquor store, for example, required that you have what amounted to a license, which meant that you purchased a book for two dollars. This book allowed you to order liquor from the Liquor Control Board of Ontario (LCBO). To do so, you had to fill out a form for the brands and quantities you wished to purchase. Then you submitted your request to the salesperson, a process that in effect was a sanctioning of your purchase by the Ontario government. Liquor could not be bought on Sundays, when all but a few restaurants were opened anyway. Everyone was supposed to know which side of the tracks he or she belonged on. In this staid environment, Black people knew their place, and acted accordingly.

Along with my community involvement, I continued my swimming activities at the YMCA. In June 1948, the swimming coach invited members of the club to the opening of Sunnyside Beach. He wanted to have some pictures of the swimming club, and this was my first experience swimming outdoors in Canada. I was told to do a few lengths of the pool, and when I dove in, the water was frigid. It felt as if I had emersed my whole body in a bucket of ice water. Feeling frozen, I immediately withdrew, and members of the swim club tried to get my circulation to its normal state by wrapping me in blankets and rolling me on the lawn. My first experience swimming outdoors in Canada destroyed my dream of competing in the marathon that was held annually in August during the world famous, Canadian National Exhibition.

I was not deterred and remained committed to the swim team and played water polo at the western YMCA. Soon after completing a life saving program, I put it to use rescuing a woman who while swimming at Centre Island, had gone out to the breakwall. On her way back, she panicked, lost her nerve and started drowning. Seeing her in distress, I dashed along the shore past a group of onlookers, went into the water, retrieved her and brought her to the shore where she was taken from me by a number of men who were among the spectators idly watching this melodrama. On another occasion, I was invited to swim with a friend at one of the pools located in a highrise building across from the Maple Leaf Gardens. Not realising that it was the deep end, my host jumped in and went to the bottom. Again, I had to come to the rescue of someone. I got into the pool and pulled her out.

Getting accustomed to one's surroundings in a new country is not easy. Adjusting to Toronto, a city that was so different from Kingston, Jamaica was difficult. My older brother Eric was disappointed that the fire had interfered with my plans to go to school, but he soon realized that I had the tenacity to bounce back. Over the years, I have oftentimes listened to new immigrants recount how on arriving in Canada, it is difficult to find affordable housing. I did not have that problem. But my housing situation was less than ideal. It was not difficult for a young single man like myself to find room and board. When I left Eric's house, I moved in with Everald who was renting from a woman who owned a boarding house on Manning Avenue. This was a practical move. Especially because Massey was located at 915 King Street West, and was within walking distance from our lodgings. I had recently started taking evening courses at Central Technical School. Our new digs were located in a row house, and the owner was known for providing shelter for students from the West Indies. After my brother showed interest in one of her daughters, they were later married.

The early years of having to settle for inadequate room and board would eventually influence my decision to later purchase my first home. When you live in someone else's house, you lose your independence, and more importantly, your privacy. Though she was a community-minded person, and very thoughtful, I had some difficulty getting along with my brother's soon-to-be mother-in-law. She could not hold her motherly instinct at bay, and this caused me a great deal of discomfort. I am not a person who takes kindly to anyone dictating to me. We paid her $25.00 each pay period. Yet we were expected to do work around the house, and share a paltry amount of food and drink for lunch. Each morning a pail with food, we had to share was handed to us. This was annoying to me.

Suffering an injury at work when a forklift ran over my foot added insult to injury. Off sick, with my leg extended, hopping on the other leg, and with little money, kept me housebound, a condition that was driving me crazy. It is not like today with television sets in almost every home and a vast array of radio stations to chose from. To make it worse, my wannabe mother placed a mark on the bottle of milk in the icebox, to ensure that when she was at work, none of the boarders helped themselves to some of it. If she returned, and the milk was below the mark, which it sometimes was, she raised hell. There was an old lady who was a boarder in the house; periodically she pinched some of the milk. Of course, I was blamed. Circumstances went from bad to worse and the only solution I told Everald, was for me to move out.

George and I took lodgings in a house near Dundas and Dufferin Streets with the Harrison family, in a location that was still fairly close to my workplace. Not long after doing so, I chose to move again, this time to 145 Augusta Avenue, where I lived with Marra Archibald who was originally from Nevis. She was like a really good mother to me and because of her I learned a lot about the West Indian community in Toronto. To get to my workplace from Augusta, I travelled on the Dundas Street car to Bathurst where I changed and went south by streetcar to King, and took another Street car west to Massey.

Massey was a huge Canadian company with a large number of employees. Of the 4500 workers, I was the fourteenth Black to be hired. It sounds like a small number in today's terms, but for the late 1940s it might not have been. I indicated earlier that when I was looking for work at some of Canada's flagship department stores, I was told repeatedly to go to the railroads since they were hiring porters. It was common practice into the early 1960s for Black men in Canada to be hired primarily as porters by the railroad companies, and many Black women were employed as domestics. However, there were exceptions. A few Black men were hired in other capacities, and at companies, other than the Canadian National and Canadian Pacific Railroads. The recently ended war had broken the stereotypical trend where Blacks were limited to only a few occupations, but it took many more years before a majority of Blacks could seriously entertain gainful employment in a wider category of careers.

Few of the Black workers at Massey did other than the dirtiest jobs in the press and forge department. It was an area requiring the most physical of efforts to put bread on one's table. The heat was so unbearable that it was necessary for us to take salt pills, especially in the summer months to cope with the hellish temperatures. There was a Black man who because of his age and seniority worked as an elevator operator, and yet another was a sweeper. "Big Jim" Matthews from Barbados had the best job among the fourteen of us at Massey. He worked the separator machine that was used for plating the parts for the combines under production. In those days Massey's workforce was a motley cast of characters, a veritable United Nations. In addition to the Ukrainians, there were Poles, English men, French Canadians, Americans, Newfoundlanders and West Indians.

I remember a man from Poland, we called him Popeye, and he did two people's work. He would put the steel on the block with one hand, and use the other to lift a fifteen-pound hammer and hit the steel. Myers, the lead hand in our area had been a Blacksmith in Jamaica, and he could wield a twenty-pound hammer. He was always dressed in a black coat, since Canada, he claimed was always cold and it could snow at anytime. He wore his winter coat, boots and a hat all year long. Even when it was roasting inside the plant, there was always one constant, Myers in his winter gear dressed from head to toe.

It was among these workers, many of whom toiled for long hours, building Massey's farm implement machines, that, I learned to work under extreme circumstances and conform to Canadian standards of productivity. It was also while at Massey that I met a Black man named Bryant who was an historian. He would tell me about the history of the world, and Bryant piqued my interest in Black history when he detailed how Whites had treated Blacks. Bryant, was like many intelligent Black people of his time. They could not get jobs downtown. From time to time as they laboured to feed their families, their bitterness got the better of them and, they displayed a great deal of resentment for what they considered to be White oppression limiting their own ambitions.

My failure to give in to the difficult circumstances I experienced on the job began to pay off. I got a ten-cent and then a fifteen-cent raise, before I knew it I was making $1.25 per hour. In the back of my mind, however, I still felt that I was coming up short. I repeatedly reminded myself of the reason why I had left Jamaica to come to Canada: to go to school. Taking night courses, I thought would not get me where I wanted to be, quickly enough. The fire at my brother's house made me change my plans, but now that I had the job under my belt, I was anxious to learn a trade. Like my father, I wanted to be a welder, and I enrolled at the Chicago Vocational school, located on Weston Road. I encountered my first hurdle when I told the foreman I was doing a welding course, and because it was a day course, I needed to switch to the night shift. "You are crazy", he said, "go get your money back. We have never had any Black welders in this company, and we ain't going to have any Black welders, so save your money!" The heat of the Jamaican sun, not as yet out of my blood, prompted me to reply, "So, I will be the first one!" "Be my guest" the foreman responded. I went to school in the day, and with little rest worked for Massey Ferguson at night.

My plate was full, and I had to coordinate all of my athletic, school, job related and community activities. On reflection what seemed to help me was rather than having too little to do, a variety of activities caused me to learn how to effectively organize my time. In this period, I developed time management techniques that have stayed with me over the course of my professional careers and personal life. My involvement in sports was also a contributing factor. Sports helped me develop a positive attitude about life. Whether it was swimming, playing water polo or soccer I really enjoyed competition. Everald, George and I played soccer with Rogers Majestics Soccer Club.

It was sponsored by the company that later owned radio station CKEY. The team was part of the Toronto District Soccer League. We were the only Black players in the League, a fact that some of the players reminded us of, when they called us "Niggers." It did not hurt our game, and the Armstrong boys developed a reputation as good soccer players. Nearing the end of the 1948 season I convinced my brothers that we should set up our own soccer club. We started looking for recruits among the students from the West Indies studying at the University of Toronto, and among a few high school students who were from Bermuda. I was now sharing a flat at 216 Lippincott Street in the home of the Jamaican-born William Peters[5], who with his wife Ruby had come to Canada early in the twentieth-century.

In our living room we established the Caribbean Soccer Club. The soccer field soon became an arena for some players to display their ethnic rivalries. In one such confrontation I was on the field with Edward Smith, the other players and my brother Everald was the goalie. We were beating the top team, an Italian soccer club in the round-robin competition. The name calling suddenly escalated into a knockout brawl. What amounted to a near riot by both teams discontinued the competition on the field. Our supporters, many of who were White, fearing that the police would arrest us, piled us into their cars and we sped away. Our team disbanded, and in 1951, a Bermudian named Eugene Cox and myself played for the Toronto and District All-Star Soccer Team. George Gross who later wrote for the *Toronto Sun* played for the Hungarian Soccer Club, and for a number of years he and I vied for the position of player with the top score. On one occasion we played together on the Toronto and District All Star Soccer Team. I wrapped up my soccer career in 1953 after playing with Malta United in the Metro Toronto Soccer League.

When the welding course was completed three months later, it was time to make good on my promise to be Massey's first Black welder. The application was filled out for a welding position, and many months went by without a reply. I had been at Massey for one year, and by any standards had performed my job well. Now with the welding course completed I was taking steps to seek advancement in the company. New welders were being hired, and this prompted me to go to personnel, and ask about my application. "It", personnel said, "could not be found." This reply would lead me to take actions that caused me to alter my course. I became more seriously involved in union activities in Canada. In doing so, a whole new world opened up for me, and I was afforded the opportunity to widen my horizons, meet people from all walks of life, contribute to, and work with and for members of Canada's working class.

Chapter 2 – Notes

1. "Drew Immigration Policy Under Fire from Hepburn." The Hamilton Spectator, May 12, 1945. See also Freda Hawkins, Canada and Immigration: Public Policy and Public Concern. (Montreal: McGill-Queen's University Press, 1972), p. 95.

2. For a comprehensive account of Marcus Garvey, his work and impact, see R. A. Hill, ed., The Marcus Garvey and Universal Negro Improvement Association Papers, 10 volumes (UCLA Press, 1983-85). Regarding documentation about the UNIA,s activities in Canada, African Canadian social historiography is still found to be wanting in this area. No known published comprehensive analysis of the Marcus Garvey UNIA led movement in Canada exists. However, African Canadian scholar Leo Bertley has written about the UNIA,s activities in Montreal, Quebec; see for example, "Montreal, the ever Loyal UNIA Division," ttp:/www.qesn.meq.gouv.qc.ca/mpages/unit6/u6p122.htm. Marcus Garvey Scholar, Tony Martin has mentioned some of the UNIA,s activities in Canada in his multitude of works on the subject. See *Race First* (Majority Press, 1986). Little has appeared in scholarly works about the Toronto UNIA,s activities. Some primary source material can be located in the archival records of the Multicultural History Society of Ontario.

3. Very little is known about the history and the important role the TUNA played in the lives of Black Torontonians. What appears on these pages is representative of the sparse documentation that exists about an organization that was active in the 1940s in Toronto's Black community. We would also like to acknowledge the information provided by Rudolpha Hood that added to our perspective of the postwar Black Toronto community.

4. Determining the size of Canada,s Black population has always proven to be a monumental task. Estimates often depended on whom one spoke to. For example, in 1946 Rabbi Abraham Feinberg estimated Canada,s Black population size as 40,000 people; see "Rabbi asks Action to End Negro Ban." *Toronto Daily Star*, February 18, 1946, p. 8. However, in 1951 the supposedly official Canada Census statistics placed the number of Blacks in Canada at 18,020. For an account of the vagaries and anomalies to consider when estimating the size of Canada,s Black population in the period before 1961, see, Daniel Hill, *The Negroes in Toronto: A Sociological Study of a Minority Group*. Unpublished Ph.D. thesis, University of Toronto, 1960.

5. William Peters had worked for Massey Harris for many years.

CHAPTER 3

Solidarity Forever

It was impossible to grow up in Jamaica in the 1930s, as I did, and not be influenced in some small measure by the abundance of trade union activities. Alexander Bustamante's efforts on behalf of working class and other misrepresented Jamaicans did not go unnoticed when in his later years he received a knighthood from the British Crown. As the leader of the Bustamante Industrial Trade Union, he was a role model and hero of mine. When I left school and went to work for R. Hanna and Sons, I did everything possible to emulate "Busta", as he was called, by trying to effectively represent the interests of the thirty-five workers in my department. In turn, they chipped in to ensure that my absences caused by my representations to management on their behalf did not affect the company's production. When I met with the foreman, an English man, whom we referred to as "Mr. Jolly" he took pains to neutralize my efforts by always reminding me that his father had been a coal miner. My response was to tell him that had his working-class father trained him well, we the workers who toiled for meager wages, and were without any benefits, would be able to tell the difference. Additionally, I constantly reminded him that being the foreman, no doubt a position of responsibility, was not license to treat hard working people as if they were serfs.

After I left Jamaica for Canada in December 1947, and went to work for Massey Ferguson, there was no doubt in my mind as to which side of the negotiations' table I preferred to sit on. As fate would have it when Massey's personnel department supposedly misplaced my request for a transfer to the welding department, a new door was opened to me. One that with the passage of time introduced me to the Canadian labour union movement, beyond being a rank and file dues paying member. I am harkening back to a period in which workers' rights and benefits were being steadfastly fought for by a budding union movement. Attempts are now being undertaken by some Canadian politicians to neutralize the gains that working class Canadians achieved in the period following the Second World War. As a consequence of little or no history being taught in the Canadian school system, many members of the postwar generation of Canadians have a meagre understanding of the gains that Canada's working class fought to secure.

The way of life that many Canadians have come to expect as a part of their birthright is still a relatively new phenomenon. In this regard, pressure was brought to bear on governments at every level of the Canadian political system. Such a social agenda was created by legislative initiatives governments put in place as a result of the lobbying efforts of ordinary Canadians. However, my reflections are now being written in a period when our efforts are being severely undermined by the realities of far right wing politics in Ontario. Furthermore, the accomplishments that were made on behalf of the Canadian labour movement are also now being brazenly clawed-back.

The old timers I met in Toronto in the late 1940s would speak with disdain of the 1930s, the years of economic upheaval in Canada. "There was little or no work", they told me, and people lined up at soup kitchens for food. Those without shelter slept in the parks, in the winter and summer; the time of year did not matter. The war ushered in better times for most Canadians. They were now working once again and therefore able to eat and support their families. Men and women who were not stationed overseas found work in the munitions plants and war supported factory system. After the war, following the lead of the British government, Ottawa began introducing measures that amounted to a welfare system. This was done to allow all Canadians to enjoy a basic standard of living. We should not forget that these gains such as the state-supported health insurance plan; employment insurance, welfare and pension benefits, for example, facilitated the design of a real social net in my adopted country. These changes, along with much of the industrial protections like a minimum wage, and a reasonable length working day, occurred because of the efforts of those amongst us with a social conscience. Canadian labour unions have led the rallying cry of ordinary workers. In the process, many workers who dared to dream of a time better than the one in which they lived, made untold sacrifices, including having their heads busted open.

When the personnel department at Massey failed to respond to my request for a transfer to become a welder, I turned my attention in earnest to the union. I needed help. Here was this massive company, with all of the protections; both legal and economic it could muster, against me, the individual. Other people were being hired as welders, and securing such jobs was a guarantee of earning more money. When I received no response to my request to move to the welding department I felt that something was wrong. I had faithfully reapplied a second time for a transfer, and again, I waited for several months without any acknowledgement. Approaching personnel was proving to be useless since each time it quite conveniently reiterated that my request supposedly was misplaced.

Truthfully, I wanted out of the heavy work that I had not mastered. My colleagues had looked after my welfare for a whole year and they had covered for me by making up my production cards. As a testament to their efforts let me be clear. What I mean is that some of my co-workers in the setting department gave me credit for work that I had not done. Cleverly, they allotted someone else's production to me, and though it was a case of good intentions, I felt guilty. Yet I needed to work, and pay for my upkeep. Keep in mind that by the end of the 1940s there was great anticipation in Canadian society. Most of the soldiers had de-enlisted, thousands of immigrants were coming to Canada, and the talk was of good times ahead. To enjoy these good times you needed money and therefore had to be working. Becoming a Massey welder was a chance for me to pull my own weight by working in an area of the plant where I could competently perform tasks that were expected of me. Three months went by, and no one called me for a test or an interview. Again I went to personnel to check out the situation, only to be nonchalantly told that my request for a transfer could not be found. It was clear to me that I was being made a fool of, especially when I was told to apply for a transfer one more time. As a boy I had been taught that it is easier to catch flies with honey than vinegar, and once again I complied.

A couple of months went by and I was not called. Once again I approached the personnel department only to find that again my request for transfer could not be found. Personnel either believed that I had the faith of Job, or somebody at Massey was trying to quietly hold me back. Deciding that I was not going to have any of it, the best thing, I thought was to take advantage of the union's open door policy. Making a quick trip to what was then a union office inside the plant I consulted with the vice-president. His name was Ellis. I told him of my difficulty in trying to become a welder at Massey. Ellis having nothing encouraging to offer made me angry and a little loud and some union members gathered around us to hear my argument. In the middle of my remonstrations, I noticed a well-dressed man who was small in stature walking toward us.

Coming forward, he wanted to know why such a disturbance was taking place. The union's vice president told him why I was beside myself, and the stranger then introduced himself to me as Steve Anko. "I am the president of the union," he politely said to me. "Why are you so disturbed and irate about not being accepted as a welder?" he continued. By the end of my explanation he realized that I was disappointed and frustrated by how I had been treated. "Brother" Mr. Anko said, looking directly in my face "you are now telling me that you have been in this plant for ten months and I have never seen you at one of our monthly union meetings." He asked me if I knew who was the union? I was dumbfounded. Only allowing me a moment's hesitation, looking at me he quickly replied, "you are the union", and pointing to someone nearby he said, "he is the union", and "all the brothers here are the union."

Anko went on to state that we were all links in a big chain and without every link doing its part the union was doomed to failure. Humiliated and ashamed, I just stood there, listened and agreed. I had been at Massey Ferguson for sometime and had not attended meetings, nor did I in anyway other than by paying my dues support Local 439 activities. What Anko was telling me was clear. I acknowledged the union's presence when I needed help, only then did it appear to be important to me. I felt as if someone had once again taken a hockey stick and hit me between my legs. Seeing the light I made a promise to Mr. Anko that from that point onward he would see me at every union meeting. I told him that he would not have any difficulty verifying my presence, because I would sit up front. I left his office with a copy of the Collective Bargaining Agreement he gave me and set about studying it from cover to cover.

In the coming weeks I learned a number of things from my repeated encounters with the union executive that helped to influence my role in Massey union politics. To begin with, at that time, the leadership of local 439 was comprised of mostly men from the British Isles and none of the union offices were held by any non-English speaking Europeans. Work was based on rank order in Canadian society, and status mirrored a similar pattern. At Massey's King Street West plant, the fourteen Blacks and most of its Southern European workers held the jobs that others refused to do. The better jobs were usually given to those who believed that irrespective of their immigrant status, having a British heritage, entitled them to positions in life commensurate with their ethnic ranking in what too, was also their adopted country. It is an attitude that was carried over to the union representing our interests at Massey.

When you are recognized in the eyes of the rank and file members as a "shit disturber" especially if your antics prove successful, rather than being shunned, you attract their support and attention. This is exactly what happened to me at Massey. While I was fighting for my right to become a welder, other workers were admiring my efforts at a distance. Because I spoke up, they saw me as being brave, and soon thereafter, I was encouraged by some of my fellow workers to seek office as union steward. However, as one of the youngest workers in my department, and maybe even in the plant, I did not think that it was prudent to do so. But their constant badgering soon caused me to run for the lesser position of assistant chief steward when I was assured that I could get the necessary support. It is a promise that they kept when I was overwhelmingly elected.

It was during this time in what was fast becoming heightened union involvement at Massey that I remember meeting someone who was to become a lifelong friend of mine. Dennis McDermott started working in the plant in 1948, and he and I agree that it was some time before we met. While we remain unclear as to the actual circumstance that brought us together, we both recollect that we had a mutual friend, Malcolm Raynard, who was half Mohawk. McDermott who later headed the United Auto Workers in Canada was ahead of me in local 439 politics, and he caught my attention by the frank, yet caring manner with which he handled human rights matters. His parents were from Ireland, but he was born in England, and had served in the British Armed Services. He was expelled from South Africa in 1941 for trying to drink at a bar with an African American Merchant Marine in Durban, South Africa. In the late 1940s and beyond, McDermott and I forged many partnerships in the interest of challenging discrimination in Canada. I will turn my attention to this subject matter later on.

The office of chief steward was soon vacant and I took the opportunity to advance my status in the union. I had my name successfully placed in nomination, and then I ran against Murray, the incumbent who was part of the union leadership. Defeating him put me on my way to a ten-year career in the trade union movement. I was now the steward for more than two hundred men in the press and forge and setting departments. It was a responsibility that I took very seriously. Thinking at the time that my success as their spokesperson would only be realized if I lead by example, I set about taking up the challenge of representing all of the workers that found themselves in difficulty. My involvement in union politics at Massey, was a good apprenticeship for my budding community ambitions.

The management at Massey had little sympathy for the rank and file workers. I cleverly took advantage of this situation during my tenure as steward by seizing on every opportunity to rile up the workers. Admittedly, it is unfair to judge Massey's working conditions at the time through lenses that have been radically altered over the past fifty years, especially on the shop floor. But working conditions at Massey were intolerable by any standards. We worked in a dirty place, where the heat caused us to sweat as if we were in hell. The foreman told us we could not use the paper towels in the bathrooms to wipe our faces, instead, we were to use toilet paper. Workers wilting in the heat emanating from the furnaces could not sit. If they did, whatever they used as seats were gone by the following day. So as steward, I did whatever was humanly possible to get on the foreman's nerves. He loved to use a stopwatch to time the workers as they took a bathroom break, so knowing this, I had them going there all day long. When he questioned their actions, I told him they had stomach aches. It was clear to me that the job as welder was placed beyond my reach, but now I had become a serious union official, and I knew how to jab at Massey's ribs whenever I thought its officials to be unfair.

Not in my wildest imagination did I think when I started my journey from Jamaica to Canada that I would play important roles in both union and Black community politics. Advancing from one elected position to another increased my influence in the plant and a year later my name was placed in nomination for the union executive. The plan was to have me run on a slate organized by members of several political factions. Initially, they asked me in 1949 to let my name stand for sergeant at arms. But I discovered that even in the union, some Whites resented an immigrant of colour running for offices that they thought themselves to be incapable of holding. It was a matter of the pecking order, and mine was a position defined by many Canadians as being at the bottom of the ladder. A case-in-point is the candidate who was selected to run for the position of guide.[1] He convinced enough union members to substitute my name with his for sergeant of arms, and mine for that of guide. When the election was held, to my adversary's surprise, more votes were cast for me than even the president of Local 439. Although popular with the membership I had little choice but to settle for the junior position of guide.

Regardless of the devious circumstances, I was honoured to serve on the union's executive and I added to my responsibilities by working on the education, political action, and the human rights committees. The latter in those days was known as the Fair Practices and Anti-Discrimination Committee. I was union guide, for a couple of years and was then asked to assume a more senior position on the slate in the next election, I stood for the position of financial secretary. My unprecedented victory was once again repeated when I received the largest plurality. Serving as the financial secretary allowed me to assist the treasurer and the executive in our local's decision to purchase its first building. We were now able to move from a little garage near King Street West and Strachan Avenue to a three-storey building further west on King. Because this property was the first of the union's holdings it was a big move on the part of Local 439. The rank and file membership later voted to strike for better pay and working conditions. It was the first strike by a United Automobile Workers' Canadian local and it preceded the Ford Local 707 strike in Oakville. I was involved in helping to organize the industrial action that lasted for eleven weeks. My responsibility was to take care of our members by responding to their welfare requests, and ensuring that they had adequate heating and sufficient supplies to meet their individual and families' needs. This was quite a task for me to administer. It was quite an experience to hear the squeaky wheels complaining endlessly about wanting additional benefits, and needing more coal in their bins to heat their homes.

During the strike we purchased a larger premises. It was an old ink factory located at 65 Shaw Street along with two houses next door that became our new union hall. The new property came in handy during the strike when it not only served as an office but in order to feed our members on the picket lines we also stored adequate amounts of food at this location. To meet the needs of Local 439 members what back then was commonly referred to as a "scrounge squad" was set up. Its mission included soliciting food from local merchants for the strikers doing duty on the picket lines. After eleven weeks we had a bounty of contributed items in our storage area, including foodstuff, bread, coffee, ham, cheese – you name it. Having so much food in our stocks allowed us to donate some of it to the local social welfare agencies. While the strike at Massey was unfolding, hurricane Hazel struck the city of Toronto and caused the loss of a number of lives and major infrastructure damage. Some of our rank and file members volunteered to leave the picket line and help with the search for bodies in various parts of the city. When the strike was over we had a surplus in the strike fund, and all of the union members received bonuses. Over the course of the strike Local 439 members and its executive had gained a tremendous amount of experience, and subsequently we were called on when workers at Ford and General Motors dramatized the extent of their grievances by walking the picket lines.

Word got around about my union activities, and about the fact that I appeared to be willing to err on the side of the little guy, and it was just a matter of time before I started receiving literature from the communist party. Everything was done to recruit me. But I just said, "listen, if you are really interested in my welfare, give me a break." In addition to being Black, the communists wanted me to be red.[2] With two strikes against me, I would not need much more to be out since this was occurring in a period when being what was termed a "commie", meant that you could not go across the Canada-US border. In the midst of the Guzenko Spy Affair,[3] Canadians, especially the Royal Canadian Mounted Police were in no mood to stomach communists, and Black ones at that. I did attend a couple of study sessions that were held by members of the communist party, and quite frankly, I found them to be educational, but that is where it ended. A lot more can be said about Toronto Blacks and Communism, but that subject is for the historians.

My next venture was to transfer from the press and forge where I had worked in what was known as the worst part of the plant. I transferred to the combine area where the lines operate and the sub-assemblies were done in departments adjacent to the assembly line. Such a move caused quite a stir. I did not hide my ambitions to become part of Local 439's upper echelon. But to do so I needed more experience in union politics. In the process I hoped that my leadership skills would improve significantly. I also wished to return later to this area of the plant where the low status rank and file members were stuck. Using the skills I had gained from the plant's more progressive wings and union establishment I could seek to more effectively represent their interests. Immediately following my transfer the chief steward in department 128, signalled to me that he was threatened by my presence in his area. I had already learned that people with power do not usually voluntarily relinquish it. This is especially true when a new face comes on the block, where every attempt is made by the status quo to indicate that despite ability one must wait for their turn.

I reflected on the similarity of this situation to my involvement in the Toronto United Negro Association and even though some of the other younger members and myself had unseated the status quo leadership, we were prevented from assuming office. Incumbency was thought of as a lifelong privilege. This time I faced opposition from a leadership, which sensed that my presence was a signal of an impending challenge. The department 128 chief steward quickly joined forces with the department foreman and together; they did everything possible to undermine my integrity. Simply put, their task was to either thwart my ambitions, or get me fired. I soon found myself doing the lowest paying jobs; meaning of course, hard work without fair remuneration. This went on for a while, but as fate would have it, in addition to McDermott's support someone else joined forces with me. As this power play unfolded it underscored the fact that union and non-union politics is about forming alliances to ensure one's survival.

A man named Dick Dickinson, who was the area committee representative, threw his fortunes in with mine. He was a big robust Canadian and though not very good at delivering his messages during union meetings, Dickinson's negotiating abilities were second to none. He was well liked by just about everyone in the rank and file. Working together with him afforded me a cloak of protection because he looked after the interests of the workers under his control. Management was out to get me, and unashamedly used every available pressure tactic at its disposal. On three separate occasions I received dismissal slips and my survival was due only to the intervention of Big Dick Dickinson and Dennis McDermott. Dickinson had the notices of my dismissal withdrawn and got me reinstated with some changes in my job responsibilities. Even so, the pressure put on me by the chief steward and the foreman continued, but eventually, I prevailed. By the time of the election for steward, I was suffering from the wear and tear of my battle to hold on to my job. Not sufficiently so, however, for me to retreat. Throwing my hat in the ring for the position allowed my supporters to cast their ballots in my favour, and I gladly accepted the position of department 128 chief steward.

As I climbed the union's executive ladder, I remembered one of my father's favourite sayings: "hard work and ambition never killed anyone." When I assumed the role as the department 128 chief steward, certain changes abounded. There was talk among the area's rank and file members about me trying for the office area committee person. This responsibility took in a major part of Massey's operations: the assembly line, department 128, the sheet metal department that was close by, the welding department and two other sub-assembly departments. Since I felt that Dickinson was a very sound administrator, I had no inclination of running against him. But when the office of vice president became vacant and he secured it, I contested his old position successfully. Now I was well on my way toward becoming part of the union's inner circle where I had a bird's eye view of how organizations function. Attending union meetings allowed me to listen to the parliamentarians who were mostly former British trade unionists from England,

Scotland, Ireland and Wales. Along with learning more about the parliamentary principles I also familiarized myself with the day to day running and building up of organizations. Those persons who dominated the floor during union meetings had to be very competent speakers. While addressing pertinent issues at great length many of them appeared to know every parliamentary procedure that was ever written.

They were the big boys of union politics, and I wanted to become more effective in my presentations on the floor so that I too, could carry out the tasks the membership expected of me. After all that was why I had been elected successively. In this regard, I purchased my first copy of *Roberts Rules of Order*. It is a how-to book about the mechanics of running meetings and administering organizations. Reading and rereading *Robert Rules of Order*, I soon concluded, was insufficient to readily improve my deficits. My wish to swim in the same waters as the big boys of union politics required that I seriously work on my personal development. My own inadequacy as a speaker, was especially telling during debates at meetings. Here I was someone who was elected to represent the interests of a significant part of the membership, yet I loathed putting my hands up or getting on the floor to make points or, counter points. At this rate, the interests of the members would not be ably served.

After seeing an advertisement in a Toronto newspaper for a ten-week public speaking course I decided to attend the information session. An initial demonstration was held in a church at St. Clair Avenue West and Avenue Road. Picking me out of the audience, the instructor called me up front and I could hardly utter my name. He asked me what I did for a living, where I worked, what were my hobbies, and how do I go about doing certain things. I remember shaking in my boots and, he kept guiding me by putting words in my mouth. Gradually, my confidence improved, and I felt more at ease. Surviving the first night led me to enrol and take the ten-week course. After the fourth week I had gained enough confidence to get up and give impromptu speeches. To encourage our progress, prizes for the most improved and best speeches were given out each week of which I had my share.

On graduation night each of us were required to give a five-minute speech on a topic of our choice. I chose to speak about the disabled, and a major part of my presentation was about the blind. Emphasis was placed on their circumstances. Everyone present was reminded of the accomplishments they had made despite the fact that they had to survive in a society where many people oftentimes treated them as second class citizens. Having completed the course, and with repeated reference to *Robert Rules of Order*, I dramatically improved both my self-esteem and public speaking. Now I was capable of taking my place among the union debaters. Attending the Toronto Trades and District Labour Council monthly meetings, I participated in debates on the future of unionism. In the process, I learned a great deal during these sessions, and my personal development allowed me to use these skills and knowledge within my own community.

My brief adventures in other areas of the plant did not break my bond with my colleagues who worked under the worst conditions and earned starvation wages in the press and forge, and setting areas. After completing my leadership preparation, I submitted my request for a transfer to go back there. My action provoked quite a debate among management and I was told that it was customary for personnel to receive requests from workers wishing to transfer to better jobs. "Nobody to date", management told me, "had ever requested a transfer to return to one of the worst areas of the plant." Yet, I felt that I owed my successes to my friends who over the years had helped me do my job. Oftentimes it is hard to describe loyalty to others, but many of these individuals had stood by me when I started out at Massey. They had made it possible for me to earn my keep in a tough working environment where production was based on one's ability to repeatedly pound a hammer, lift heavy pieces of steel, and withstand the rigors of heartless foremen. If this was not enough, when I sought elected office in the union, they stood with me against more powerful forces in the plant. Like the prodigal son when the day came I returned to my old department, confident that I could continue where I had left off, a few years before.

I had to stick around for a while before there was an election for office. The opportunity was given to me to gain some hands-on experience. I was able to reacquaint myself firsthand, with the deplorable conditions my colleagues faced in their daily quest to make a living. Although still holding office as the union's financial secretary, this was an administrative portfolio that did not give me the opportunity to work directly with the membership. It took nine months before an election was called for the chief steward's position. I eagerly stood for the office, and anxiously awaited the results. After receiving the mandate, I immediately started a campaign to improve working conditions and wages for workers in the press and forge and setting areas.

Aided by my improved knowledge of union activities, I now had a better grasp of my capabilities. In my monthly column for the union paper I made sure that stories were published about the happenings and poor conditions under which the workers laboured for example in the press and forge area. When the general manager got wind of what was happening, in September 1955 he gave the foreman notice. Telling him that too many grievances were originating in his department, the general manager indicated that something had to be wrong, which meant that production was affected. Returning to his office, the foreman summoned me, indicating that I had destroyed his career, and he proceeded to take a few strips off my back. But it was too late for him. He had done the workers under his charge a disservice. It was his pattern to treat them as slaves to wage labour. Timing their washroom breaks was one of many incidents he used to intimidate them. Since he was considered to be part of Massey's management team, he was without any representation. There was no one to fight on his side. Accepting his fate, he left the plant and went to work for General Motors in Oshawa where he later retired.

Chapter 3 – Notes

1. Guide was a lowly union executive position and as the need arose the person elected to this office assisted other members of the executive with their duties.

2. With the passage of time members of certain ethnic groups in Canada who became familiar with Canada's communist party agenda have developed amnesia. By the 1960s, it was no longer fashionable to openly admit one's communist leanings. The rise of the new liberalism in North America also railroaded the communist agenda. There was however a longstanding connection between communists in Canada and in the United States. Individuals such as the late Lenny Johnson who owned the Third World Bookstore openly admitted to Sheldon Taylor that he was a card-carrying member of the communist party in the 1940s. In his book, *Black Bolshevik: Autobiography of An Afro-American Communist* (Chicago: Liberator Press, 1978), Harry Haywood mentions the Canadian communist party. In the 1920s, Haywood was a member of the US communist party. As one of the founders of the American Negro Labor Congress (ANLC), in the 1920s the FBI became interested in his activities. He had to leave for Europe by way of Canada. As he made good his escape, his safety was secured by some of the deans of Canadian communism. Haywood remembers meeting Jim McDonald and Tim Buck at the Toronto headquarters of the communist party. McDonald and Buck are names that were quite familiar to some members of Toronto's Black community. In the early 1950s, the Toronto wing of the Canadian communist party held study sessions for Blacks in an

apartment building on Augusta Avenue. City Alderman, Joe Salsberg was one of the organizers. After visiting Russia in the 1950s, he become disillusioned and denounced communism.

3. The defection in 1946 in Ottawa of Soviet spy Igor Gouzenko revealed the existence of organized communist spy rings in Canada.

CHAPTER 4

No Racism Here

By the early 1950s, the age of Canadian liberalism had not as yet set in. But in what was the post war years, everyone's attention in Canada was focused on the politicians' promise of: better times ahead. "Better times" was a phrase that appeared in the media, to indicate that now that the war years were over, everyone could expect an improved standard of living. The magazines and newspapers of the day foretold of happier times. The happy kitchen filled with gadgets for suburban housewives, well-paid jobs for their husbands, and unbridled economic boom for Canadians ushered in a new prosperity. The war years had allowed some Black Torontonians to improve their standard of living, but not sufficiently so to equal that of many Whites. An indicator of a growing economic base for some Toronto Blacks was reflected in the state of affairs in their churches. For the first time in decades, the First Baptist Church located on University Avenue and Edward Street was not operating in the red. Several years hence, its congregation would move to a new building, not much more than a decade after the church had held its mortgage burning when nearly all of its members were earning an income.

Some of the younger Blacks, including myself were becoming increasingly impatient. Steady paying jobs did not add up to equal treatment for us in Canada. We wanted what many other Canadians seemed to be enjoying. In the words of

Martin Luther King Jr. we "wished to be judged based on our abilities and the content of our character, and not the colour of our skins." Our world was changing rapidly, and the newspapers we read told us that nationalism was on the minds of many subjugated peoples. The United Nations Universal Declaration of Human Rights in 1948 signaled to many of us in the trade union movement that the time was right to seek positive changes in a world that had not always been fair to the poor and the powerless. In Canada, the question of French Canadian rights and redress for the World War Two internment of Japanese Canadians were topical subjects. In the United States A. Philip Randolph's Brotherhood of Sleeping Car Porters had fought successfully to improve working conditions for Black porters on the railroads. In the 1940s, the Brotherhood of Sleeping Car Porters in Canada had also negotiated more pay and secured a reduced number of hours that Black porters were required to work each month. These outcomes convinced us that a better future for our community lay in organization, agitation, and activism. The examples were clear. Mahatma Ghandi's non-violent activism had aided his efforts to wrestle India from the jaws of the British Raj. In Jamaica, and elsewhere in the West Indies, a new generation of leaders was actively seeking to chart their countries' destinies.

Although I had found a job that was paying me a good wage, as a Black person living in 1950s Canada, my soul was not well. Canadian racism and prejudice caused me to operate in an environment with narrow margins. The signs around me suggested that I could only go so far. For although Black men and women had helped to fight Canada's battles during two World Wars, in the early 1950s, many Canadian-born Blacks were forced to continue accepting jobs primarily on the railroads or in other service sector areas. It was not a question of a glass ceiling; it was the reality of a brick wall that we as Black people faced each day. Our community too, had its brighter lights, some of whom had seized the opportunity and attended various Canadian and American post-secondary institutions. Promising leaders such as Lincoln Alexander who later became the province of Ontario's Lieutenant Governor, and Leonard Braithwaite the first-known Black to be elected to the Ontario legislature in the 1960s, were showing in the 1950s that they too, had the right stuff. They excelled academically and continued to maintain a strong identity with their local Black community. But even with a first-class education, I saw that they still faced an uphill battle. In this period, the winds of change though not with the same force, had already begun blowing in our direction. And it was just a matter of time before the ills of Canadian racism and prejudice were to be effectively challenged by some of us. Leaders like Ghandi had shown us that we were actors capable of setting a course toward defining and achieving our own advancement.

As far as I was concerned, my activities in the trade union movement at Massey set me on a similar course like Alexander and Braithwaite. My own involvement in Toronto's Black community provided me with a ticket to be part of the budding human and civil rights movement that had predated my arrival in Canada in the late 1940s. In the 1950s, because of the efforts of groups like the Toronto Joint Labour Committee for Human Rights, the Government of Ontario recognized that racism and prejudice were evident in Canada's largest province.[1] Accordingly, to fight these evils it was necessary for those of us involved in human and civil rights initiatives to use the bully pulpit of government legislation, community organizing, communication strategies and alliance building. An outcome of our efforts was the Ontario government's establishment of a broader human rights code and the institution of the Ontario Human Rights Commission in 1962.² It was the first of its kind in Canada.

A lot has been made of the postwar civil rights agenda in the United States, but some Canadians who identify with the era that I am writing about, can also take pride in their efforts to right the wrongs of discrimination and racism that were evident in their midst. However, one required a lot of nerve to undertake such initiatives in the cold war era. As I have stated before, the immediate postwar period in Canada was less about righting social ills and more about moving on with an economic agenda. Canada's social ills when discussed publicly were usually commented on by left of centre politicians and labour leaders. In 1953, during the onslaught of the cold war, Cooperative Commonwealth Federation (CCF)³ Ontario provincial leader, Donald McDonald reminded Canadians that: "[a] t a time when the fate of the world may hang on the building of good relations among people of different colour, [they were continuing] flagrant discrimination against fellow-Canadians solely because they are Negro".⁴

McDonald's statement alludes to the fact that in the cold war period countries like Canada's Achilles' heel was race relations. This was a period when the West was pointing its finger at the Soviet Union, accusing it of subjugating countless numbers of people, especially minorities within its political and geographic boundaries. While Canada's Black population was small, its members, representing a distinctive minority were not treated well. Many Canadians ignored racial discrimination in their midst and paid attention instead to how badly African Americans were treated in the US. The apogee of the American civil rights movement was still a decade away. However race relations' studies such as the one commissioned by the Carnegie

Endowment entitled *An American Dilemma*[5] by Gunnar Myrdal, ensured that some attention was paid to the pervasive discrimination south of the border by an increasing number of Americans. The National Association for the Advancement of Coloured People (NAACP); some African American Church congregations, and a plethora of organizations dedicated to the cause of improved US civil rights had begun to push for change.

The problem was not just one of trying to keep Canada White, in fact, it was the extent to which Blacks, Jews and Native people, amongst others were being treated as second class citizens. The discussion of Ottawa's immigration policy in the next chapter underscores this point. Many bars, restaurants, and places of employment openly discriminated on the basis of race. This was not just hearsay. Organizations like the Toronto Joint Labour Committee To Combat Racial Intolerance and Local 439's Fair Practices and Anti-discrimination Committee had strategies in places to fight such bigotry. In 1948, the Youth Employment Centre undertook a study of the problems certain minority groups encountered while attempting to secure gainful employment. This study supports my contention that while White Anglo Saxon Protestants enjoyed certain privileges, Jews, Blacks and persons of Japanese ancestry for example, were not as fortunate.

The number of Jewish employers in the late 1940s had increased overall, yet Jews were still having problems finding gainful employment.[6] Although many members of Toronto's Japanese community had success in finding work, they felt that their placements prevented them from "making maximum contributions to their community." This was just a polite way of saying that the colour of their skin prohibited their upward mobility in Canada. Blacks on the other hand had a great deal of difficulty irrespective of their qualifications. Traditionally, work for most of them lay in menial occupations. What was then called the National Employment Service (NES), the forerunner to the modern day Human Resources Development Canada was found to be discriminatory by many Black Canadians. Seventy-five percent of Black females in Toronto in the late 1940s could only secure the help of the NES to obtain Domestic Work. In its recommendations, the survey indicated that both legislation and inducements to employers were required to overcome the blatant prejudice in employment.[7]

The political climate was less welcoming to the efforts of those of us who tried to improve race relations in Canada. Not much had been done historically in terms of legislation to alter Ontario's race relations' situation. When Harry Gairey Jr. was prevented in 1945[8] from skating at the Icelandia rink because of the colour of his skin, his father Harry Gairey Sr. protested to Joe Salsberg, a city of Toronto Alderman. Salsberg with the help of forward thinking individuals like Rabbi Abraham Feinberg pushed to have more favourable accommodation for all Torontonians. The Fair Employment Practices Act (1951) was still only an idea in 1948. During this time Leslie Wismer, MPP, and publicity director for the Trades and Labour Congress, Albert G. Watson, a member of the Fellowship for Reconciliation and the Reverend J.T. Dawson of the British Methodist Episcopal Church sat on a non-violent action committee for the Race Relations Institute.[9] One of that committee's tasks was to monitor Toronto hotels, restaurants and clubs that were suspected of practicing discrimination on the basis of race, creed, or religious affiliation. Black people knew where we were and where we were not welcomed.

Dance Halls like the Old Mill, Playters Hall, the Embassy, Palais Royale, Palace Pier, Masonic Hall and Columbus Hall kept us out. The management of hotel dining-rooms in the

King Edward, Windsor Arms, Royal York, Prince George, New Barclay and Park Plaza allowed us in via the employees entrance to do the dirty work, but not at the front entrance to be served. The plight of Black Canadians provoked human rights leader Rabbi Feinberg to compare their circumstances with those of Black Americans. "Negroes in Canada have been victimized by the same contempt. Their plight is less dramatic and noticeable but not a whit less challenging to the decency and democracy and destiny of free Canadians."[10]

Members of the Tory or Conservative Party in Ontario usually numbered among the well heeled, the monied, and those who preferred to keep Canada lily-white. Yet, ironically, it would be the Tories who introduced legislation leading to the creation of various civil rights protections like the Fair Accommodation Practices Act and by 1962, the Ontario Human Rights Commission. Ontario Premier Leslie Frost met in 1950 at Queen's Park with representatives from seventy groups who were part of the budding civil rights movement in Ontario. I was included in the deputation to Frost who listened attentively to notables in the Canadian civil rights movement like Irving Himel, executive secretary of the Association for Civil Liberties. The premier was noncommittal but he accepted our brief in which we outlined our requests including a recommendation that a board should be set up to investigate complaints of discrimination. We indicated to Frost that although the Ontario government had passed the Ontario Racial Discrimination Act in 1944, not much more had been done since then to fight racial and religious intolerance. The premier was friendly but members of the delegation realized that changes would only result from our ongoing vigilant efforts.

As Joseph MacKenzie, the representative for the Ontario Federation of Labour (OFL) told Frost, "trade unions have been fighting for years to bring about the changes in the brief that was given to him."[11] Members of the disenfranchised, including, Jews, Blacks, representatives of Labour, and some members of the Japanese community, for example, united under the umbrella of the Joint Labour Committee to Combat Racial Intolerance. Its agenda remained the same, that is: fighting against religious intolerance, prejudice and racism. Fighting discrimination and racism in Canada in the late forties and fifties was no easy feat. We had to put ourselves on the line. Which usually meant that when reports were received by the Joint Labour Committee to Combat Racial Intolerance about a certain establishment discriminating against minorities, test cases were carried out by its members and associates to determine the validity of such claims.

On Friday, June 05, 1953, Dennis McDermott and myself went to the Mercury Athletic Club in Toronto. Getting past the door check, I took the lead and moved toward a seat at the bar. Suddenly, the hostess appeared and approaching me she asked if I had a membership card. Looking at her, I replied, "no!" I asked her, "do I require a membership card to enter?" She nodded her head [in the affirmative]. There was no doubt, her answer was "yes." While the hostess was speaking with me I saw White patrons entering and they were only being asked, if they "required beer or cocktails?" McDermott and I were there to do a test case. The point had been proven, but we had to be sure. I left the Mercury Club and met McDermott outside. He then returned to the club with another White person, named George Clyde. Asking the doorman if they required a membership to enter, he politely replied to McDermott, "that's OK sir, let me show you to your table." He was the chairperson of Local 439, Fair Practices and Anti-Discrimination Committee. Not long after a letter was sent to the Liquor License Board of

Ontario. The Board headed by Judge W. T. Robb had previously received a number of similar complaints from persons throughout Ontario. The Board's help was necessary since it oversaw all Ontario establishments that were legally selling liquor. The Liquor Licensing Board, if it chose to, could have taken measures to see that clubs and taverns it licensed ensured that all patrons received fair treatment. Since liquor sales were essential to the overall profitability of such establishments we naturally wished to see the Mercury Athletic Club's license suspended as a deterrent to other institutions that knowingly discriminated against minorities. But four months later, in October 1953, the Liquor Licensing Board, as a Board member of the City of Toronto Board of Control put it, "was refusing to face up to its responsibility."[12]

The only option left to us was to take the matter into the public arena, which meant, repeatedly calling it to the media's attention. Our Joint Committee to Combat Racial Intolerance provided a report documenting similar incidents going back to 1949. The *Toronto Star* picked up on our claims that the Liquor Licensing Board was more interested in seeking "refuge in technicalities rather than addressing the issues of racist discrimination." Various reports of these developments in the media caused Sammy Luftspring, former boxer and co-owner of the Mercury Athletic Club to deny charges in the *Toronto Telegram* of discrimination at his establishment. Infuriated by his recalcitrance we decided to turn up the heat. With the help of Donna Hill who was now the committee's executive secretary, a letter writing campaign was undertaken to enlist the aid of as many sympathizers as possible. Additionally, we continued to take sworn statements from patrons at the club to emphasize the point that, although many of them were not members, being White ensured that they were not turned away. Donna who was

White and her husband Daniel Hill who later headed the Ontario Human Rights Commission went to the Mercury club in 1953. While removing his coat, Dan Hill who was Black was asked for proof of membership; having none they both left. The Liquor Licensing Board eventually dismissed the case against the club, but the message was clear, discrimination of any kind in Ontario would not go unchallenged.

Our human and civil rights agenda required an unrelenting attitude on the part of those of us who were committed to righting such wrongs in the early 1950s. With the passage of time, it would be easy for me to state that we felt that all of our efforts to eliminate racism in Ontario were done on behalf of future generations of Canadians. On reflection this is only partly true. For we also wished to secure a better life for ourselves. How does one explain to the Hip-Hop or the so-called Generation Xers what it was like to live in society, in a period, when to be Black was to be numbered amongst the powerless. Operating in an Anglo-Saxon world our every move was calculated. We were always assessing the situation: Yes we can go into this neighbourhood; no we cannot go to see the Jazz band since it is performing at a club which discriminates; it is no point applying for that job since we are going to be told that the railroads are hiring. Our lives were guided by the limitations Whites placed on us. The task was monumental. Actions for change and our betterment required not just our efforts, our personal ambitions, but the sympathies of a minority of Whites who chose to stand and fight along side us.

The feeling we had, meaning those of us who fought in the trenches for rights and freedoms that are now taken for granted by many Ontarians, was that our victories should be measured centimeter by centimeter. Even after the Ontario Legislature's passage of the Fair Employment Practices Act in

1951, nothing really changed. The company that I worked for, Massey Harris contravened the spirit of the Act when in 1953, it "caused to be published, in the *Toronto Star*, an advertisement ...that specified that tool designers must be Canadian born or British subjects."[13] Ontario provincial legislation with an aim of altering the way things had traditionally been done was not taken seriously by a majority of Whites. This attitude was not just steeped in ignorance; more so, it was entrenched in a failure to accept the fact that racism was as Canadian as hockey. This point was soon driven home by media reports of the manner in which Dresden's Black residents were treated.

There is no other way to say it than to describe Dresden in the late 1940s and 1950s as Canada's Alabama. It was situated in Southwestern Ontario with a Black population of approximately twenty-percent of the total. Dresden is located in an area of Ontario directly in the path of the Underground Railroad. It is ensconced in the nineteenth-century legacy of Harriet Beecher Stowe's characters in *Uncle Tom's Cabin*. It was a town in which discrimination was openly practiced against people with Black skins, and as is usually the case, there were many vivid examples to prove the point to the contrary. Black and White kids attended the same schools, engaged in Boy Scouts' and Girl Guides' activities. However, they went their separate ways when it was time to have ice cream or a soda in local restaurants. The hostility toward Blacks went beyond the usual subtleties of Canadian racism. With the exception of the Catholic Church, religious services were segregated. All of this was taking place in a town in which the only soldier from Dresden, Ontario who was killed during active war duty in Korea in 1953 was Black.[14]

Dresden's Black population historically, was forced to grin and bear the awful treatment based on the principles of

Canadian segregation. Restaurants and barbershops had blatantly refused to serve Black patrons, actions for which there was little or no recourse. The nature of the attention Dresden was receiving in the early 1950s divided the community along racial lines. In a 1953 editorial, the *Windsor Star* agreed with Toronto's Rabbi Abraham Feinberg when he "warned that incidents of racial discrimination in Dresden and elsewhere in Canada furnished material for communist propaganda in other parts of the world."[15] However, like many of its readers, the newspaper was unwilling to accept the fact that racism was a pervasive feature of Canadian society. The newspaper thought it best to blame a handful of troublemakers living in Dresden. It also stated: "that most of the headaches [came] from outsiders refusing to accept some of the understandings of the community."[16]

Dresden's Black population numbered in the hundreds, and with limited political clout, their complaints about unfairness sometimes caused them to receive threats against their lives, families, and property. In 1949, local Black leader W. J. Carter and his nephew Hugh Burnette were warned by letter that they would be destroyed. It was signed "Danger, with a skull and cross-bones."[17] It was also in 1949 that Dresden residents voted 517 to 108 to oppose a by-law that would have made it illegal for that town's businesses to refuse to serve Blacks. When I met Burnette, he was one of the leaders of the National Unity Association. It was an organization fighting racism on the local front, and the association provoked the ire of the *Windsor Star* and many residents in Southwestern Ontario. Burnette, the secretary of the association owned a carpentry business and he was being squeezed economically by a local wood mill. Not just for his refusal to meet the demands of one of its manager's who allegedly wanted kickbacks in exchange for contracts. More importantly, Burnette was being punished for showing Dresden to be a racist place to the rest of the world. The *Toronto Telegram* newspaper reporter Gordon Donaldson was shocked by the treatment Gladys Grizzle and Julian Brooks of Toronto received when they visited a Dresden restaurant. Donaldson concluded: "Dresden doesn't like the publicity because publicity is slowly killing the prejudice that has flourished there for so long."[18]

The National Unity Association focused its attention on discrimination practiced by two of the three local restaurants, the town's five barbershops, its three poolrooms, and one beauty parlour. Dresden's Black residents had seen positive results when discrimination was fought successfully. In fact, the White owner of Martin's Dairy Bar claimed to have seen his business improve considerably when Blacks were provided with nondiscriminatory service.

In May 1954, the US-born Sid Blum replaced Donna Hill as the executive secretary of the Toronto Joint Labour Committee for Human Rights. Hill was about to give birth to Daniel Hill Jr., the now famous Canadian singer. We were fortunate to have Blum as part of our team. He had fought discrimination and as a Jew had felt the harsh realities of anti-Semitism in the US. His experience agitating and controlling the scenarios for test cases were immensely useful to those of us who had to put our friends in harms way. When Blum visited Dresden in July 1954, he was told by a White minister that: "all Negroes wanted was to marry with Whites." Blum mentioned in his report that the minister "was terribly anxious" for him to meet "the *right* kind of Negro who would tell him "the right kind of story."[19] To make matters worse "outsiders" as the *Windsor Star* called us, began focussing attention on Dresden.

In 1954, the Leslie Frost government set out more clearly the Fair Accommodations Practices Act provisions. We were keenly interested in Chapter 28, Sections 2 and 6 that read:
> "No persons shall deny to any person or class of persons the accommodation, services, or facilities available in any place to which the public is customarily admitted because of the race, creed, colour, nationality, ancestry, or place of origin of such person or class of persons."

The Joint Labour Committee for Human Rights' efforts in Dresden were a continuation of the 1953 initiatives against Judge Robb and the Ontario Liquor Licensing Board. By the time we were finished, it was not just a matter of us being called "outsiders." As the Ontario minister, Charles Daley whose Labour Department was mandated with the responsibility of enforcing the Fair Accommodations Act put it, we were members of " a communist group." Before any charges could proceed under the Fair Accommodations Act, the minister responsible had to give his permission. Daley was adamant in his refusal to prosecute Dresden business owners, accused of discriminating against Blacks.[20]

I had the experience of working with Dennis McDermott in test cases including those at the Mercury Athletic Club. To put the Dresden situation to the test, I joined forces with Hugh Burnette and University of Toronto graduate, Canadian-born Ruth Lor whose parents were Chinese. We were wary of Daley's claims that our efforts were communist-directed, and given the minister's prejudice against our efforts, we were careful to ensure that an already tense situation in Dresden would not be further inflamed. At one point, the threats made against Burnette's life included the following in a note sent to him: "Be careful" it read, "No more of this publicity. There is a place in the graveyard for you." [21] Burnette fearing the worst armed himself with a revolver.

When Sid Blum and I visited Kay's Cafe, owned by Morley McKay on September 30, 1954, the atmosphere was very tense. We were there as a test group, and our aim was to determine if the restaurant staff would serve a Black patron. Arriving at 5.45 p.m., we sat down in one of the booths and waited to be served. Other patrons were seated in the restaurant. I was the only Black person there. After we sat down, the waitress went immediately to the back, and after two additional White patrons entered, a man wearing a white apron emerged, pulled down the blinds and locked the front door. He also turned some of the restaurant's lights off. The two persons who arrived after us were soon served, and for the next twenty-five minutes there was a steady stream of traffic through Kay's Cafe. Entering or leaving meant that the door had to be locked and unlocked each time by restaurant staff. Without being served we left at 6.10 p.m.

A second test case was undertaken on October 1, 1954. It was on a Saturday evening at around 7.15 p.m., Sid Blum, two other persons from Windsor, Ontario and myself entered Kay's Cafe. There were other patrons in the restaurant, whose needs were attended to. When Blum asked proprietor, Morley McKay, if we would be served, he nodded his head, and continued walking to the back of the restaurant. Again, I was the only Black person in the restaurant. We left at 7.40 p.m. without receiving any service. As difficult as it was we kept our frustration in check. Keeping the faith, we returned to Kay's Cafe on October 5, 1954 at about 2.50 p.m. Arriving ahead of Blum and myself were two White acquaintances of ours from London, Ontario. When we were taking our seats, they were already being served. Once again, I was the only Black in the establishment, and after not being paid any attention by Kay's Cafe staff, Blum and I left at 3.15 p.m. To do so, I unlocked the restaurant's door.

Morley McKay had been given every opportunity to demonstrate that Blacks could be served in his cafe. We had now experienced what untold numbers of Blacks from Dresden and surrounding areas knew for a long time: Black patrons were not wanted in McKay's Cafe. Dresden was not the kind of place that Blacks from surrounding areas wished to be stuck in overnight. Many of them would go out of their way to avoid being there at that time. For in some of their minds it was the Alabama of the North. McKay had asked for a fight and despite the non-support of Charles Daley, and many others, we were going to make sure that he got one. Ruth Lor, Hugh Burnette and I went to Kay's Cafe on October 29, 1954, and when I ordered coffee, McKay told me that he was too busy. We also went to another restaurant operated by Matthew Emerson, and found the doors closed when we tried to enter. It was time to cut to the chase.

Minister Charles Daley appointed a one-man Commission to investigate discrimination in Dresden. Judge William F. Schwenger from Hamilton, Ontario, was asked to write a report in what amounted to one of Daley's stalling tactics. We were getting no where. The Ontario minister of Labour either lacked the will, or chose not to enforce, either the spirit, or the letter of the law, set out in the Act which was legislation enacted by his government. The recourse we had was that of filing an official complaint under the Fair Accommodations Act (1954), to the same minister who had labeled our activities in Dresden as "communist-inspired." The Joint Labour Committee and the Dresden based National Unity Association decided to put the law to the test to determine its validity. Using the above incidents and a number of complaints from local Dresden and surrounding area Blacks we sought redress in the courts. Complaints were registered with the Department of Labour, and the media were informed of our activities.

During the test cases at McKay and Emerson restaurants fate was on our side, when Ruth Lor, Syd Blum and I accompanied by a *Toronto Telegram* reporter and photographer were refused service.[22] At the heart of the matter was whether or not the province had the power to enforce such an Act–with criminal penalties attached. We knew that those found guilty under the Act could only suffer a maximum fine of $50. But more importantly was the publicity such persons attracted during the court battle that helped to draw attention to our cause. The sordid revelations about their discriminatory behaviour would have a direct impact on their ability to keep their businesses economically viable. Daley ran for cover, but each time ways were found for him to take the heat. His boss, Leslie Frost, the premier of Ontario, said in January 1955 that he stood by what he called "the finest piece of legislation [that] is constitutional."[23]

We knew that our efforts would yield results that would have to be measured in centimeters, and not meters. The task was tiresome, and our efforts were mainly volunteer-based. We had our allies and detractors in the media, but ultimately, we had faith that we were standing on solid ground. An added benefit was the support of Kalman Kaplansky who in his capacity as the director, of the Montreal-based Jewish Labour Committee of Canada took every opportunity to study the arguments put forward by McKay's and Emerson's defense counsels.

A number of court cases charging discrimination in Dresden restaurants got on the way in late 1954, and not surprisingly, the lawyers representing the accused sought to use every leverage, including, accusing the *Toronto Telegram* and *Toronto Star* with setting up the cases. Mrs. Anne Emerson, Matthew's wife was charged with refusing service, namely: of not serving pop and milk to Mrs. Bernard Carter in Emerson's Restaurant. Morley Mckay was similarly charged with allowing the waitress on duty not to serve me coffee. Emerson's lawyer argued that since the Act was criminal law it was the responsibility of the federal government. We fought on. I remember being cross-examined by Emerson's lawyer. In his questioning, he asked, if I had gone to his client's restaurant to get food, or to create a situation? Unabashed, I told him: "I went to get food and at the same time I was making a test case for the Joint Labour Committee for Human Rights to see if McKay's restaurant was complying with the [Fair Accommodations Practices] Act." McKay and Emerson were engaged in fighting for a way of life, albeit, one that was misguided, and built on their supposedly racial superiority. Paradoxically, these developments were taking place in Canada, not just in the cold war period, but in an era immediately following a war that had been fought, to preserve democracy and eliminate Germany's claim of being the "master race."

When Magistrate Ivan B. Craig found Morley McKay and Mrs. Emerson guilty on January 14, 1955, we thought our side had won. More importantly, we believed that the Fair Accommodations Act had withstood the test of those questioning its constitutionality. The guilty verdict only carried a maximum fine of $50.00, plus court costs that they were both ordered to pay. However, we saw the decision as vindication of our efforts. Our celebration was fleeting. Magistrate Craig's decision was appealed. After much hoopla in the media, on September 09, 1955, Judge H. E. Grosch overturned the decision thereby, quashing both convictions in the County Court, in the County of Kent, Ontario. The judge ruled in effect that the evidence was not presented to support our claims of denial of service. At all cost, he avoided the question of whether or not the Fair Accommodations Act (1954) fell within the jurisdiction of the provincial legislature.[24]

Without impugning the judge's reputation, this is the same judge whom the *Toronto Star* reported had supported a restrictive covenant barring "Jews and [Blacks] from owning property in [the Beach O' Pines,] Lake Huron summer resort area."[25] At least, the judge had an appearance problem. Even if his denials that both issues were unrelated, were taken at face value, Mister Justice H. E. Grosch should have excused himself from the case. He did not, and the media on both sides of the issue had a field day. Premier Frost was clear in his denunciation of the decision reported a week later by some Ontario newspapers, when he said: "The fact that others were being served in the restaurants while the Negroes were ignored should have indicated discrimination. It shouldn't be necessary for a written notice telling them why they weren't being served."[26] No legislation... can overcome faulty judgement or appraisal of evidence"

For sometime to come, other charges were levied against McKay, and the legal seesaw unfolded in the courts that was becoming increasingly costly to his business. McKay was again accused of refusing service in his restaurant to two students because of their colour. Jacob Alleyne and Percy Bruce, U of T students from Trinidad had taken time out from their studies and they were part of a test case in Dresden, Ontario. McKay was accused of serving two of their White colleagues and refusing to take their orders of pie and milkshakes. McKay was found guilty, but true to form he appealed. On May 23, 1956,

Mr. Justice Lang after hearing the appeal dismissed it. We had fought arduously over the years for such a decision. As we had hoped, Judge Lang responded directly to McKay's lawyers' claims that racial discrimination had never been a crime in Canada. "Now it is a new kind of crime."[27]

Over the years we have come to associate the terms "civil rights" and "human rights" with events taking shape in the postwar US. African Americans struggled within the vast expanses of Florida to the Canadian border, from the Atlantic to the Pacific oceans to integrate lunch counters, establish fair housing practices, and obtain fairer employment practices. I am proud to say that a small group of determined individuals also rallied for similar changes in Canada. Ours was a struggle that was fraught with difficulty, especially, since protections under the law were at best nebulous. When Ottawa enacted the Canadian Bill of Rights in the early 1960s, during the John Diefenbaker era, such unprecedented legislation came about because of a budding human and civil rights agenda that we had helped to foster at the grassroots level. I believe that changes like these occurred because by that date the climate had been altered sufficiently by those of us, who joined forces, established alliances, worked with labour, religious groups and other vested interests to help make Canada a more tolerant and just society. "A society is not genuinely free which tells a Protestant Negro that he cannot strive for any position beyond that of a Pullman porter, or a Catholic Italian that God designed him for manual labour." [28]

Chapter 4 – Notes

1. In 1954, the chair of this Committee was Ford Brand, and the vice-chair was Eamon Park. Committee members were Lloyd Fell, Bert Groves, William Jenoves, W.D. Kerns, Dennis McDermott, Gordon Milling, Robert Myles, Harry Simon and Percy Yaffe, and the executive secretary was Donna Hill. The Committee was sponsored by the Toronto District Trades and Labour Council (TLC) and the Toronto and Lakeshore Labour Council (CCL)

2. For a chronology of the various components of the Ontario government's legislative initiatives that set out the province's human rights agenda in the 1950s and led to the establishment of the Ontario Human Rights Commission in 1962, see "Human Rights Code Broadened." *Human Relations,* vol. 1 no. 2 (March 1961)

3. The CCF, Corporate Commonwealth Federation was the forerunner to the New Democratic Party

4. Statement by Donald McDonald following a meeting of the Ontario CCF Provincial Executive at Woodsworth House, 565 Jarvis Street, Toronto, NAC MG 28 I173 vol 12-1 File 1.

5. *American Dilemma: The Negro Problem and Modern Democracy* (New York, 1944).

6. For full details see Race Relations Institute documents MG 28 I173 vol. 23

7. Ibid.

8. With the passage of time and fading memories, the date of this incident is sometimes given as 1947. However, in a *Toronto Star* article dated February 18, 1946, p. 8, "Rabbi Asks Action To End Negro Ban," reference is made to the incident as having taken place "last fall, meaning the fall of 1945.

9. This body was set up by individuals and groups whose interest and mandate was civil and human rights issues in Toronto, Ontario and Canada.

10. Ibid.

11. For an account of the deputation to Premier Leslie Frost, see "Brief From 70 Groups Asks Wider Legislation To Fight Discrimination." *Globe and Mail* January25, 1950, p. 1.

12. Ford Brand to Eamon Park NAC MG 28 I173 vol 39

13. See correspondence between Dennis McDermott and the director, Fair Employment Practices Branch, Ontario Department of Labour, August 14, 1953. Copy of correspondence with Bromley L. Armstrong.

14. For an account of what it was like to live in Dresden in the early 1950s see *Hugh Burnette's Remarks on Dresden,* January 18, 1954 NAC MG 28 I173 12-2

15. Ibid, see *Excerpt From Editorial, Windsor Star*, December 22, 1953

16. Ibid

17. See "Common law Mischief or Inciting Riot." *Ontario Provincial Crime Report*, April 30, 1949, Detachment File C.R.-49

18. Gordon Donaldson, "Fear 'Martyr' Atmosphere If prosecutions In Dresden." *Toronto Telegram*, September 3, 1954.

19. *Report on Visit to Dresden*, July 22, 23, 1954. NAC MG 28 I173 vol 12-2

20. "Daley Backs faith But Color bar Stays." *Toronto Telegram*, October 30, 1954, p. 1

21. "Dresden Negro Warned Gets Gun For Safety," *Toronto Telegram*, June 19, 1954 copy located NAC MG 28 I173 F12-1.

22. "Ontario's Anger Forces Government To Act on Racial Discrimination," *Steel Labor*, December 1954, p. 2

23. Jack Gale,"Draw Blind, Lock Door MacKay's System of 'No Service' – Crown," *The Varsity*, January 18, 1956, p. 4

24. See "Reasons For Judgement." *In The Matter of Fair Accommodation Practices Act, Revised Statutes of Ontario*, 1954, Chapter 28, Section 2 and 6. Anne Emerson, Appellant and Regina, Respondent. See also, *In: The Matter of Fair Accommodation Practices Act, Revised Statutes of Ontario*, 1954, Chapter 28, Section 2 and 6. Morley McKay, *Appellant and Regina Respondent.*, August 31, 1955. NAC Mg 28 I173 vol 38.

25. Pat McNenly, "Charge Judge Known For Race Prejudice Want Ruling Appealed," *Toronto Star*, September 13, 1955.

26. "Say Dresden Invalidates Ontario Law," *Toronto Star*, September 16, 1955.

27. Ronald Collister, "Guilty In Color Case Won't Change Stand," *Toronto Telegram*, p. 1

28. "Rabbi Claims Can Legislate For Intolerance," *Globe and Mail*, November 01, 1947. Rabbi Abraham Feinberg made the cited comment when he disagreed with the Ontario Attorney General, Leslie Blackwell's comments that "legal action cannot eliminate discrimination."

CHAPTER 5

Banging on the Door

In 1950 a rather stern looking man introduced himself to me. Donald or Don Moore as he was commonly called was from Barbados, and he had been a resident of Toronto's Black community since the years of the First World War. Moore was an intellectual, and the proprietor of a tailor shop and dry cleaning business in Toronto's west-end near Dundas and Dufferin Streets. When I met him, I was living close to his place of business, and in order to get home after work, the streetcar would let me off in front of his establishment. Moore timed my arrivals, and would come out of his shop and greet me. Of course, he did not hesitate to ask me about my ambitions, and during our first meetings he made sure that he gave me unsolicited but much-appreciated guidance and advice. Because of his influence, I even agreed to become a member of his Odd Fellows Lodge. I recall attending a lodge initiation meeting at which the proceedings undertaken by its members were full of symbols and rituals. The whole affair seemed a bit scary to me and soon thereafter I discontinued my membership.

I enjoyed my discussions with Moore. He had seen his community move through a number of important stages in its growth, yet he remained despondent that little progress had been made in the area of its financial development. Though nearing sixty when I met him, he still professed a commitment to the radical politics of Marcus Garvey and the UNIA. In fact, the Toronto branch of that organization was founded in 1919 in his tailor shop when it was located on Spadina Avenue. Moore was a progressive man, but he kept to himself. I tried to get him involved in the Toronto United Negro Credit Union, an extension of the Toronto United Negro Association. He readily signed up by giving me the $5.25 for his book. However, when I brought his name up at the next meeting a majority of the members wanted to throw me through the window. It turned out that a significant part of the so-called Black leaders of the day shunned Moore. Like his colleague Reverend Stewart, they found him threatening, because he was ahead of many of them, in both thoughts and deeds.

My growing familiarity with Moore led me to the realization that he provided a useful service to many disenfranchised persons in our community. Blacks in need of help oftentimes turned to him for counsel and support. In addition to his wide breadth of knowledge, as a businessperson, he could close his shop, and accompany people with problems to visit politicians with a reputation for being sympathetic to the Black community. He also had little compunction in challenging Immigration Branch officials when the need arose. Moore concentrated a major part of his activism and representations on issues relating to the recently arrived Blacks in Toronto. At the time, he reminded me of the difficulties a sizeable number of Blacks had in their efforts to come to Canada, either as landed immigrants, or as visitors.

I had heard of similar stories in the community, and it was not difficult for me to relate to discussions about barriers Ottawa deliberately placed in the way of many potential Black immigrants. My own situation had been a case-in-point when I attempted to get to Canada from Jamaica. In addition to my job, sports activities, other community endeavours, and trade union involvement, I soon found myself involved in initiatives on behalf of Blacks who had been shunned or mistreated in their attempts to enter Canada. It was ironic that so many Blacks were having unimaginable problems with immigration officials in a period when tens of thousands of White immigrants from around the globe were being invited to Canada.

By the early 1950s, Ottawa's blatant discrimination against Black immigrants was common knowledge. Just prior to my arrival in Canada, Prime Minister Mackenzie King had set the tone in 1947 as to which immigrants were welcomed. Rising in the Canadian House of Commons, Mackenzie King outlined changes in Canada's Immigration policy. In particular, he insisted "no fundamental alteration was to be made through immigration, in the character of the Canadian population and large scale Asian immigration was rejected."[1] Such an edict also meant Black immigration as well. Ottawa's unwillingness to open the doors to Blacks, Canadian politicians and bureaucrats claimed, was due to the inability of dark-skinned people to tolerate the Canadian winter. But actually the imposed prohibition on any significant Black immigration to Canada went beyond this mythical construct. Interestingly enough, Ottawa was not pretentious about its immigration colour bar. Many official government documents still exist to support Moore's point about racism in Canada's immigration policy. To add fuel to the fire, the issue was a regular topic of debate in the newspapers of the day. These attitudes date to the nineteenth century when many Whites thought Blacks to be "incorrigibly lazy, explosively passionate, pliable and credulous."[2]

Such characteristics, it was commonly believed by some Canadians made [Blacks] by nature fit "for life in warm climates and they could not flourish in northern latitudes."[3] The director of the Immigration Branch then located in the

Department of Mines and Resources reinforced such a stereotype about Blacks in a response to a query about the importation of servants from the West Indies. "Canada's coloured population has not increased rapidly, and while this is to some extent due to our climate it is also due in no small measure to the immigration policy that had been pursued for years."[4] The director also acknowledges that although one would be hard-pressed to perceive Canada's immigration policy in terms of "a colour line, there is something that comes close to a racial line."[5]

I have already indicated that when I went to work at Massey Harris in 1948, I found thirteen Black workers there. The majority of them hailed from the Caribbean, and had worked at Massey for some time. They told me that intermittently, small numbers of unskilled labourers were brought in from the Caribbean as porters, and in the old days women were brought in periodically as maids. This amounted to informal recruitment drives. Ones that yielded factory workers who were employed in menial jobs at Massey Harris, the railroads, and at other companies such as Toronto Foundry and Parker Pen or in the homes of well to do Canadians. By the late 1940s, work shortages in the Caribbean and the existing small population of Canadians of Caribbean descent with relatives here, precipitated a growing number of applications from those now wishing to come to Canada and work or further their education.

Ottawa bureaucrats behaved as if by ignoring what they perceived as "the coloured immigration problem," it would go away. To the letter, the direction set out by successive Canadian governments, was followed by the Immigration Branch which did everything in its powers to ensure that "persons within the prohibited classes [could not] be admitted to Canada as immigrants except by an Act of Parliament."[6] After May 1947, the bureaucrats were abrupt and dismissive with regard to sizeable Caribbean immigration. Responding to queries about the possibility of Blacks immigrating to Canada, A. L. Joliffe, the director of Immigration would express his regrets, followed by a brief statement in clear and concise terms that, "such persons are not admissible under existing regulations."[7]

After the Second World War, some Black Torontonians remained hopeful that changes to the Immigration Act would remove the prohibition that prevented many of their relatives from entering Canada. It was a common practice during the 1940s for Ontario farmers with Ottawa's assistance to secure the labour of tobacco workers from the American South, but the Canadian government stipulated that African Americans were to be excluded from the selection process.[8] Its Immigration Branch's concern was not so much over the settlement of unskilled migrant workers in the country, but rather the settlement of 'Black' unskilled migrant workers."[9]

In the 1950s Order-in-council P.C. 2856 deferred the development of any significant Black delayed family migration because, the Immigration Branch, not having a preference for immigration from the Caribbean and the US did its best to prevent family unification. This practice of racial exclusion by the Canadian State was perplexing for many Caribbean nationals. They had seen relatives migrate to Canada after the Second World War when restrictions were temporarily relaxed to allow former Caribbean enlistees in Canada's Armed Forces to become Canadian residents. P.C. 2743 had made their entry possible. Both of my brothers Eric and Everald who had fought in the Canadian Armed Forces took advantage of this stipulation. But after June 9, 1950, P.C. 2856 once again entailed meticulous adherence to regulations, which only granted entry to Caribbean nationals who were the "husband or wife and/or unmarried children under twenty-one years old of legal residents of Canada."[10] Yet through a temporary easing of the policy, whose net effect allowed in only several hundred persons from the Caribbean, expectations had been raised by what was thought might become a permanent receptiveness to the entry of Caribbean immigrants.

But while P.C 2856 put in effect more stringent regulations for Caribbean applicants, it removed at the same time most prohibitions for Europeans wishing to come to Canada. In effect facilitating the entry of relatives over a period of time from countries such as Italy.[11] P. C. 2856 further complicated the intended maize constructed by Ottawa officials to keep Canada White. In so doing, it was made almost impossible for other than a few close relatives to come to Canada from the Caribbean. Some exception was made for Caribbean students who entered Canada "under temporary status providing that they were in full daytime attendance at a recognized trade or vocational school with the means to support themselves."[12] The well-known Canadian politician Rosemary Brown[13] remembers arriving in Canada in 1950 from Jamaica to attend Montreal's McGill University. She points out that, "at the end of the spring semester West Indian students had to go to the immigration office to ask for an extension of [their] students' visas over the summer. [A]t the beginning of the academic year [they] had to show a balance of $1000 in [their] bank accounts to cover the years tuition fees and living expenses."[14]

It had been a long-standing practice by the Immigration Branch to discourage migration from non-preferred countries, and through careful selection invite immigrants from countries in which immigration offices were maintained. In other words in the 1950s a Black person resident in Britain would have encountered similar difficulties in his or her attempts to come to

Canada, as a Black West Indian did. No official immigration offices in the Caribbean, in the 1950s, was used as a deterrent to discourage Caribbean immigrants wishing to come to Canada, from having the necessary first hand contact with regular Canadian immigration representatives. "To ensure that the bulk of immigrants to Canada would come from [White] British Commonwealth countries, the United States and Northern Europe, most Canadian immigration offices were established in these countries, and most of the immigration propaganda was concentrated there as well.[15] Local responsibility for Canadian immigration matters in the Caribbean therefore came under the mandate of the Trade Commissioners' offices that were themselves the representatives of the Foreign Trade Service. While such arrangements were practical in the 1940s and the preceding years when applications from Caribbean residents were manageable, in the early 1950s this practice proved to be cumbersome. In fact, Canadian Trade Commissioners stationed in the Caribbean were expected by their superiors back in Ottawa to maintain dual loyalties. On one hand maintaining good economic ties with a small but lucrative customer, and on the other with regard to local susceptibilities, maintain the Canadian government's policy of rigid control of non-White immigration from the region into Canada.

In 1950, the Department of Mines and Resources ceased to be responsible for the Immigration Branch. Instead, the newly created Department of Citizenship and Immigration (DCI) took over the immigration mandate. Immigration matters continued to present major challenges for the Canadian government. As the decade of the 1950s unfolded governments at both the federal and provincial levels remained rather nervous about the impact of immigration on the Canadian economy and character of the country. Immigration restrictions had eased somewhat, but the federal government held meetings with their provincial counterparts in an attempt to monitor the overall impact of immigration on Canadian society. They generally agreed "that immigration must be selective, keeping in mind job opportunities, so that immigrants brought to Canada will be readily assimilated."[16]

In the 1950s the trade union leadership participated in what was called 'cap in hand sessions', to tell the politicians labour's position on various matters. This was just a formality, and the government graciously accepted our advice and gave us nothing. Moses McKay, the president of Local 439 came to me after such a trek in 1950. He indicated that during discussions with Ottawa politicians, union representatives had protested the manner in which West Indians of African origin were being restricted from coming to Canada as immigrants. But the politicians were unimpressed, and looking at the delegation asked, "where are all these people you are talking about? We don't see any of them with you here. We don't even see one of them in your midst." Walter Harris, the minister of the DCI, in his comments to the labour representatives, said, "persons of Caribbean origin in Canada were not represented either in the labour movement or in its leadership." McKay was both shocked and embarrassed by the response of Ottawa politicians, and he was bent on responding appropriately to them. He gave me a copy of the Immigration Act and sought my help in putting a group of people together from Toronto's Black community. The group's purpose was to allow study sessions dealing with Canada's immigration policy to take place, with the objective of taking action against restrictive immigration regulations. McKay was well meaning but he placed a formidable task in my hands.

I met with Don Moore on the matter and we both agreed that the McKay initiative should be pursued. A number of persons representative of the community that was made up of American, West Indian, and Canadian-born elements were brought together to discuss Canada's restrictive immigration policy as it applied to West Indians of African heritage. As Moore tells it in his book, "On a cold and crisp Sunday afternoon...a group of such nationals met in my home."[17] Included in the gathering were persons who were themselves descendants of immigrants from the Caribbean, and they were quite familiar with Canada's Whites-only immigration policy. Moore's difficulty with a sector of the Black leadership did not prevent his attracting young Turks, the likes of Daniel Braithwaite who later lead the challenge to the Toronto Board of Education's usage of the book *Little Black Sambo* in its schools.[18] Other members in our group were Dr. Norman Grizzle, who in 1951 was a practising chiropractor, and Edsworth Searles, then a university student and future lawyer. We joined forces with Moore and other well-respected community members such as Harry Gairey Sr., and E. A. Davis, an executive member of the Toronto United Negro Credit Union.[19]

All thirteen persons in attendance at the January 1951 meeting decided that further consultations were necessary and several study group sessions and planning meetings were subsequently held.[20] The minutes of the first meeting cannot be found, but a record of the second meeting held on the following Sunday, February 4th, shows that Don Moore officiated in the role of acting chairman.[21] These minutes make reference to the first meeting when it had been decided that those of us present would contact representatives of other Toronto Black community organizations.[22] There was also agreement that information-sharing with other organizations should occur, and mindful of the human rights records of the Canadian Congress of Labour, the Jewish Immigrant Aid

Society and the Civil Liberties Association, George King[23] suggested that they should be immediately approached.[24] Members of our group agreed that a new organization would not be formed. Instead, that the individuals assembled who represented a number of different community groups establish a body called the Negro Citizenship Committee (NCC), with Don Moore as chairman.[25] The NCC's constitution stated that its objective was "[m]ainly to petition the Government to enlarge the section of the Immigration Act, in order to permit freer entry of Negroes into the Dominion of Canada."[26] By the second meeting research was initiated for the purpose of clearly identifying the reasons why the overwhelming majority of non-White West Indian applicants were not being allowed into Canada as immigrants.[27] These findings would confirm what was already known: "that persons of African origin from the Caribbean, or those of colour any place in the Commonwealth, were not deemed to be British subjects...only White Commonwealth citizens were considered to be [eligible for entry to Canada as immigrants]."[28]

The NCC's activities in its first year were later chronicled in a newspaper published in Toronto called *The Canadian Negro* and they were described as "trying." A fire partly destroyed the location where we met causing us to move our meeting place to the office of the Home Service Association. As is the case with many community initiatives, the membership dwindled from thirteen to five. "However those who remained were convinced that they were supporting a just cause; and refused to despair."[29] Support was received from a few politicians. Senator Arthur Roebuck, formerly a minister of Labour and Attorney General for Ontario,[30] is remembered by Harry Gairey Sr. as attending meetings in Toronto's Black community at "four year intervals usually at election time."[31]

Nonetheless, his early contacts with the NCC provided us with sound advice on how research should be conducted and information prepared for the presentation of our case to the general public and politicians.[32] I remember Harry Gairey Sr. reporting to us that Roebuck suggested that we "research the problem, from the first Black immigrant's presence in Canada."[33] This task would eventually take sixteen months, but the initial phase took three months. During which time, consultations were carried out with other Black organizations to ensure that we all spoke with one voice on immigration matters of relevance to Toronto's Black community. In this we were successful, and indeed, for much of the 1950s the voice that was heard was the NCC's. It's name was later changed to the Negro Citizenship Association (NCA).[34]

During its nascent stage the NCA was involved in data gathering on the problems of Caribbean immigrants who were refused entry to Canada. To support our claims that Black immigration was beneficial to Canadian society, a comprehensive study was also undertaken regarding the history of African Canadians. Analysis of the NCA's constitution reveals that we did not see ourselves as participants in radical politics, but thought that our initiative was of constructive benefit to Canada and to our community. Increasingly, we regarded Canada's racial barriers in immigration as an impediment to our own progress. Yet with encouragement from the Canadian Congress of Labour, and a number of other mainstream organzations, we were still willing to assist Ottawa in any matter which would arise through the entry of Black immigrants. Ottawa's, and our definitions of ideal immigrants diverged, because most Canadian politicians perceived Black immigration as anathema to their country's way of life, we strongly disagreed with such a wrong-headed policy.

Toronto's Black population was about 4,000 in 1951, and it was not long before the news of the NCA's work got around. Moore was accessible to the public in his store and he had become well known as a trouble-shooter on deportation cases. Persons in distress who were looking for advice and assistance on immigration matters repeatedly contacted him. P.C. 2856 was effective in keeping the so-called "unwanted" beyond Canada's borders, and Black immigrants wishing to come here were put in a position of having to satisfy immigration officials that their movements were meritorious. If unable to do so, non-White West Indians were made ready for immediate deportation. The first step in that process was to lock them up in a hotel room on Jarvis Street. When such cases were brought to us as members of the NCA, our intervention involved the securing of legal counsel, or the provision of a paralegal. In a number of instances release was obtained of individuals previously judged by the Immigration Branch as having entered Canada illegally. By fighting deportations the NCC gained important support both within and beyond the Black community. Although most politicians were unmoved by our plight, the CCF and certain Liberal politicians were brave enough to speak out against the disbarment of Black West Indians by the Immigration Branch. In the case of the CCF such outcries were indicative of the party's willingness to "become a serious national force because of its outspoken concern for social justice and reform in post-war Canada."[35]

The efforts of John Braithwaite, the father of NCA member Daniel Braithwaite, to have his granddaughter admitted as an immigrant in Canada in 1951 received wide attention in Toronto's Black community and brought critical support from the CCF. After leaving Barbados and working on the Panama Canal, John Braithwaite settled in Sydney, Nova Scotia in 1911.

In 1926 he moved to Toronto, where he became a popular community worker and civil rights leader.[36] Having failed in his bid to convince the Immigration Branch that his granddaughter would not suffer because of climatic conditions, in 1952 he sought the assistance of Joe Noseworthy, CCF M.P. for the Toronto riding of York South.[37] Noseworthy referred the matter to Walter Harris, the minister of Citizenship and Immigration under whose jurisdiction the Immigration Branch fell.[38] Responding to Noseworthy's requests for further information, Harris quoted what by then was the much rehearsed statement of his department: "...It would be unrealistic to say that [persons] who have spent the greater part of their life in tropical or sub-tropical countries become readily adapted to the Canadian mode of life which to no small extent, is determined by climatic conditions."[39] In tune with his government's position, Harris reminded Noseworthy that "such immigrants [had] a great deal of difficulty succeeding in a competitive Canada."[40]

P.C. 2856 bound Canada's Immigration Branch, but the minister, if he wished to, could have exercised his prerogative and granted Braithwaite's relative her landing on humanitarian grounds. He and his officials in the Immigration Branch believed, however, that the paramountcy of a Whites-only immigration policy had to be maintained, even at the expense of a grandchild's wishes to be with her grandfather. It was issues such as this that provoked members of Toronto's Black community into action in the 1950s. After we completed a study of Black West Indian immigration to Canada, a community meeting was called on Sunday June 22, 1952 to report the results of the findings. Those persons attending were asked to: "remember what is done to other Negroes affects you directly. You are being discriminated against by your government. Let us raise our voices together in objection to this injustice."[41] The meeting place was the Carlton Street United Church, where the presiding minister, Reverend J. M. Findlay, had become involved in the immigration issue because a few Blacks in his congregation had solicited his support. He was included among the guest speakers. Two of the three major Toronto newspapers in attendance reported that letters were read from the University of Toronto supporting our claims that Blacks "are able to meet the rigors of Canadian climate as easily as White people."[42] In a public display of disagreement with the government of Canada, its Department of Health was quoted at the meeting as supporting both the NCA's and the University of Toronto's declaration.[43]

The new Immigration Act of 1952 did not take effect until June 1, 1953, but its contents signalled little in the way of changes that we had lobbied for, since setting out on this mission in January 1951. The St. Laurent government refused to allow sizeable Black immigration from the Caribbean and elsewhere in the Commonwealth by denying that they were British subjects. Some of us in Toronto's Black community displayed our disappointment over Ottawa's refusal to grant landings to other than a handful of Black West Indians. We did what was in the limits of our power to do, and sent "a petition to Ottawa, complaining of discrimination and Mr. Harris' attitude."[44]

The immigration issue became personal for me in 1953 when my mother's visit to my brothers and I in Canada started off on the wrong note. As she disembarked at Toronto's Malton Airport my mother was detained by immigration officials, who accused her of entering Canada without proper authorization. She was detained in the St. Regis hotel, and we were advised that she would be held there until transportation could be arranged to send her back to Jamaica. Immigration officials indicated that only family members were allowed to see her. It is recorded in the Immigration Branch's files that on a previous occasion I had applied for permission to bring my mother to Canada as a permanent resident. My request was turned down on the grounds that my father was still in Jamaica. The Immigration Branch's claim was that since my father was sick, and could not travel, no attempt should be made to separate the family.[45] It would require the intervention of W. R. Baskerville, the District Superintendent of the Immigration Branch, for her to be released. Later that year, at a union conference, federal Labour minister Allen Gregg was on the platform when my friend Dennis McDermott told the gathering what had happened to my mother. Infuriated by the course of events, he also criticized the Canadian government's policy of preventing sizeable Caribbean immigration because of climatic considerations. "A government that endorses the Universal Declaration of Human Rights should clean up its own policy." McDermott told Gregg to "go back to Ottawa and clean up our policy as far as Negroes are concerned!"[46]

I was determined to have my mother remain in Canada. Ignoring the refusal of the Immigration Branch to accept her as a potential immigrant again I applied to sponsor her. One year later she was granted landed immigrant status. We were fighting on many fronts. Our enemy was Canadian racism, oftentimes a subtle foe. Bringing this fact to life on these pages has been rather challenging. Especially, since many Canadians, subscribe to the notion that, there is no racism here. How does one, therefore, fight a foe that lurks in the dark? Especially, when racism Canadian style is masked with the usual smiles and denials.

W. E. P. Duncan, who was the Toronto Transit Commission's (TTC) new general manager in 1953, reminded Black Torontonians of how they were thought of by many Whites.

In responding to a question about his views on washrooms for the new Toronto subway, during a televised press conference aired on October 21, 1953, Duncan stated that he had visited the washrooms in Chicago's subway "but what he didn't like was that they were staffed by niggers."[47] There was a rash of responses to his remarks from the trade union movement, including local 439. Dennis McDermott and members of Toronto's Black community including the CPR's Brotherhood of Sleeping Car Porters registered protests with the TTC. Duncan responded that there was no discrimination in the hiring of Blacks and claimed that the term "nigger" to him was "just Latin for Black and that he didn't know it had any derogatory meaning."[48]

In December 1953, we scored a major success when the Canadian Immigration Branch granted permission to Beatrice Massop to enter Canada and work as a registered nurse. Massop since that time has been touted as "Canada's first West Indian immigrant nurse."[49] Her initial attempts to be accepted as an immigrant from Jamaica had been refused by Ottawa in late 1952. She contacted Don Moore in October 1952 and asked for the intervention of the NCA.[50] It would take Massop fourteen months before the Immigration Branch recognized her as a worthwhile immigrant and allowed her to enter Canada through Malton Airport under the exceptional merit category. The Registered Nursing Association of Ontario aided her efforts. It sanctioned her credentials, and the Mount Sinai Hospital in Toronto offered her a position on its nursing staff. Her entry nonetheless did not signal a change in attitude to immigrants from the West Indies. As 1954 dawned the Canadian government with few exceptions remained firm in its resolve that Black British subjects still fell within the restrictive class of immigrants, and their entry, therefore, remained the exception rather than the rule.

Nearing the mid-1950s it was becoming increasingly difficult for Ottawa to remain so nonchalant about its immigration policy of racial exclusion. Britain was accepting many Black West Indian immigrants, and the British Colonial Office was openly supporting the initiatives of Caribbean governments to have Canada alter its exclusionary immigration policy that directly affected their citizens. Commonwealth solidarity was used to pressure and embarrass Ottawa to agree tacitly that Black West Indians were in fact British subjects. In relenting, Ottawa did so grudgingly; such a change was likely in the early to mid-1950s, an era of new beginnings for the downtrodden. In Africa, the Caribbean, and elsewhere colonized people were starting to throw off their yokes of oppression. Although African Canadians were never colonized they too had a role to play in this new movement toward world wide Black upliftment. For them, reforming Canada's immigration policy proved to be a formidable task.

In early 1954, we intensified our activities and Don Moore was instructed to request a meeting with Prime Minister Louis St. Laurent. The purpose of this meeting would be to allow us "to place before the government...certain facts and suggestions [that] would be of benefit to [both parties.]"[51] Moore's attempts to involve St. Laurent in the process met with little success, and Walter Harris, the minister responsible for the immigration portfolio, was designated to represent the Prime Minister. He agreed to meet with the delegation on April 27.[52] News of the Ottawa meeting caused a flurry of activities in Toronto's African-Canadian community. Nearly two hundred copies of a brief outlining the NCA's position were prepared for distribution, and they accompanied invitations that were sent to organizations and churches across Canada asking them to be a part of the April 27th delegation.[53]

To demonstrate the level of support for the immigration issue in Toronto's African-Canadian community, we organized a meeting at the Carlton Street United Church in Toronto on Sunday, April 25, 1954. More than 200 persons were in attendance.[54] Details of our brief were given to the association's members and supporters, and events relating to what by then was the familiar pattern of discrimination in Canada's immigration policy were outlined. Moore reminded the audience that many attempts had been made on previous occasions to institute a fairer immigration policy for Black immigrants. Harris's claim that Black British subjects were unable to tolerate the Canadian winter was refuted.[55] Each speaker took issue with the Immigration Branch's treatment of Black immigrants from the West Indies.[56] The main thrust of the brief chided Ottawa for not only establishing two classes of British subjects, but it cited the pronouncements by the new British monarch, Queen Elizabeth II, regarding an equal partnership of all Commonwealth nations and races. There were to be no surprises for the St. Laurent government. Harris and the Cabinet had heard it all before, either publicly or in the numerous letters between the NCA, the Immigration Branch, and the Department of Citizenship and Immigration. But by marshalling our forces and demonstrating a willingness to go to Ottawa as a delegation, we were making good on our promise to double our efforts in seeking further changes in the Immigration Act to have other West Indians admitted.

On April 27, 1954, 35 delegates representing the NCA, various Black community organizations, labour, and mainstream religious denominations assembled in Ottawa after a train ride that involved further deliberations and strategy sessions.[57]

Because of the efforts of NCA treasurer Harry Gairey Sr., a porter-instructor for the Canadian Pacific Railway, his employer provided sleeping car accommodation at no cost. Soon after arriving in Ottawa, Donald Macdonald, the executive secretary of the Canadian Congress of Labour, led the delegation to meet Harris. Officials had been expecting a small group and were taken aback somewhat by the large size of the delegation.[58] After reading a summary of his organization's brief, MacDonald introduced the members of the delegation. Then it was our turn to speak. Reading from the final draft of the NCA's brief Moore requested that the St. Laurent government amend its understanding of "British subject" to include all British subjects and citizens of the United Kingdom and Commonwealth.

Harris was told that "racial restrictions should be removed from Canada's immigration policy; that the word 'orphan' should be deleted from the regulation which provide[d] for the entry of nephews and nieces under 21; that the term 'persons of exceptional merit,' should be explicitly defined; and that the Immigration Branch set up an immigration office in a centrally located area of the British West Indies for the handling of prospective immigrants."[59] In supporting briefs, the contributions and statistical data of persons of African descent in Canada were outlined by Stanley and Norman Grizzle.[60] Since its inception in 1951, the NCA had set out to remove racial biases from the Immigration Act. With the appearance of the delegation before Harris, its case had been brought to the capital in the hope that the St. Laurent government would introduce more favourable enactments aimed at doing away with the policy of excluding Black immigrants. Ottawa bureaucrats, however, were like the Rideau Canal in winter, ice cold, and the NCA's efforts met with little sympathy.

One month later in a memo to Laval Fortier, the deputy minister of the Department of Citizenship and Immigration, C.E.S. Smith, the director of the Immigration Branch, having reviewed the briefs, responded privately to our deputation to the St. Laurent government. Simply put, the director was methodical, and in classic bureaucratic style he dismissed the calls for a fairer immigration policy. Smith's advice to Fortier was to the point: "nothing can be said regarding our policy with respect to coloured and partly coloured immigrants that has not already been said and I would not advocate any change a [sic] this time."[61] The director also cautioned against broadening the class of relatives since this would result in "an increase of sponsored applications from all sources." He defined the 'case of exceptional merit' as conditions decided on "humanitarian grounds, by executive direction or for public benefit such as cases where special qualifications or achievements of prospective immigrants, their admission is in the public interest." In other words, where "they will contribute appreciably to the social, economic or cultural life of Canada."[62]

J. W. Pickersgill replaced Harris on July 1, 1954 as minister of Citizenship and Immigration. A change in ministers delayed any official response to our delegation's requests for a fairer immigration policy for Black West Indian immigrants wishing to venture to Canada. Smith's analysis of the delegation's requests had been made available to the upper echelons of the federal government a month after the April 27th meeting. But no official reply nor formal contact was made by Harris with the NCA after the Ottawa meeting. It took Pickersgill several more months after assuming the post before he made contact with the Toronto Black leadership. In the interim, Moore had to settle for a simple letter of acknowledgement from Pickersgill's secretary after a follow-up copy of the brief was forwarded to him.[63]

It was evident through his ministers' lack of response that Louis St. Laurent considered immigration to Canada from the Caribbean an unimportant matter. Moore wrote to Pickersgill in November reminding him that the NCA was "patiently but anxiously awaiting an official statement ...as to what action [his department had] taken, or proposed to take to relieve the situation."[64] Pickersgill, drawing on his many years as a mandarin in the Ottawa bureaucracy, finally replied to Moore, telling him that nothing had changed. Like his predecessor "[he] could offer no encouragement for the broadening of the categories of persons admissible to Canada from the British West Indies." The minister was quick to reiterate the Immigration Branch's claim of being willing "to consider any individual cases which appear to have outstanding merit," ones that qualified for admission on "humanitarian and compassionate grounds, and ...special qualifications an applicant may have."[65]

News got back to us in Toronto that representatives of the Barbados government had journeyed to Ottawa and had met with C.E.S. Smith, the director of the Immigration Branch in August 1954. They were in search of a safety valve for their country's growing population. With a population density of "1300 persons per square mile, and an economy that was extremely dependent on sugar cane, many of its inhabitants were underemployed or unemployed."[66] Present at the meeting was A. H. Brown, Canada's deputy minister of Labour, and the Barbadian representatives in attendance were R. G. Mapp, minister of Trade and Labour, and Arthur Pickwood, commissioner for Labour. Smith and Brown were advised that Barbados wished to establish mutually a scheme for seasonal workers and domestics and some procedure that would allow for the training of student nurses from Barbados in Canadian training institutions. The governments of Barbados and the

United States previously had entered into such an agreement, and in 1954 there were 6000 Barbadian migrant workers in the US.[67] Of course the Canadian representatives, by themselves, could not change official immigration policy, and in any case they showed little interest in the proposal.

Such an undertaking was delegated to Smith, who was a known opponent of Black immigration. He was insistent in reporting, "the disadvantages outweighed the advantages."[68] Not wishing to mince words, Smith reminded the deputy minister Lavel Fortier, that it was not by accident that "coloured British subjects other than negligible numbers from the United Kingdom [were] excluded from Canada. Coloured people in the present state of the White man's thinking are not a tangible community asset."[69]

By now however the handwriting was on the wall. The time was fast approaching when a review of the policy would have to be done and some concession would have to be offered. A nominal easing of restrictions seemed the only plausible solution. Fortier and Pickersgill understood this fact and in December 1954 they instructed that a review of immigration regulations as they affected West Indian immigrants be initiated: "...[I]n view of the pressure exercised in Canada as well as from the British West Indies, and the representations made by the Trade Commissioner, it is considered that it would be worthwhile reviewing this situation again."[70]

As a follow-up to the August 1954 Ottawa meeting with Barbados representatives, another meeting was held in London in early 1955. It was one where the Barbados government in cooperation with British authorities announced the setting-up of a plan for 200 women to be trained as domestic workers in Barbados and Britain. When the candidates had completed their training, they were to be placed in British households. At the meeting held at Canada House, London, and attended by Mapp, Pickwood, and a Mr. Anderson from the British Colonial Office, details of the plan were unveiled, and discussions followed with Canadian officials, Frederick Hudd of Canada House and C. Wallace of Canada's Immigration Branch Services in London. The Barbados government representatives now playing hardball were the same R.G Mapp and A. H. Pickwood who had met previously with C.E.S Smith, director of the Immigration Branch, and A. H. Brown, deputy minister of Labour. Egged on by Anderson, they enquired "as to whether the Canadian government had any scheme comparable to the one now being proposed by the United Kingdom, and, if not, would the Canadian government favourably entertain a similar scheme?"[71] There was no such scheme at the time in Canada for women from the West Indies.[72] Shortly after the meeting ended, the request from Barbados was referred to the Department of Citizenship and Immigration and the Department of Labour. In early March, the British Colonial Office wrote Canada House, London, about the request put forward by the Barbados representatives.[73]

Norman Manley met with NCA members at the Steel Workers Offices at 11½ Spadina Road, and he agreed to pursue with Ottawa fairer immigration regulations for Black West Indians. Manley's party, the People's National Party (PNP) came to power in Jamaica in January 1955. In May 1955 Pickersgill met with Wills Isaacs the Jamaican minister of Trade and Industry in Ottawa. It was at this meeting that Isaacs proposed to him that Canada "admit Jamaican women as domestic servants under a form of indenture that would require them to return to Jamaica at the end of the period."[74] Pickersgill claims in his biography that he refused to agree to what he called "a form of slavery."[75] Ottawa was under mounting pressure to take action; something had to be done and done soon.

To the outside world Ottawa appeared calm. After all, West Indian immigration hardly mattered to Canada. But from the volume of documents it is obvious that a day did not go by without the immigration authorities receiving a petition, letters, or other forms of communication regarding the issue. The time had come for a glimmer of hope. On May 6, 1955 at a meeting a directive was issued to the ministers of Labour and the Department of Citizenship and Immigration. The Canadian Cabinet instructed: "investigate the possibility and the desirability of working out an arrangement to admit a certain number of domestics from Jamaica for a trial period of one to two years."[76] It was also agreed that "consideration be given to the desirability of establishing an immigration quota for the British West Indies at a later date."[77] On June 10, 1955 Laval Fortier informed his director of the Immigration Branch, that the Cabinet had decided "to admit a certain number of domestics from the British West Indies on an experimental basis. 75 of these domestics to be selected from Jamaica and 25 from Barbados." Instructions in the director's memo also pointed out that "these domestics are to be admitted as immigrants upon arrival."[78]

It had taken us in the Negro Citizenship Association and our supporters more than four years to come this far. Furthermore, it had taken Black people nearly 100 years to have Ottawa begin a process of recognizing them as a tangible asset to Canada. It was only during the period of American slavery that Blacks were usually allowed into Canada as refugees. As members of the NCA we did not get all that we had wished for. Yet with the West Indian Domestic Scheme, a formalized arrangement between Ottawa and certain Caribbean nations, the doors were being inched open. In the process, Ottawa politicians and bureaucrats were sensitized in some small measure about the dangers of their racist immigration policies. The many tens of thousands of immigrants from the Caribbean now living in Canada are a testament to our efforts.

Chapter 5 – Notes

1. Freda Hawkins, *Critical Years of Immigration: Canada and Australia Compared*. (Montreal: McGill Queen's University Press, 1989), p. 117

2. Allen P. Stouffer, "A 'restless Child of Change and Accident': The Black Image in Nineteenth Century Ontario," *Ontario History*, vol 76 no. 2 (June 1984), p131.

3. Ibid.

4. Memo from the director to Gerald Wilks, April 8, 1942. NAC, RG 76, vol 838 File 553-36-644. The referenced letter is a copy and there is no indication of the name of the sender other than the fact that it was sent by the director. Frederick Charles Blair had been the assistant deputy minister of immigration since 1924 and in 1936, he became director of the Immigration Branch, with full deputy-minister status. He retired in 1943. See Irving Abella and Harold Troper's brief account of Blair's career in *None is Too Many* (Toronto: Lester E. Orpen Dennys 1983), pp. 7-10.

5. Ibid.

6. Hugh Llewellyn Keenleyside, "Canadian Immigration Policy." *Empire Club Addresses 1948-49* (Toronto, 1949), p. 201.

7. Memo from A. L. Joliffe to Beverly Matthews, December 19, 1945. NAC, RG 26 File 3-32-16 pt. 2, vol. 123.

8. Vic Satzewich "The Canadian State and Caribbean migrant farm labour." *Racial and Ethnic Studies*, vol. 11 no. 3 (July 1988), p. 295. See edn 87, it cites a memo from C. E. S. Smith, Assistant deputy minister, to the deputy minister of the Department of Citizenship and Immigration, October 18, 1960, PAC, RG. 26, vol. 145, File 3-41-15, pt. 3.

9. Ibid.

10. See Chairman of Committee on Admissions to Secretary of DACI, August 16, 1950 PAC RG76, interim 16, vol. 830 File 552-1-644.

11. Robert Harney, "If One Were to Write A History of Postwar Toronto Italia" In: If One Were To *Write* A History (Toronto: MHSO, 1991), pp. 63-89. The author identifies the post-Second World War II flow into Canada as "partly induced by renewal of earlier chain migration."

12. Memorandum to minister from the director, "Admission of Coloured or Partly-Coloured Persons.September 12, 1951." PAC RG76, interim 16, vol. 830 File 552-1-644.

13. Rosemary Brown was born in Port Antonio, Jamaica in 1930. She had been a member of the British Columbia legislature and in 1975 she ran unsuccessfully for the national leadership of the New Democratic Party. See Rosemary Brown's book, *Being Brown: A Very Public Life*, (Toronto:Random House, 1989).

14. Ibid., p. 31.

15. G.A. Rawlyk, "Canada's Immigration Policy,1945-1962." *Dalhousie Review*, vol. 42 no. 3 (Autumn 1962), p.288.

16. Memo from F.W. Stanley, Office of the Department of Planning and Development, Immigration Branch, to the Col. The Hon. Wm. Griesinger June 1, 1950. Archives of Ontario RG9-6 Access 3249.

17. Don Moore, *Don Moore: An Autobiography* (Toronto: Williams-Wallace, 1985), p. 88.

18. Braithwaite spearheaded the fight against the Toronto Board of Education in 1956 to have the book, *Little Black Sambo* removed from that city's schools. He gives an account of the events leading to its removal in *The Banning of Little Black Sambo from Toronto Public Schools* 1956. (Toronto: Overnight Typing and Copy, 1978). Braithwaite was also a founding member of the Library of Black Peoples' Literature, established in Toronto in 1962, and its librarian from 1971-76.

19. Esau A. Davis was one of the leaders of the Toronto's Black community. His name appears in the July 31, 1945 application for letters patent of the Toronto United Negro Credit Union.

20. Moore identifies the persons in attendance in addition to himself as Bromley Armstrong, Daniel Braithwaite, Joseph Bailey, Cecil Duncan, Esau Davis, Harry Gairey, Sr., Dr. Norman Grizzle, Louise Hewitt, Julius Isaac, George King, Edsworth Searles, Charles Mills and M. Williams. Moore, op. cit., p. 88.

21. The minutes of the first meeting held on January could not be found. Copies of the two subsequently held meetings are on file with the writers.

22. Minutes of the second in a series of organizational meetings called by Mr. Don Moore on Sunday February 4, 1951.

23. In 1962 George King became the first secretary of the Jamaican-Canadian Association.

24. Ibid.

25. Ibid.

26. Copy of the draft constitution is with the writers. It was produced on the letterhead of the Negro Citizenship Committee and it lists Don Moore as Chairperson, Harry Gairey as Treasurer and Dr. Norman Grizzle as Secretary.

27. Ibid.

28. Ibid.

29. Cecil Duncan, "Citizenship Body Strides Ahead." *The Canadian Negro*, June 1953, p. 2.

30. Roebuck at that time was the former Liberal Member of Parliament and is described by Abella and Troper in *None is Too Many* as "a friend of Jewish causes," op. cit., p. 183 and 229. Roebuck was elected to the Ontario legislature in 1934 as the Liberal member for Toronto-Trinity; in 1940 he was elected to the House of Commons and he entered the Senate in 1945. See Parliamentary Guide (Ottawa, 1954), p. 100.

31. Moore, op. cit., p. 89.

32. Ibid., See also Harry Gairey's book, *A Black Man's Toronto 1914-1980*, (Toronto: MHSO, 1981), wherein he states that members of the NCA visited Roebuck in his office on Richmond Street and they were given an hour and a half of his time, p. 34

33. Ibid. p. 34.

34. "Claim Ottawa Hinders Negro Immigration." The *Globe and Mail*, June 23, 1952, p. 5. See Also Gairey, op. cit., p. 34. A survey of newspaper reports between 1951 and 1957 reveals that the NCC and its successor, the NCA, represented Toronto's Black community's immigration concerns. Labour, and other affiliated organizations voiced their opinion in support of the repeated calls by the NCA for a non-discriminatory immigration policy for West Indians of African origin.

35. John Bullen, "The Ontario Waffle and the Struggle for an Independent Socialist Canada: Conflict within the NDP." In: *Interpreting Canada's Past. vol 2: After Confederation*. J. M. Bumsted, ed. (Toronto: Oxford University Press, 1986), p. 430.

36. Interview, Danny Braithwaite, October 1986 and November 17, 1992.

37. J. W. Noseworthy, formerly a Toronto school teacher, beat Arthur Meighen, the then leader of the Federal Conservative Party in the York South 1942 by-election.

38. Walter Harris was minister of Immigration from the time of the inception of the Department of Citizenship and Immigration, January 18, 1950 until July 1, 1954, when J.W. Pickersgill took over the portfolio.

39. "Immigration by Discrimination." *The Black Worker*, March 1952, p. 1. This was a Black newspaper, and was described as the official organ of the Brotherhood of Sleeping Car Porters. It appears that only one issue was produced and it was devoted to Canada's discriminatory immigration policy in the early 1950s.

40. Ibid.

41. Black community members in Toronto were notified of the meeting by letter from N. W. Grizzle, Secretary NCC to Negro Citizens, June 16, 1952. A copy is with the writers.

42. See "Canada too Cold for BWI Citizens, Harris is Quoted." The *Globe and Mail*, June 23, 1952, p. 5; "Claim Ottawa Hinders Negro Immigration." *Toronto Star*, June 23, 1952, p.3.

43. Ibid. *Globe and Mail* article referred to above.

44. "'Unchristian' Gov't Rule Bars West Indies Negroes." The *Toronto Telegram*, June 23, 1952, p. 1.

45. See record entitled, "Mrs Armstrong, mother of Bromley Armstrong, 219 Lippincott St. Toronto, may 16, 1953." MG 28 I 173 vol. 38

46. Exclamation mark is the writers' emphasis. "Charge Canada Bars Negroes Unjustifiably." *Toronto Telegram*, September 16, 1953.

47. "Charge TTC Head Showed Jim Crow Attitude on TV." Toronto Star, Tuesday, October 21, 1953, p. 11.

48. Ibid

49. Lois Hines "Nurse Wins Long Fight To Enter." *The Canadian Negro*, February 1954, p. 1.

50. Don Moore, *Don Moore: An Autobiography*. op cit., p. 139.

51. Letter from Donald Moore, director, Negro Citizenship Association to the Honourable Louis St. Laurent, Prime Minister of Canada, March 3, 1954, and Letter from J. S. Cross, Secretary, Office of the Prime Minister, to Donald Moore, director, Negro Citizenship Association, March 9, 1954.

52. Letter from Don Moore to Walter Harris, March 03, 1954, copy is with the writers.

53. Ibid. p. 105.

54. "Immigration Law Rapped At Citizenship Meeting." *The Canadian Negro*, April-May 1954, p. 1. See also letter from Donald Moore to James M. Finlay, March 24, 1954.

55. Ibid.

56. By 1954 it was becoming commonplace for the Immigration Branch to return Caribbean nationals to the Caribbean after placing them in detention, usually in places such as the Don Jail in Toronto. By its own account, the Immigration Branch quite often dragged out cases that involved either prospective Black immigrants from the West Indies, or those who had the misfortune to have been detained at points of entry. Whatever the reason, and in all such instances the individuals were left in a state of uncertainty. Beatrice Massop's case took fourteen months after the intervention of Moore and the NCA in October 1952. In other examples this duration appeared to be the norm. In some instances even when supporting relatives were willing to vouch for persons held in suspicion by the Immigration Branch, its procedures were in keeping with the letter of the law. For example, a young student from Jamaica who was born May 16, 1935 was refused admission at Malton Airport on August 26, 1952, after "she claimed to be coming forward as a student." Although having an aunt in Canada at the time she was refused admission on the grounds that she was "likely to become a public charge." The Immigration Branch's decision

was appealed, but was dismissed at a hearing. She left Canada, April 24, 1953. See "Cases in which the Negro Citizenship Committee or similar associations are interested." NAC, RG 76, vol. 830, File 552-1-644.

57. Trade Union representatives had been instrumental in setting up the April 27, 1954 meeting. Pat Smith and I represented Massey-Harris, Local 439 and were accordingly included among the delegates. See letter from Thomas Paton, president Local 439 of the International of the United Automobile-Aircraft-Agricultural Implement Workers of America(UAW-CIO) to D. Moore, director, NCA, April 22, 1954. Additionally, local 439's Fair Practices and Anti-Discrimination Committee's Report summarized the April 27th meeting. The delegates listed were from twenty-five different organizations, including the Canadian Congress of Labour the Toronto and Lakeshore Labour Council, United Automobile Workers (CIO-CCL), Locals 439 and 303, Toronto: and Local 222, Oshawa, the United Church of Canada, the Church of England in Canada, the Brotherhood of Sleeping Car Porters, C.P.R. Division, Toronto, the Canadian Negro Women's Club, Toronto, the Home Comfort Club, Toronto, the Negro Citizenship Association, Montreal, the Universal Negro Improvement Association, Montreal, the National Unity Association, Dresden; Dresden, Chatham and Buxton, the Toronto Negro Veterans Association and the Canadian Brotherhood of Railway Employees, Local 123. Norman Dowd represented the Trades and Labour Congress. Although there was no representation from the United Church of Canada, permission was given to Moore to say that it endorsed the NCA's briefs. See Moore, op. cit., p. 108.

58. Interview, Rachael Mills, January 19, 1993.

59. See Brief, op. cit.,

60. *Statement of Stanley G. Grizzle, regarding Canadian Immigration Act and P.C. 2856 dated June 9, 1950 as amended, in support of brief submitted by Negro Citizenship Association to the Honourable Walter Harris, minister of Citizenship and Immigration, Tuesday, April 27, 1954, at Parliament Buildings, Ottawa.* See also *Remarks of Norman W. Grizzle, D. C., in Support of Brief.* In Stanley Grizzle's remarks, mention was made of a letter from Dr. A. F. Peart of the Department of National Health and Welfare, Ottawa, in which he pointed out that "there [was] no record to show that climatic conditions [had] affected immigrants from tropical areas." Grizzle also pointed out that Dr. D. Y. Solandt, head of the Department of Physiological Hygiene, University of Toronto, and Dr. Fleming of the Faculty of Medicine, McGill University, "have both stated in reply to questions put to them with regard to the climatic effects on immigrants, that although there has been intensive study made, there is not on record any proof that our climate is a hazard to tropical immigrants."

61. "Comments on Brief presented to the Prime Minister by the Negro Citizenship Association," from C.E.S. Smith, director to deputy minister, May 26, 1954. NAC, RG 76, vol. 830, File 552 1 644.

62. Ibid.

63. Letter from Donald Moore to J. W. Pickersgill, minister, Citizenship and Immigration, July 10, 1954. PAC, RG 76, vol. 830, File 552-1-644.

64. Letter from Donald Moore to J. W. Pickersgill, November 3, 1954. PAC, RG 76, vol. 830, File 552-1-644.

65. Letter from J. W. Pickersgill to Donald Moore, November 29, 1954. PAC, RG 76, vol. 830, File 552-1-644.

66. *Proposal for controlled emigration from Barbados of specific types of Workers.* NAC, RG 76, vol. 830, File 552-1-644.

67. Memo for file, from the director. "Meeting with deputy minister of Labour and minister, Trade and Labour and Commissioner of Labour, Barbados, August 9, 1954. NAC, RG 76, vol. 830, File 552-1-644.

68. *A Review of Immigration from the British West Indies.* From the director to the deputy minister, January 14, 1955. NAC, RG 76, vol. 830, File 552-1-644.

69. Memo from Laval Fortier to the director of Immigration, December, 1954. NAC, RG 76, vol. 830, File 552-1-644.

70. Ibid.

71. Memo from C. Wallace, A/director, United Kingdom to Chief, Operations Division, Ottawa, February 28, 1955. NAC, RG 76, vol. 830, File 552-1-644.

72. At the time there was a shortage of domestic workers. Between 1947 and 1953, Displaced Persons were brought to Canada and 15,000 of them were employed as domestic workers. See Blair Fraser, *The Search for Identity*. (Toronto: Doubleday, 1967), p.117.

73. In a March 3, 1955 memo from the Office of the High Commissioner For Canada, London signed by Frederic Hudd to the Under-Secretary of State for External Affairs, Ottawa reference is made to a letter sent from the Colonial Office to Canada House in London. Two copies of the letter were then forwarded to Ottawa but were not made available to the writers since they fall under the restrictive documents section, because they originated from a foreign government. It is clear from the covering memo written by Hudd that the Colonial Office was following up on the February 14, 1955 meeting. NAC, RG 76, vol. 830, File 552-1-644.

74. J. W. Pickersgill, *My Years with Louis St. Laurent: A Political Memoir*. (University of Toronto Press, 1975), p. 238.

75. Ibid.

76. Memo from Laval Fortier to the director of Immigration, May 31, 1955. NAC, RG 76, vol. 2, File SF-1-1, pt. 2.

77. Ibid.

78. Memo from Laval Fortier to the director of Immigration, June 10, 1955. NAC, RG 76, vol. 830, File 552-1-644.

CHAPTER 6

A Fork in the Road

A survey was carried out to determine the success of the initial movement of women involved in the West Indian Domestic Scheme. The Department of Labour did such an undertaking, and it illustrated the positive impact these women from the Caribbean were having on Canadian households. Accordingly, in 1956 the Caribbean Domestic Scheme became a regular and continuing program under the joint management of the Canadian and various governments in the region. In March 1956, all 100 domestics were still actively meeting the terms and conditions under which they came to Canada. Thirty-four of the women were working in Toronto, twenty-seven in Ottawa-Hull, and 39 in Montreal.[1] Wages on average ranged from $60 to $125 per month. The overwhelming majority of both employees and employers were satisfied with the arrangements. Indeed immigration officials found employers satisfied to the extent that a number of them felt safe enough to leave their children in the charge of domestics while they took winter vacations.[2]

It should have come as no surprise to anyone that by early 1956 the program was meeting with success. Many of the Black women from the Caribbean who ventured to Canada via the scheme saw it as a ticket to improve their circumstances. But not all of them who came via this method were either impoverished or undereducated. Some of the women selected for domestic work in Canadian households took the opportunity to enter Canada through the West Indian Scheme since few other options were available at the time. Some of their relatives on previous occasions had gone to the United States, Britain and elsewhere, and these women entering Canada saw the experience of going "foreign" as offering them the opportunity to follow in their footsteps.

The late Eva Smith, who was a good friend of mine, came to Canada from Jamaica as a domestic worker under the 1956 quota. After studying as a dental technician for two years in the United States, she returned to her native land in 1954 where she worked for a while, but wanted to emigrate.[3] Eva applied in 1955 to come to Canada with the initial batch of domestic workers, but was turned down because she had no experience in domestic service. A referral by someone at the Jamaica Labour Board, which was responsible locally for the scheme to Canada, led her to Amy Bailey's School of Training for domestics.[4] Realizing that this was probably her only opportunity to come to Canada, Eva took the course, and subsequently obtained the necessary experience by working as a domestic in Kingston, Jamaica. Arriving in Montreal in October with the second batch of domestics from Jamaica, she remembers meeting other women in the service from the Caribbean who were either well educated or whose parents were members of the middle-class and/or the political elite in Jamaica.[5] For them and others, she said, the Domestic Scheme "in those days was the only way [to] put your feet on [Canadian] soil."[6]

Members of the Negro Citizenship Association (NCA) did everything possible to support these women selected for work in Canada. Life for many of them was rather lonely. They worked in households where each day they had to be up at the crack of dawn, and were the last ones to retire nearing midnight. Their employers gave them Thursday afternoons off, but with few friends and family in Toronto they congregated in support of each other. A gathering point for those domestics who worked in Toronto and surrounding areas was Yonge and Queen Streets in the heart of the city's downtown. They attracted the attention of onlookers because some of them were dressed in bright colours with white running shoes, and a few of them even donned cricket caps. When they met on Thursday afternoons, all of their frustration from being isolated in alien households came pouring out. However, a group of Black women engaging in loud conversation at the corner of Yonge and Queen Streets was something that 1950s Toronto "the good" was not ready for. Some NCA members agreed that a welcome house, one equipped with temporary quarters for new arrivals, meeting rooms and kitchen facilities would help to alleviate the settlement and adjustment problems for many of the domestics on their days off.

When Moore told us he saw a building for sale on Cecil Street that was advertised in the paper, we jumped at the opportunity to make an offer to have it purchased. Finding a suitable place, we thought at the time was a blessing in disguise. We were especially concerned about the complaints many of the domestics made that the kind of food they wanted to enjoy was frowned on when they took the ingredients back to their households. Their employers were not accustomed to the odours of mackerel and green bananas, for example, that these people from the Caribbean relished. Additionally, members of the NCA were concerned that at times new arrivals to Toronto had nowhere to stay. Therefore we wanted our own premises, one that could accommodate people on a temporary basis and have space for a hostel. We were also concerned with the process of adjustment for the women in the scheme, and hoped, that they would learn more about the Canadian way of life. After the Cecil Street building was purchased Moore approached Toronto author and journalist Kate Aitken and convinced her to come to what we called the Donavalon Centre. Aitken was very gracious and helpful. She spoke with the domestics and gave copies of her cookbook to the new arrivals.

Unfortunately, as is the case with many community organizations, in the midst of our success, the members had to find something to disagree about and the purchase of the centre soon became one of the more disturbing issues for the NCA. The organization's status was enhanced by the recognition it received from politicians and bureaucrats at the federal and provincial levels. Additionally, many letters requesting help were being received from persons in the Caribbean who wished to come to Canada. The NCA was both an arbiter and a sounding board depending which side of the immigration issue one stood on. Some hospitals in Toronto, and other parts of Canada, actively sought our assistance after 1954, in the recruitment of prospective nurses from the Caribbean region. But with all of these positive developments dissatisfaction reared its ugly head, and led in 1956 to the ruination of the NCA. Some members of the executive were daunted by our move to purchase the Cecil Street property. The scope of the problem centred on their feelings that it was too big a project for us to successfully undertake and manage, and major disagreement set in. In early 1956, the NCA's executive was divided into two camps. One camp supported the Cecil Street purchase, therefore Don Moore, and the other camp was opposed. The latter group withdrew its support for the organization's activities and abandoned the NCA.

I too, had a slight row with Moore when I learned the details of how the building was purchased. It was clear to some of us in the organization that at the outset, we did not adequately scrutinize the details of the offer to purchase the Cecil Street property. Because of his reputation as a businessperson, and his involvement with the purchase of properties in other capacities, many of the details were left solely to Moore. In this regard his reputation was stellar. For in the mid-1940s, Moore along with Reverend Stewart had made a major property purchase of what later became the British Methodist Episcopal Church building, located at 460 Shaw Street. The members of the NCA knew that in purchasing the Cecil Street building, we had difficulties in meeting our obligation for the down payment that was to be discharged in three instalments. When I learned of the difficulty I loaned the NCA half of the down payment, but it was my understanding that the property would be purchased in the organization's name. To my surprise, six months later I discovered that the building was purchased in the names of Donald Moore and Bromley Armstrong. I acted immediately to ensure that my name was removed as one of the owners of the Cecil Street property. But my actions were viewed by some of Moore's supporters as intolerable. A lengthy and heated discussion ensued at a meeting that lasted until the early hours of the morning.

 Needless to say, I fell in disfavour with the majority of the remaining NCA members and its executive, who saw no difficulty with the building being in Moore's and my name. I however kept my resolve. After being a member of Toronto's Black community for nearly nine years, and having heard countless stories and accusations about how previous community initiatives had been affected by greed and ruthless individuals, I was not about to have my name added to that list. I could not afford to have my reputation sullied by anyone who would later charge when the building was sold, that the persons whose names were on the deed personally benefited from equity realized by the sale. Relations between Moore, the NCA membership and myself had been damaged, and I determined that my only recourse was to withdraw from the organization. It took a number of years before I received a partial repayment of the amount of money I loaned to the NCA. But given all that we had accomplished, the many persons we had helped, and the degree to which Moore and the NCA had advanced the cause of community building, I rationalized at the time that it was a small price to pay.

My life was in transition in 1956, and my ties with some community organizations were lessened. My experience with Moore and the NCA had disillusioned me somewhat. Yet, I remained a disciple, and a friend of his, because I had seen the sacrifices he had made to foster a vision toward the betterment of Toronto's post-war Black community. My own personal assessment led me to conclude that it was time to leave my employment at what was now called Massey Ferguson. In addition to its name change, after a company-initiated time and motion study was completed, management brought in what was supposed to be a new and more efficient system of operations. It was a system that was less-labour intensive, and its implementation meant that Massey would lay off thousands of people. I had worked over the years with many of them, and I felt that Massey's attitude to its workers was heartless. After relying on the workers blood, sweat and tears, capitalism proved once again, that it was without a conscience, and had little consideration for the workers. Like colonialism, what mattered, was the vast amounts of money the few derived at the expense of the many. My years at the plant had afforded me what was called super seniority. This meant that I would not be affected by the pending lay-offs. But I was yearning for a change of scenery and more challenge.

Approaching management I indicated that I was willing to take a voluntary lay-off. I wanted to leave Massey in the summer of 1956, but the factory was closed for retooling, and for the introduction of the new time and motion system that was supposedly designed to increase production. I took the opportunity to visit Jamaica on the invitation of Ken Sterling, the island supervisor for the National Workers Union (NWU). We met in 1953 at the Canadian Congress of Labour convention when the United Steelworkers of America, Canadian section, brought him to Canada. His purpose for being here was to observe the operation of local unions and study their structure and function. The Steelworkers Union was interested in the development of the bauxite industry in Jamaica and Guyana. In particular, indiscriminately low wages and poor working conditions, members of the union executive thought, would undermine the structure put in place by this international union in North America.

Sterling arranged for me to meet some of the leaders in Jamaica. On arrival there, I spoke with Thossy Kelly whom I believe at the time was the president of the NWU. I also spoke with the future Jamaican Prime Minister Michael Manley, then a popular union organizer. They all seemed to be impressed with my trade union credentials for I was soon offered a position as a NWU union organizer. I turned down the offer. This was not an easy decision for me to make. After what was nearly a nine-year absence from Jamaica, and having made up my mind to leave Massey, I needed an opportunity that would take me to higher ground. But my discussions with several Jamaican politicians and union officials left me unimpressed with the distance that post-war Jamaica had not travelled. I remember being at a party in Mona Heights, a suburb of Kingston, where members of the emerging indigenously born bourgeoisie were replacing their British colonizers in both tastes and appetites. I stood in someone's upscale home listening to conversations that reeked with insensitivity and classism, and decided that I was not ready for Jamaica. Or maybe it was not ready for me. Jamaica should have travelled much further after the 1865 Morant Bay rebellion, when the poor and downtrodden fought to secure a future for themselves. Our struggles in Jamaica were always about mounting intense efforts to remove the colonial yoke. The 1930s and 1940s seemed to be about broadening the base of political participation and economic stability, and here we were in the 1950s mimicking the mores of the colonizers. Maybe during my 1956 visit to Jamaica I met the wrong people, but I concluded that I needed more time before going home.

On my return to Toronto I resigned my position at Massey Ferguson. I had a discussion with David Archer, president of the Ontario Federation of Labour who told me that if he had it all to do over again, he would have chosen a field other than one in the trade union movement. Archer suggested that at my age, I could do well in another chosen field. My experience as an employee and union representative in Local 439 at the Massey plant, had given me the opportunity and the experience I had dreamt about when I left Jamaica for Canada in 1947. I thought initially that I was coming here to go to school, but the fire at my brother's house caused me to find a full-time job at Massey. As a result it provided me with a wealth of experience that I could not otherwise pay for. Many friendships had been forged during my years at Massey. Some of these friends had helped me to mature and survive during my early days at the plant. In the process, I also learned to relate and work with people from many backgrounds. The multicultural Canada that was to be officially acknowledged in 1971 by the Pierre

Elliot Trudeau government had been a reality for me a generation before, during my Massey years. After leaving Massey Ferguson, I joined forces with my brother Everald, and we went to work for the Mann and Martel Real Estate Company located at St. Clair Avenue West and Avenue Road. I was able to secure a number of listings, but had difficulty with sales because of my concerns that some potential purchasers would not be able to make regular monthly payments. After three months, most of my savings had been depleted and I had no choice but to start looking for other ways of earning a living.

From time to time I visited the Donavolan Centre which became one of the hubs for Toronto's Black community events. It was more than a meeting place. The diverse needs of the community soon fostered an atmosphere that allowed the centre to be a place where many West Indians and their friends visited. They read Caribbean newspapers and magazines, enjoyed the festivities of a Caribbean atmosphere, and developed a sense of belonging in a city that was still unfriendly. The decade of the fifties was a time of ongoing change in my life. Many of us in Toronto's Black community welcomed some of the changes we were experiencing. Home ownership was an option that led some Blacks to move out of the downtown core to suburban areas like Scarborough. Jobs, other than portering and domestic work were gradually being accessed by a small, but increasing number of Black men and women.

Some Toronto Blacks were pleased with the election of John G. Diefenbaker as Prime Minster in 1957. A number of sleeping car porters remembered the "Chief", as he was called, as a politician who was approachable. He had a reputation in the 1940s as a supporter of human rights when he was a Saskatchewan lawyer. As he travelled across Canada by train, Diefenbaker had listened to the porters' stories in earnest when they related incidents of discrimination in Canada's immigration policy. Now, as Prime Minister, those Blacks who knew him hoped that he would reflect their concerns in his new government's policies. Concerns about the issues of immigration did not wane in the latter years of the 1950s. If anything, immigration problems intensified in Toronto's Black community. The Chief found himself in a quandary, because, for much of his adult life he had identified himself as a civil libertarian and a champion of the underdog.[7] As Prime Minister, groups like the Canadian Bar Association expecting that he would act accordingly, chose to present immigration matters to him in a human and civil rights context.

When the West Indian Federation took effect in 1958, one of the first items Ottawa considered was the prospect of negotiating with the West Indies' government to establish an immigration agreement, "similar to those with India, Pakistan and Ceylon."[8] This decision was not based on any desire to have more non-White Caribbean immigrants in Canada. It was another example of Ottawa's smoke-and-mirrors policy for the so-called coloured sending areas. India and Pakistan were allowed in 1951 to send just 150 immigrants each, and Ceylon only 50. It was an accord that did little to encourage immigration from those sending areas. In the 1958 Omnibus submission on immigration to the House of Commons, the minister of Immigration, David Fulton noted, apparently with embarrassment, the sharp criticism from Canadians of East Indian ancestry. They too were prohibited from bringing relatives to Canada. Fulton indicated: "Their criticisms are difficult to answer when they point out to us that they come from a Commonwealth country and yet it is more difficult for them to get their relatives into Canada than it is for people who come from non-Commonwealth countries."[9] R.G.C. Smith, who in

1958 was appointed Canadian Commissioner to the West Indies, advised Ottawa that its immigration program with the West Indies should be expanded because such a gesture would serve to strengthen the federation. Canada's good-natured imperialism was a policy aimed at convincing many of the poorer nations that it was a viable alternative to both Britain and the United States. But because of its colour-bar Ottawa bureaucrats had difficulty doing so. For as Canadians aspired to assume major leadership in the British Commonwealth of Nations that international organization's makeup was becoming increasingly non-White.

The NCA with only a handful of members became less effective in its dealings with Ottawa bureaucrats and politicians. As a consequence calls were coming from various sectors of the community for an organization that more ably represented the interests of Toronto's Black population. These demands were indicative of a maturing community, one whose members had the desire to see their community's position grow stronger in an increasingly ethnically diverse Canada. Some of us continued to push for the fairer treatment of Black-West Indian applicants who were being repeatedly turned away by the Immigration Branch. But the disintegration of the NCA caused us to lose most of our effectiveness. Soon however, the mantle of leadership was picked up by the newly formed, Canadian Association for the Advancement of Coloured People.

The St. Kitts-born Sydney Williams who became the association's executive secretary arrived from Chicago in the late 1950s. He proclaimed that God told him in a vision "to go to Toronto and save the downtrodden Black people there." For a period of time Williams was popular in the so-called mainstream community, and he served as a political consultant in the early 1960s. It is in this capacity that he momentarily commanded the attention of both Prime Minister John Diefenbaker and his successor, Lester Pearson. I am not sure who introduced Sydney Williams to me, but in deciding to go along with his vision, a number of individuals got together to establish the Canadian Association for the Advancement of Coloured People. George Carter, who is now a retired judge, was the organization's first president. Leonard Braithwaite was the vice-president and Williams was the executive secretary. I served as the organization's treasurer.

Our efforts summoned the attention of other prominent members of the community, and Reverend Williams, pastor of Toronto's AME Church became a board member. Energized by Williams' spirit, we all hoped that for the first time in its history, Toronto's Black community, in terms of the indigenous and immigrant Blacks, were coming together to forge a commonweal. Our aim was influenced by developments in the US. The rising tide of nationalism displayed by African Americans in their attempts to eliminate racism in the late 1950s found attraction within our ranks. Martin Luther King's actions in the South, along with the Southern Christian Leadership Conference's growing responses to American racism were featured regularly in Canada's media. We had our own problems with racism, Canadian style, and so Sydney Williams, with his erudite manner helped to renew our efforts. What we wanted then, a point that was still the rallying cry in Canada's Black communities in the 1990s were unity and equality. In 1958 and beyond a few of us living in or identifying with Toronto's Black community decided that the Canadian Association for the Advancement of Coloured People could help us work toward achieving this goal.

For a brief moment the Canadian Association for the Advancement of Coloured People did pick up where the NCA left off. Its members championed a variety of causes. The newly formed association helped some Blacks who were experiencing difficulties after arriving in Canada. It lobbied on behalf of those domestics who were in search of gainful employment after their year-long contracts ended. The association fought for others who were having difficulty finding employment after arriving on Canadian shores without the proper papers. By 1959, Ottawa bureaucrats recognized Williams' tenacity, for he had become a thorn in the side of Ellen Fairclough, the new minister responsible for immigration. His insistence that Black West Indians were being treated unfavourably by Canada's immigration regulations was disturbing to Ottawa bureaucrats and they were not sure what to do with him. After one of his representations to the deputy minister, Laval Fortier, the latter was exasperated with the executive secretary. Fortier advised his department: "From our past associations with Mr. Williams and his organization, I feel that regardless of what argument we put forward, we will not be able to convince him that our present policy respecting West Indian immigration is the most realistic one under the circumstances."[10]

But as was the case with the NCA, our dreams were soon dashed. Tensions developed between the association's members and Williams because of his style of operating as our executive secretary. He was a one-person show. When meetings were called to address specific issues, members of the press, we learned, knew the items on the agenda before the rest of us. Different strategies were instituted to alleviate this problem, but Williams had already entrenched himself with some members of the Toronto media. A decision was made that, as president of the association, George Carter, would be the only person to speak officially to the media. We all agreed with this decision, but were unable to keep the executive secretary in tow. Without any other recourse, the organization's executive decided to remove Sydney Williams from office. To our dismay, he refused to turn over the organization's records to his successor. We discovered that there were two groups representing the Canadian Association for the Advancement of Coloured People. Finding other willing individuals to hold offices as president, vice-president and treasurer, he left with the association's records. The legitimate members of the executive saddled with the problems of no records, no membership list, nothing to show except a bank account with a small balance, decided to disband. Once again the demise of a community organization was brought about from within. It is a story that was told to me when I arrived in Canada in the late 1940s. Sadly, because of my many experiences with community organizations, it is a story that I can now recount as recurring over the years.

After leaving Massey in the Fall of 1956, I responded to an advertisement in the local newspapers seeking canvassers. A number of companies had started canvassing households to determine the type of appliances Torontonians were using. Natural gas was introduced to Toronto in the mid-1950, and stoves, furnaces, refrigerators and other appliances using this type of energy were rapidly coming on the scene. After visiting the company on Rogers Road, I received an offer of one dollar per hour to canvass Toronto households. With clipboard in hand, I set out on a new career. A location was assigned to me and I went to households and asked persons answering my knock at their doors what type of furnace they had in their homes. In the mid-to-late 1950s, most Toronto homes with basements had coal or wood-burning furnaces. Homes without basements usually used what we then called "Quebec heaters." Toronto has been marketed as a world-class city for many years, but in the 1950s and beyond, it was in some respects not more than a small British-styled city. Its Anglo-Saxon ethos kept everyone defined along lines of ethnicity, religion, race, creed and gender. Even in such an environment, there is a natural tendency for people to develop a sense of connection with others and determine how many of their kind were actually occupying the same space as they were.

Many new Black residents to Toronto in the 1950s oftentimes queried the number of Blacks resident in the city. This may have had something to do with a need for contact comfort and a feeling of not being alone in what was sometimes less than hospitable surroundings. I did an unofficial survey in 1956 to determine how many of them I saw going to and from work in downtown Toronto. Within a thirty-day period I saw no more than thirty, and it is likely that in arriving at that figure, I probably counted some Blacks more than once. What is now Canada's largest city has come a long way, as has Canada in the 1990s, toward being classified at present by the United Nations as one of the "best places in the world to live."

Toronto in the late fifties and early sixties was a city whose apartment buildings were usually not higher than three storeys. Hotels were the only high rise buildings and both the King Edward and the Royal York were the only two Toronto hotels with international reputations. East of Victoria Park Avenue was all farmland, travel beyond Toronto's Sunny Side in the south west-end meant that one encountered vacant land, and what was classified municipally as "New Toronto" was sparsely populated. A friend of mine received a plot of land located in the Lawrence and Warden Avenue area, from his father who was in the trucking business. It was farmland in Scarborough and both father and son dug the basement, placed blocks in the hole, and covered it up with a floor that became the roof. My friend lived in that basement with his wife and children for more than four years, and shared a well with a neighbour whose property was half a mile away.

When I was an insurance broker in the sixties there was an occasion when I visited a home in Pickering, Ontario, just east of Toronto. I was there to sell an automobile insurance policy, and I asked the owner to allow me to use the washroom. He showed me to the back of the kitchen where there was no running water, and directed me to what we knew in Jamaica as a pit latrine. The difference being that he used a chemical similar to white lime that was regularly sprinkled in it to keep the stench down. Urinating in it was like throwing water on carbide. The fumes shot up! It was in such a world that I began what was to become an extended career in sales. Reflecting now on my decision to leave the security of a job with seniority at Massey and embark on a career that required face-to- face and one-on-one contact with the public, I consider myself rather daring. Especially since failure meant that I would not be able to support my growing family.

On my third day of canvassing homes, the manager called me into his office. He asked me if I would take a heating and air conditioning course, and after its completion, assume new duties with the company. I happily and anxiously accepted. At the same time Tom Mboya, a future minister of Labour in Kenya was brought to Canada as a guest of the United Steelworkers of America. I was invited to a reception that was held for him in Don Mills, then located on the outskirts of Toronto. When I met Mboya, along with a number of trade unionists, my reason for being there was apparent to me. Having been in Canada for several days he had not seen anyone who looked like him; no Black faces. Mboya was scheduled to speak at Varsity Stadium the following evening. As fate would have it, during the Mboya visit I met an old friend and trade unionist, Francis Edie, who had come to Canada from France. Edie informed me that he had just taken up a new position with a company called Wholesale Typewriters that was hiring new employees. The company sold typewriters and adding machines manufactured in Italy. My friend thought that because of my trade union contacts securing a job as a sales representative with Wholesale Typewriters would be an ideal position for me. I acted on Edie's advice and applied for a job at the company that was then located at Toronto and King Streets.

My application was accepted and I was employed as a sales representative; payment was on a commission basis. After a few days on the job, I went to the office to report my progress, and I met Jack Tramiel, one of the principal owners of Wholesale Typewriters. He needed a ride to his new Yonge and Wellesley Street location and I volunteered to take him there. On the way, Tramiel wanted to know about my background, where I had previously worked, and where I was born. Nearing his destination, he suddenly turned to me and offered me a job to establish a repair and parts department at the new store. Negotiations led me to agree to a wage of $65 per week and a twenty-percent commission on any typewriters and adding machines I sold. Anxious to demonstrate that I was worthy of the trust my boss had placed in me, I immediately set up a card system, instituted a recording system for inventory purposes, and hired a number of typewriter and calculator mechanics. I found my new duties to be challenging, but the rigors of the job restricted my ability to move about and sell. I had little opportunity therefore, to earn my twenty-percent commission. After bringing the matter to Tramiel's attention, my wages were increased to compensate for my loss in commission.

Six months later, some friends of mine who were trade unionists in Jamaica, came to visit me on their way back from the 1957 World Trade Union Movement Conference held that year in Banff, British Columbia. I introduced them to my boss, and he took us out for dinner. However, after a hearty meal we were returning to the store only to discover that the fire department had cordoned off the entire block where the store was located. A major fire, which had begun in a restaurant, had engulfed many of the area's businesses and our store was in disrepair. We had no choice but to move our operations elsewhere, and a suitable location was found on Dupont Street. The business was expanding and to meet local demands we now imported adding machines and typewriter parts from Czechoslovakia, and radios from Japan.

Working with Wholesale Typewriters provided me with the opportunity to learn about business from the perspective of management. During my years at Massey, my perspective had been from the position of being an employee; one who responded to decisions made by others. I also acted in concert with our union's objectives. Now, I worked as a manager, and performed well enough to be promoted to hold the combined positions of production, general and personnel managers. I was sent to Chicago on a six-week course to learn about the manufacturing of platens that were used in typewriters. While I was in the Windy City, I had the opportunity to study assembly and manufacturing systems. Wholesale Typewriters developed into a major business venture in Toronto and we were soon selling thousands of typewriters and portable radios to retail chains and department stores across Canada. Many large shipments were being received from Czechoslovakia and Japan. The company's name was changed to Commodore Typewriter Company and later to Commodore Business Machines.

A FORK IN THE ROAD

In late 1960, Jack Tramiel asked me to go to Kingston, Jamaica and supervise the setting up of a factory and assembly line there. This initiative was part of an incentive program established by the Jamaican government to attract business ventures as a means of stemming the ongoing brain drain from that country. My assignment in Jamaica allowed me to introduce a number of changes on how a factory should be managed. It was commonplace in the 1950s for many Jamaican factories to function under what I called a padlock system. The workers usually operated in an environment wherein security and locks on every gate were the norm. As a consequence I observed a high degree of alienation from management. I introduced an open factory system wherein the workers who were assembling typewriters felt some sense of ownership and took pride in the fact that they were partners in this new Jamaican endeavour.

After a ten-month stay I returned to Toronto in September 1961, and was immediately frustrated with Commodore's Toronto operations. I wanted to resign my position. I expected that I would once again take over the operations, but the president told me that the job I had previously done required the efforts of three people. Which meant that after I left for Jamaica, the company's operations were stymied for a period of time, as replacements had to be found, and trained while I was away. I discovered that Commodore Business Machines now had a general manager, a production manager and a personnel manager. The company was willing to offer me a job as trouble-shooter. Commodore was growing rapidly. In 1961, it had offices and plants in New York, and Ireland. Accepting the offer meant that I would travel with the president to many parts of the world, but I felt that I had had enough. Resignation was the only option for me and I started looking elsewhere for employment.

Someone referred me to the Teskey Cement Company where I applied unsuccessfully for a position as a truck driver delivering cement. Another referral led me to a company where I was interviewed for a job loading and unloading trucks. That job was also put beyond my reach. No one seemed to want to hire me despite my many years of Canadian work experience. Desperate and frustrated I applied to what was called Manpower[11] in those days, but never received any referrals for job interviews.

My involvement in community organizations, the trade union movement, and a variety of athletic activities had put me in contact with a lot of people. Some friends of mine tried on several occasions to get me involved in the insurance business. Even a manager of a major Toronto insurance company badgered me for many months in the late 1950s after I repeatedly sent him prospective clients. He kept telling me I was an ideal candidate for that industry. Now that I had left Commodore Business Machines, I began weighing this option seriously. I called the insurance manager, told him of my intentions to take him up on his offer, and began doing an insurance course. I obtained my life insurance agent's licence after six weeks of daily training and taking a medical, and was then invited by my new boss to his home to meet my fellow employees. We played charades and chatted. After supper, a number of awards were given out to the most productive of the sales staff. The second place winner, who was disturbed about not being number one in sales, went out on the balcony where I joined him in a conversation. He intimated how disgusted he was that he had lost the top award. I promptly told him that I would be starting on the Monday, and I felt that I would not want to be second to anyone, so he would have two people as rivals to outsell in the coming year.

I am not sure if this was the reason for my receiving an envelope by special delivery the following day. A cheque was enclosed for my insurance licence and a letter informed me that I should not present myself at the office on Monday as the company had decided not to hire me as a salesperson. To say the least, I was very upset and depressed about the turn of events. I went to see my friend Francis Edie who told me that he thought I was not accepted because of my colour. He telephoned Andrew Hebb the general manager at Co-operators Insurance, explained what had happened to me and inquired if there were any vacancies at his company. "Send him to me at 30 Bloor Street West was the response." I was there as quickly as I could, and met with Hebb who in turn, introduced me to Earnie Moore, the personnel manager. After conducting an interview Moore told me that he had no objections to hiring me. But before doing so, I needed to take an aptitude test. After completing the test, I waited for an hour, before he informed me that I had passed the test with flying colours. My excitement was dashed, however, when Moore advised me that there were still some feelings of apprehension about offering me a position at Co-operators. I was asked to go to the McQuaig Ferguson Agency at Yonge and King Streets where an assessment would be done to determine my suitability for employment in the industry as a sales representative. The assessment lasted eight hours each day, and was done over a five-day period. A number of projects were assigned to me, and I was put through a series of gruelling interviews about my family background, my childhood, my ambitions, my aims in life and my employment activities to date. At the end of the process, I was told that a report would be sent to Co-operators and thereafter, someone would be in touch with me.

It took almost three weeks for Moore to contact me. By that time Co-operators had already received several copious assessments from the agency. Moore told me that he still had some concerns in a few areas, and highlighted the fact that the assessment revealed that I was both a determined and an argumentative person. He told me that I was someone who could be successful in whatever endeavour I pursued, but that it was difficult for me to retreat from strongly held points of view. Moore wanted to know if I would be argumentative with customers. I tried to assure him that although I was strong-willed it was not my nature to be rude or burdensome to anyone. In selling Co-operators insurance policies, I realized that I would be representing the company, and everyone would expect that I would govern myself accordingly. This job was one that I fought for. But before Co-operators made me a final offer, I was invited to have lunch with twelve of its insurance managers, and following our meeting eleven of them recommended that I should be hired.

The twelfth was apprehensive because as he told me, my initial salary would be $125.00 per week, along with a car and expenses, and he was concerned that I may not be able to live within my means. As politely as I could, I told him that I started working in Canada at Massey Harris for 62 cents an hour, and when I left that company I was being paid more than $2.00 per hour. Whether I worked in a factory or in a managerial position, I assured him that I was always capable of living within my means. He told me that at the time he was making $35,000 per year, and found it difficult to make ends meet, especially since his wife wanted to purchase so many things. All I could say to him was that he needed to have a better handle on his household situation. In accepting the position at Co-operators Insurance I was in effect starting over. But my immigrant experience in Canada had taught me to be fearless of the future, and to take the uncertainties of life and treat them as lessons in living. As the 1960s unfolded, my career in the insurance industry, in conjunction with my community involvement would offer me untold opportunities and challenges.

Chapter 6 – Notes

1. NAC, RG 76, vol. 830, File 552-1-644

2. Ibid.

3. Interview, Eva Smith, January 18, 1993

4. Ibid.

5. Influence sometimes proved to be an important asset for Black West Indian nationals who were attempting to obtain their landings in Canada. In one such instance the Canadian Trade Commissioner in Jamaica intervened on behalf of a Jamaican wishing to emigrate and work for Bell Canada. She was recommended to the Trade Commissioner by her cousin, an executive with one of the largest business firms in Kingston, Jamaica, and by the nominated member of the Jamaican Legislative Council. And although the Immigration Branch had determined that the woman in question did not fall within the admissible categories, the Trade Commissioner asked that her application be treated favourably because of the "public relations angle." The memo of recommendation, dated 18/12/56, from the director of the Immigration Branch to Laval Fortier, Deputy minister of the Department of Citizenship and Immigration was approved 19/12/56. NAC, RG 76, vol. 830, File 552-1-644.

6. Ibid.

7. Ibid., p. 103. See D.V. Smiley, *Canada in Question: Federalism in the Eighties*, 3rd ed. (Toronto: McGraw-Hill Ryerson Ltd., 1980), p. 44.

8. *Report to His Excellency the Governor General in Council*, from the Acting minister of Citizenship and Immigration, March 12, 1958. PAC, RG 76, vol. 830, File 552-1-644.

9. "Immigration from India, Pakistan and Ceylon." *Omnibus submission on Immigration Policy and Procedures*, May 10, 1958. NAC, RG 76, vol. 830, File SF-1-1, pt. 2, p. 16.

10. Memo from Laval Fortier to Ellen Fairclough, minister, Citizenship and Immigration, November 12, 1959.NAC, RG 76 vol. 830, File 552-1-644.

11. A federal government job recruitment centre, commonly referred to in the 1960s as Manpower and Immigration, more recently called Human Resources Development Canada (HRDC).

CHAPTER 7

Shedding the Old Coat

I n 1960, Ottawa was indicating that it was willing to reconcile some of its domestic and international policies. By that date John Diefenbaker in his capacity as Prime Minister of Canada had become rather outspoken on South Africa. In June 1960, he also introduced legislation to the House of Commons for a Canadian Bill of Rights. On the eve of doing so, Diefenbaker caught my attention with his language of the moment when he said:

> The hallmark of freedom is recognition of the sacred personality of man, and its acceptance decries discrimination on the basis of race, creed or colour. Canadians have a message to give to the world. We are composed of many racial groups, each of which must realize that only by forbearance and mutual respect, only by denial of antagonisms of prejudice based on race, or creed, or even surname, can breaches in unity be avoided in our country.[1]

In his message to the nation, Diefenbaker carefully outlined his reasons for introducing a Canadian Bill of Rights. He reminded us that such legislation had been previously introduced, but that it had been held over so that his government could receive representations from interested individuals and organizations in Canada.[2] In some small measure, it seemed to me that the Chief was sanctioning the efforts of those of us who had long fought for justice and freedom and dignity for all Canadians. Each word seemed to personally address us, and in turn, I could not help but hope that we were witnesses to the birth of a new Canada. Nonetheless, we still had much work to do. The immigration issue had provided me with a clear example of how Ottawa had remained unwilling to be ahead of Canadian public opinion. I however, viewed Diefenbaker's Canadian Bill of Rights as embodying the 1948 United Nations Universal Declaration of Human Rights. Thus, I was encouraged when the Canadian Bill of Rights received royal assent in August 1960.

Though small in number, the increasing Black presence in the late 1950s and beyond did not go unnoticed in cities like Toronto. Accordingly, there was something of a backlash by those White Canadians who were themselves fearful, disdainful or suspicious of what appeared to be growing numbers of Black strangers in their midst. As a consequence, it was common for newly arrived Black immigrants to speak of difficulties when looking for apartments to rent. Some White Canadians in Toronto and other Canadian cities had long shown their unease for the so-called newcomers. The Joint Labour Committee for Human Rights included the issue of discrimination in housing as an essential part of its agenda. Since the end of the Second World War, some newspaper articles pointed to the difficulties that Jews and Blacks had encountered in their attempts to either find rental accommodation or purchase homes. What made the situation even more sorry was that this problem extended to homes that were being built under agreements set out by Canada's National Housing Act.[3]

Oftentimes application forms for rental units included sections to be filled in for "nationality of self and family, religion or faith."[4] I found the process very frustrating; especially after having worked with my colleagues in the human rights movement to effect changes so that rental accommodation would be included in the Fair Accommodation Practices Act. In a brief to the Ontario government in early 1961, a coalition of groups representing churches, labour unions, and over 40 organizations led by Eamon Park, a former politician, reminded premier Leslie Frost that: "racial discrimination is sufficiently widespread to necessitate remedial government action."[5] More than ever I was convinced in 1960 that we were right. Continuously fighting an uphill battle, we counted ourselves among the children of Sisyphus. There were so many fronts to fight on, so many battles yet to be won; rental accommodation issues, immigration matters, discrimination in employment and the like. What seemed clear was that those of us involved in human and civil rights issues needed the backing of both the federal and provincial governments. The Canadian Bill of Rights was a good start but Ottawa and Queen's Park needed to take more of a proactive role in alleviating racism and religious intolerance. As members of the Toronto Joint Labour Committee on Human Rights we continued to conduct surveys, and provide various governmental bodies with our findings about the evils of discrimination. For example, "in the summer of 1957, G. Williams, a [Black] minister and social worker, seeking accommodation for his wife and child said that he faced discrimination in 25 apartment buildings."[6]

Throughout the 1950s and into the 1960s I was involved in a number of test cases dealing with discrimination by landlords in the rental of apartment units. A survey conducted in Toronto by university students, members of the Black community and the Labour Committee for Human Rights authenticated Williams' experiences. From apartments advertised for rent in

Toronto's daily newspapers, "thirty-seven were randomly selected. Of that number, sixteen rental agents were found to be discriminatory, eleven stated they accepted people irrespective of race, religion or nationality and ten expressed doubts or equivocated."[7] Eventually our efforts and the shifting political tide convinced premier Frost to place amendments before the Ontario legislature in 1961 to the Fair Accommodation Practices Act. The purpose for these amendments was to "prohibit discrimination in the renting of apartments in buildings containing more than six units."[8]

The above and other related initiatives would set out a 1960s agenda for the Ontario government in an era when Canadians were becoming more familiar domestically and internationally, with issues of human and civil rights. In particular, this latter Act was one of a series of legislative initiatives begun in 1944 when the Ontario government proclaimed its Racial Discrimination Act. What had followed since that date were amendments to the Conveyancing and Law of Property Act to nullify any discriminatory covenants in the sale of land (1950). Amendments were also enacted to the Labour Relations Act to deter collective agreements that discriminated against a person on the basis of race or religion (1950). The Fair Employment Practices Act was put in place in 1951 and the Fair Accommodation Practices Act was proclaimed in 1954. In 1958, the Ontario Anti-Discrimination Commission Act allowed for the establishment of the Ontario Anti-Discrimination Commission set up in 1959. It was the precursor to the Ontario Human Rights Commission. In effect, these Acts proclaimed if not in all of Canada, certainly in Ontario, some semblance of an understanding by the provincial government that the rights of individuals needed protecting. In doing so, both the federal government with its 1960 Bill of Rights and in Ontario, the Leslie Frost government with the various legislative initiatives mentioned above, at least on paper were acting as change agents.

What is to be remembered is that the Frost government was conservative in its ideology and its politicians subscribed to right of centre principles. In 1962, under Premier John Robarts the Ontario government established the Ontario Human Rights Code that was enforced through the establishment of the Ontario Human Rights Commission. This was an important time in Canada's history. For it set the tone for the emergence of a different Canada, one that was becoming increasingly less Eurocentric, and one that over the next several decades appeared to become increasingly committed to the concept of multiculturalism. By ourselves, Black Canadians found it difficult to effect change. Our numbers were insignificant. But by joining forces with other groups, supporting their causes, and in turn receiving support for our own programs, we helped to build a common cause wherein our voices could be heard.

The Black struggle for survival in Canada had naught to do with Ottawa's pretence of granting landings to only those who demonstrated that they "counteracted their climatic abilities with ...exceptional qualifications."[9] Notwithstanding their supposed exceptionality, on arrival, Black immigrants soon discovered how quickly the doors of landlords and employers were shut in their faces. Though it was often said that there was no racism here, some Canadians could not temper their prejudice to allow Blacks to earn a living and put a roof over their heads. The national president of the Jewish Labour Committee of Canada declared in 1959 that "racial discrimination in housing ...is bringing humiliation and suffering to members of minority groups."[10] The human rights coalition of labour, community, and disadvantaged ethnic groups remained intact, and some landlords and employers who blatantly discriminated against minority groups were openly challenged in the 1960s. Despite the discriminatory attitudes of some Canadians, many Caribbean residents longed to come to Canada. Growing difficulties that led to riots by Whites and Black West Indians in several British cities caused many West Indians to look in Canada's direction.

The Diefenbaker government, twice elected by 1960, was still not publicly supporting any significant increase to Canada's Black population. While pushing away Black immigrants, who wished to settle in Canada, the Chief was openly challenging South Africa's apartheid policy. In this regard, he was able to distinguish between his domestic and foreign policy objectives. At its March 1961 conference, the Commonwealth seemed to me to be at a vulnerable point in its history. The older Commonwealth member nations were being challenged by the newer, non-White members to discard many of their colonial attitudes, and accept them, the former British colonies, on an equal footing. The task for Britain was in finding a way to maintain old loyalties by preserving the character of the Commonwealth's traditional membership, while concomitantly giving some leeway to its new non-White partners.

In the meantime, from all media accounts of the situation, the Chief displayed a willingness to place on the world stage his reputation earned at home in the 1940s for being a champion of the downtrodden. Diefenbaker publicly displayed his discomfort with the Sharpeville Massacre when in November 1960, he warned the British Prime Minister, Harold Macmillan, "that unless significant changes occur in the Union government of South Africa's racial policies, Canada's support could not be counted on."[11] This was an instance when the Chief was comfortable in moving beyond White solidarity and siding instead with his country's international objectives in the hope of making Canada more acceptable to the developing world.

The South African Union government had refused to back away from its apartheid policies, and Diefenbaker was resolute that it must. I was very pleased when I read local media accounts of how Diefenbaker had held steadfast at the conference. He insisted that no compromise was possible in the face of South Africa's bloody crimes and treatment of its Black majority. In the end the British Prime Minister's policy of "understanding, patience, and persuasion"[12] was defeated when South Africa withdrew from the Commonwealth. Ironically, Diefenbaker's position on South Africa caused Ottawa bureaucrats to walk a tight rope. In this instance his high moral position on the world stage required a balance in terms of Canada's own domestic and foreign policy objectives. The External Affairs officer in the Prime Minister's office, H. Basil Robinson, recorded that concern was expressed by some senior bureaucrats that "if [Canada] was too outspoken on South Africa, and brought about its exclusion, Canada would invite serious immigration problems; a large flow of non-white applicants."[13] The question for people like myself however, was why should the same high ethical standards in Canada's foreign policy not be similarly reflected in its domestic policies? And how could Canada's immigration policy, one which had long subscribed to the concept of White superiority, remain intact?

The federated West Indies, itself a member of the Commonwealth was in trouble from its inception in 1958. By the early 1960s it was doomed. Parochial concerns were at the heart of the matter. Even after several years, the units of the Federation were without any firm resolve that the new political union would at least facilitate their economic betterment.[14]

It was an era of growing Black Nationalism in many parts of the world. One read of Ghana's efforts to maintain its independence; of other African nations' attempts to secure their autonomy, and of the daily battles fought by African Americans to achieve equality in the US. Thus the "British-imposed" solution for West Indian problems further delayed rather than encouraged a concord.[15] Diefenbaker in his memoirs indicates that he received a visit on the eve of the Federation's destruction from the premier of the Federation, Sir Grantley Adams. Adams apparently implored him to make a trip to the West Indies to help save the Federation. But by then Diefenbaker felt that his efforts would be to no avail.[16] By 1961, Adams' political reputation in his own country, Barbados, and in the rest of the West Indies, like the Chief's in Canada, was beginning to wear thin. In Barbados, Adams and his Labour Party would go down to defeat at the polls in 1961. In his biographer's words: "one of the damaging indictments made against Adams' leadership of the Federation was that it did not put forward a plan for economic development of a federated West Indies."[17]

The strongest links in the Federation had been Jamaica, Trinidad, and to a lesser degree Barbados. One year after the Federation took effect there was growing opposition to it by many Jamaicans, who believed that the economic burdens of smaller areas of the Federation would be carried by the larger. Trinidad, already suffering from unemployment and a shortage of housing, was feeling the effects of increasing immigration from the smaller Caribbean areas.[18] The poorer areas of the region, remaining suspicious of the larger units, refused to be dominated by what they perceived to be "the exchange of one colonial power for another." These developments culminated in "the general breakdown of confidence ...among the various units of the Federation."[19] In terms of the relevance of such moments of change for us as Canadians, we later witnessed hundreds of thousands of West Indians vying for the right to enter Canada. There was growing uncertainty that was brought about by the ongoing shifting sands of political and economic developments in the Caribbean region. A development that caused over a million West Indian nationals, among them the best and brightest, to seek refuge in far off places in the Sixties and Seventies, as I had previously done.

Ottawa finally relented somewhat in 1962, when changes were made to Canada's Immigration Act. Ellen Fairclough, minister of Immigration introduced new immigration regulations in the House of Commons that supposedly removed Canada's "White's-only" immigration policy. At the time my review of the situation was less optimistic about the pending changes. I interpreted the new regulations as favouring only, "persons who by reason of their education, training, skills or other special qualifications were likely to establish themselves successfully in Canada and who had either prearranged employment in Canada or sufficient means of support to maintain themselves while becoming established."[20] Nonetheless, I rationalized that any changes to Canada's Immigration Act, no matter how small would bring a response in the West Indies. This was especially true for those Caribbean residents who were bent on seeking a foreign experience. They interpreted Fairclough's proposed changes as an attempt by Ottawa to establish a level playing field for Black West Indians. The feedback from Canada's Trade Commissioner stationed in Jamaica in 1962 supported my thinking. Reporting to Ottawa, he indicated that by early February of that year on a daily basis, his office was receiving twenty-five visits and seventy telephone calls from Jamaicans. In a two-week period over 1000 applications were handed out. Between May 1 and September 30, 1962, there were 957 deferred applicants for personal interviews in the West Indies; of this number 649 originated in Jamaica. Another 1455 files in the pipeline were not as yet at the stage where a decision could be made, and 688 of this number also originated in Jamaica.[21]

From the above, it is possible to understand why the Jamaican population in Toronto is currently approximately more than half that city's Black population. In search of opportunities, Jamaicans by the thousands looked to Canada in the early 1960s. A fact that those of us already living in Toronto began taking seriously. As we continued to tackle problems of adjustment and settlement there was talk by some persons about the possibility of setting up an organization for Jamaicans living in Toronto. With the dissolution of the West Indies Federation, and a date identified for Jamaica's independence, the idea seemed more favourable to some Jamaicans. The move toward Jamaican self-determination was an objective that both Norman Manley and Alexander Bustamante had worked toward for a number of decades. Jamaicans had already begun the internal process of separating themselves from Britain. Universal Suffrage in 1944 and the existence of the two-party political system proved to be important steps in moving Jamaicans on the road to a democratic system of government. They also began the process of redefining themselves and their country by establishing important structures like the Jamaican Broadcasting Corporation (JBC) in 1959.

By the time the news spread in the community that Jamaica would formally separate from Britain on August 6, 1962, I had already decided in my mind that I had had enough of an experience with the rigours of community organizations. Apart from my volunteer work in the wider community, I continued my involvement in the trade union movement, and my efforts as a member of the Joint Labour Committee for Human Rights. Since January 1948, I had given my time and money to many Black community organizations, that included, the Toronto United Negro Association, the Toronto United Negro Credit Union, the Universal Negro Improvement Association, the Negro Citizenship Association and the Canadian Association for the Advancement of Coloured People. When I reflected on the progress of the Black community in early 1962, I called to mind my initial meeting in the early 1950s with Don Moore, and how disillusioned he was with his community's failure to establish a blue print for its development and success.

The problem historically appeared to be that too few of us were working to effect real change. In the process, we became disillusioned, overburdened, and oftentimes not recognized for our efforts. The prevailing competition among Canadian and immigrant Blacks made it difficult to work toward the forging of a common agenda. The added sociological problem of inner tensions between fair skinned and dark skinned Blacks only compounded the problem. Organizational rivalries, and a willingness by some of us to forsake the big picture, looking instead only at personal gain suggested to me that it was time I left Black community affairs alone. So I thought to myself, no more. I have had it with such thankless work! But as is usually the case, circumstances intervene and one becomes caught up in the tide of historical events.

In early 1962, my friend E.S. Ricketts invited me to be part of a group to help arrange an event to mark Jamaica's independence. I told him that I had had enough of community groups and that I was not interested. But this stalwart of the community, someone who had laboured intensely to help keep the UNIA alive, and had given of his time to teach young people to appreciate music, had heard it all before. My impatience was no deterrence to him, and several months later his sustained badgering caused me to give in to his wishes. A meeting was held at the Home Service Association located at 941 Bathurst Street. Those of us assembled agreed that a dinner and dance should be arranged to commemorate Jamaica's historic break with British colonialism. Our committee was made up primarily of students and other individuals, many of whom I did not know. I was asked to play a key role. Securing an appropriate venue and arranging the entertainment were essential to the successful outcome of the event. Fortunately, my friend George King whom I had worked with at Massey Ferguson and served with on various community organizations was also involved.

My first task was to go to the King Edward Hotel, and after guaranteeing 250 persons for dinner I secured it as the venue for the August 6, 1962 event. Next I arranged with my brother Eric who performed under the name Lord Power II, to have his band play, and his daughters dance the limbo. We needed a guest speaker and because of my involvement in the trade labour movement, I approached the late David Lewis, who at the time was a federal member of parliament for York South. He later became the leader of the national New Democratic Party. Lewis agreed to be our guest speaker, and invitations and flyers were printed with the assistance of the United Steelworkers of America and the United Automobile Workers of America, Local 439. The president of the Ontario Federation of Labour, David Archer agreed to attend and sit at the head table. Through his connections in the Canadian army, George King managed to obtain the assistance of a Colonel Legg. His duty was to ensure that we followed the necessary protocol such as head table seating, and the proper unfurling of the new Jamaican flag. We sold more than 250 tickets by the date of the function, and everything seemed to be in place as planned. On August 6, 1962, politicians from the three levels of government, other dignitaries and people from all walks of life came together to celebrate the ending of more than 300 hundred years of the British domination of Jamaica. I was stationed at the door, and Roy Williams, then a student at the University of Toronto represented our committee among the head table guests.

Lewis pointed out in his remarks that Canada had two duties to Jamaica: "one was to give all possible economic assistance: the other was to erase from Canadian immigration law all vestiges of racist and colour discrimination." In the spirit of the flag debate that was topical at the time, Lewis reminded the audience that Canadians could learn from Jamaicans about "securing a distinctive flag."[22] Stanley Haidasz, Liberal MP for Parkdale told the crowd that "Canada was proud to welcome Jamaica as a sister nation, sovereign and equal."[23] My nieces Donna and Sandra Armstrong held the audience's attention with their limbo dancing feats. The evening seemed to have gone as planned until I approached David Lewis at the head table to congratulate him for his sincere message, only to be rebuked. I noticed that the tablecloth was soaked through with red wine. Apparently, the King Edward Hotel had served our head table guests South African wine, and they were not amused. Some of them spilled the wine in protest, and I was admonished for not paying closer attention to the catering details. The discomfort I felt served as a valuable lesson for me that evening. Since then, I have played a leading role in the planning of numerous public functions and have mastered the art of checking and rechecking each detail.

The following day, Toronto newspapers reported the event as a success, and we were all very happy to have been associated with it. Energized by the event and the media recognition we received, some of those people who attended the function underscored the point that we should establish an organization for Jamaicans living in Toronto. Both the success of the recent celebration, and the existence of a core group of people who had served on its planning committee made the task easier.

Our early gatherings where we discussed the formation of the Jamaican Canadian Association (JCA) were held at George and Viola King's home located at 1072 College Street. In addition to the Kings, my brother Val and brother-in-law and sister Frank and Mavis Magnus, my cousin Roy Heron, Amy Nelson and Phyllis White both of whom were nurses, E.S. Ricketts, Roy Williams and Ira Dundas, were all present at these initial meetings.[24] After a number of serious and painstaking deliberations the JCA was launched in September 1962. At a meeting at the College Street YMCA held on September 23, 1962 the association's officers were elected. Roy Williams was elected president of the JCA, I was its vice-president, and George King was the executive secretary, Ira Dundas, treasurer and Mavis Magnus, recording correspondence secretary. Other officers were J.B. Campbell, Owen Tennyson, Phillis White, Violet Carter and E.S. Ricketts.[25]

We had already arduously established our constitution, with specific aims and objectives. Including: "developing and maintaining closer ties between Canadians and Jamaicans; the establishing of closer relations with Jamaicans living in Canada, and the moulding of this group into an effective and influential voice in community affairs."[26] The association had no money. However, I ran in to Sydney Williams and he informed me that there was still a small balance left in the Canadian Association for the Advancement of Coloured People's bank account. After discussing the matter, and drawing on the fact that my name was still listed as treasurer of the defunct association, we both agreed that the JCA would benefit from these funds. Soon thereafter, as he promised, Williams turned over money totalling less than a hundred dollars to the new organization's account. This is how we began, and it was an instance where cooperation by many people from a variety of backgrounds helped to bring to fruition the Jamaican Canadian Association.

Establishing the JCA turned out to be a very good idea, and it was in place at a critical moment in the history of Toronto's Black community. The early Sixties proved to be an important era for the formation of what I refer to as the "Newer Black community."[27] Because by 1963, Black immigration showed signs of picking up, and the Jamaican Canadian Association was able to advocate on behalf of Jamaicans and others wishing to come to Canada. In particular, other West Indians who did not have access to an effective advocacy group. Other community organizations in Toronto that reflected on the Canadian-Caribbean experience were still a decade away.

In Canada, and more specifically, when the era of the Sixties in Toronto is mentioned, Yorkville, Hippies, Draft-dodgers, and uncertainty come to mind. Much of that however, had little to do with the Black community. Uncertainty for us was nothing new, and all of those moments of change associated with such upheaval would be more prevalent from 1962 onwards. Growing numbers of Black immigrants, and in particular more and more Black students studying at post-secondary institutions created a new vitality in our midst. Yet, it was one thing for those with nature's passport to claim disillusionment with the system, but one way or the other they had ownership of the system. Even for those Black folk whose ancestry dated to the eighteenth-century, Canada seemed less of a home, and more of an overstayed stop on the Underground Railroad. What

Black Canadians experienced in-house, many Black immigrants experienced on arrival at Malton Airport. Repeatedly, immigration officials looked at them and sent a clear message: "there is no room at the inn."

An effective organization is as good as its membership. More important to the process is the nature of the leadership an organization is able to attract. When Roy Williams was elected JCA president, he had recently completed his graduate studies at the University of Toronto. Initially, Roy and I had a lot of disagreements with each other. It was a classic case of how different personalities come together to work toward achieving a common purpose. In the process, conflict develops when there are different points of view of how the association's course should be charted. My involvement in community and organizational development has taught me that when you have a leader who borders on being overly strong willed, it is vital that if the organization is to thrive that a strong executive be put in place. I have already recounted my experiences with several community organizations in which certain individuals saw fit to continuously run with the ball at the expense of the other members.

Roy felt that as the JCA president he had the authority to make certain decisions without the hindrance of the executive. He saw nothing wrong with making purchases for the organization without receiving the approval of the executive. In such instances he tendered bills for items we had not approved for purchase. Roy bought a duplicating machine at a fire sale for over $100.00, and the JCA incurred additional costs of a similar amount to fix it, and it was still unworkable. He also bought a fan at the fire sale that did not work, and so his purchases, though well intentioned, were frustrating our coffer in a period when there was very little money. While respecting his zeal, some of the members had difficulty with such an approach and found it necessary to put a $50.00 limit on the amount the president could spend without authorization.

Roy was resistant to what he perceived as our attempts to restrict his authority. I had to take on the role of opposition leader, a position that was rather difficult since I was vice-president. Roy was a charismatic leader and he had the support and trust of the majority of the executive. Thus at times, he was able to bypass my opposition. Through all of the turmoil, however, we maintained the respect and a friendship we shared for each other. We disagreed at meetings, but we knew that our actions were being carried out in the best interest of this fledgling organization. It never reached a stage where Roy and I disliked each other. He was a good president, and the membership placed him on a pedestal. His education and sound business knowledge helped the JCA in its infancy, and most of us were happy to serve during his tenure.

Being part of the JCA executive turned out to be hard work. In an era of growing immigration from the Caribbean, we were constantly called on to intervene on behalf of new arrivals from that region. We soon discovered how important viable organizations like the JCA were, and still are to Toronto's Black community. As chairperson of the general purposes committee, I was kept busy attending meetings and responding to phone calls from community members, newly arrived immigrants, bureaucrats, civil servants and politicians. The lessons I learned from these encounters convinced me that any viable community is only as strong as its ability to advocate and represent its own interests. For in the end, it is not the meek who inherit the earth, but those who are in a position to sit at the table with the power brokers and command their attention.

In November 1962, the Social Planning Council of Metropolitan Toronto and the Immigration Branch invited me to sit on a panel and represent the JCA. The forum took place at the International Institute, which was located on College Street, and the topic was: "The Integration of non-White Immigrants and the community's role." Alan Borovoy who was then the director of the Toronto and District Human Rights Committee was among those on the panel, and U of T professor Freda Hawkins, who later wrote a number of seminal studies on Canadian immigration, chaired the panel. Out of this process, those organizational representatives in attendance agreed to work more closely together. During the following decade, we consulted and supported each other on a variety of social and political issues. The growing popularity of the JCA was underscored when after the meeting I was approached by John Eckert of the Immigration Branch, and he told me that it was his department's intention to repeatedly call on our organization for assistance.

On the heels of this panel discussion, the Social Planning Council's Family and Child Branch invited me to attend a meeting. The late Wilson Head was brought to Toronto by the Social Planning Council of Metropolitan Toronto in 1965 to serve as its director of planning and research. He recollects in his book, *A Life on the Edge* that he discovered that the council was run by a board of directors: "comprised primarily of middle class men and women who had an interest in meeting the community's most pressing needs."[27] This, I soon discovered when the council's representative, Mrs. Marshall expressed her organization's concern that many problems were being experienced by social workers who were trying to find adoption homes for children of non-White parents. She told me the problem was so acute that the City of Toronto could no longer cope with the problem.

In early 1963, we learned that new arrivals from the West Indies were not receiving appropriate treatment at the hands of immigration officials at Malton Airport. Some of the newly arrived immigrants from the West Indies were being taken from Malton to the city for medical examinations. They were then returned to the port of entry and held for up to three hours without being allowed any contact with their relatives or friends who were waiting to greet them. Just imagine going to the airport to await your sisters' arrival, only to see every one else except your relative come through the gates. As members of the Jamaican Canadian Association we were repeatedly asked or at times we took it upon ourselves to go to the airport and assist new arrivals from the West Indies who were being treated disdainfully by immigration and customs officials. Some immigration officials relished the opportunity to quiz new arrivals from the Caribbean about their sex life. In my capacity as the JCA vice-president, I complained publicly in 1963 about this problem. During an immigration conference, I pointed out to the audience that West Indian women applying to bring their fiancés to Canada had to answer a sex quiz given by immigration officials: "How many times they [had] kissed their boyfriends?" They were also asked to indicate, "how intimate they had been with their boy friends." The Immigration Branch later denied the charges as the *Toronto Star* put it of, "Our Crazy color bar where kisses count."[28] The branch however, indicated that the women were being questioned to determine if there was a genuine relationship.[29]

There were also other heinous accusations. A number of people claimed for example, that some immigration officials had tried to kiss some of these women. Furthermore, that in instances where they were detained in a hotel as was usually the practice, immigration officials showed up at their doors and tried to have intimate relations with them. The Immigration Branch denied that any of this was happening. But some individuals did come forward and verify that unsavoury things did happen to some of the West Indian women.

Some Black West Indian women also claimed that they fared no better at the hands of officials in the Caribbean. We had reports where women were coerced to have sexual relations with men in authority in exchange for approval to be included in the quota for the West Indies Domestic Scheme. At one of our JCA membership meetings I spoke of how some of the women from Jamaica claimed to have been treated by some officials in that country's Department of Labour. Someone took the liberty of taping my remarks that were later played for the Jamaican minister of Labour. He denied that any such behaviour had taken place. Of course, he was not happy with my comments and someone in his department went out of his way to say that I was crazy and that my facts were not right. My facts were right. It was a shame that some decent women, having no other choice, were forced to subject themselves to such cruel and inhuman treatment in exchange for a foreign experience. Coming to Canada put many of them at risk, for the Immigration Branch held them in high suspicion. When the scheme was begun in the mid-1950s, the Canadian Medical Service determined that a pre-screening medical exam was not sufficient for these women and a further step was instituted by administering a sample Wassermann tests when they arrived at Dorval. The claim was made that this decision was "due to the large percentage of syphilis in the West Indies." However, the director of the Canadian Immigration Branch decided that "West Indies authorities were not to be notified that the tests were being conducted."[30]

As an organization, the JCA must have been doing something right, because we not only attracted the attention of politicians and bureaucrats, but the police as well. There was some collaboration with the Toronto police when its representatives came to us in the early 1960s, and asked for our help in finding potential Black recruits for the force. But there were also instances where our suspicions led us to believe that as members of the JCA, we were under surveillance by the Metropolitan Toronto Police Force. Some of us were followed, our phones appeared to be bugged, and there was even a White police officer that took out membership in the association. Whenever we sent correspondence to his home, his wife would respond by phoning our offices and with the worst possible rancour, she would tell us that she did not want any Black material being sent to her address.

It is apparent to me of the extent to which the State held me close to its chest, especially in the 1970s, when I repeatedly spoke out about the police shootings of Blacks in Toronto, and of the inhumane manner in which Black people were sometimes treated in Canada. When research was being undertaken for this book, several attempts were made to access whatever information may be contained in the files of the RCMP. Needless to say that although it is my right to know what is on file, efforts to access this information through the Freedom of Information Act were met with complete silence. After all, in "The True North Strong and Free," those who fight for rights and freedoms are usually forced to suffer a heavy price by having our freedoms curtailed, and our abilities to earn a living severely limited.

Despite the clandestine behaviour by government officials, when circumstances warranted, representatives from all levels of government came knocking at our door. Members of the JCA continued to work vigilantly on behalf of their community, and those in authority had to take us seriously. After its formation, our representatives attended conferences, forums and government briefings. We met with Caribbean government officials, and had no apprehension about representing our community's interests.

In 1967, the JCA responded to the federal government's 1966 White Paper on Immigration. In this period, the Lester B. Pearson government had introduced pending changes to Canada's Immigration Act. Advocating for change to Canada's immigration policy was nothing new for those of us who had continued to do so since the early 1950s. Although the 1962 changes to the Immigration Act had allowed a crack in the door, Canadian immigration regulations still discriminated on the basis of geographic location. Section 31d continued to allow for the retention of a wider range of European immigrants to Canada. Additionally, the Governor General's Order-in-council underscored the importance of section 61 that still "prohibited or limited the admission of persons by reason of nationality, citizenship, ethnic group, and geographic area of origin."[31] Because immigration officials were not readily accessible to those persons wishing to apply in the region, in our brief, the JCA recommended that the practices of sending immigration teams to the Caribbean should be terminated. Instead, permanent immigration offices should be established in the region. We were encouraged by some of the changes enacted in 1967. For the first time what is commonly referred to as the "points system", allowed potential immigrants to Canada from the Caribbean to be assessed on the basis of "education and training; personal assessment, by an immigration officer; occupational skills; arranged employment in the area of destination."[32]

In 1967, immigration offices were opened in Jamaica and Trinidad. This new system did not mean that Canada had the intention of opening wide its gates to Black immigrants. Nor did a change in Ottawa's policy signal a lessening of racial tendencies in Canadian society. Racism in Canada was as Canadian as maple syrup. But through our efforts to effect change, those of us in the JCA, in trade union movement and involved in various human rights endeavours were able to sensitize many Canadians to the evils of racism.

At least into the 1970s we also helped to establish a human and civil rights agenda that would advance the status of Blacks and other minorities in Canada. There was a growing awareness that Black people had been part of the Canadian fabric, sufficiently so, that Robin Winks wrote a book entitled *Blacks in Canada* (Montreal: McGill-Queen's Press, 1971). Winks' account acknowledged the Black Canadian presence dating back to the early 1600s. This was a fitting rebuttal to those who had laboured long and hard in Canada's Immigration Branch to prove that because of their skin colour, Black people were unfit for Canada's supposedly harsh climate. Blacks had long endured the hostility of Canada's winters. The problem we had was the damage that Canadian racism had done to our psyche.

Chapter 7 – Notes

1. John George Diefenbaker, "Address on the "Nation's Business", June 30, 1960. Refer to document at internet site http:collections.ic.gc.ca/canspeak/english/jgd/sp1.htm

2. Similar legislation had been introduced in September 1958

3. "Race bar Charged in NHA Projects." Toronto Telegram, August 27, 1954, p. 41

4. See copy of Chibaw Securities Limited, Toronto, Ontario in: MG28 I173, vol. 36

5. See copy of brief included in NAC files under "Apartment Housing Surveys." MG 28 I1173 vol. 36

6. Daniel G. Hill, "Discrimination in Apartment Buildings." *Ontario Housing*, (August 1963), p. 6.

7. Ibid.

8. "Human Rights Code Broadened." *Human Relations*, vol. 1 No. 2, March 1961 (Toronto: Ontario Anti-discrimination Commission)

9. Wilson Head, *The Black Presence in the Canadian Mosaic: A Study of Perception and the Practice of Discrimination against Blacks in Metropolitan Toronto*. (Toronto: Ontario Human Rights Commission, 1975), p. 18.

10. "Racial Discrimination in Housing Charged," *Globe and Mail*, December 5, 1959.

11. Alistair Horne, *MacMillan: 1957-1986, Vol. II of the Official Biography* (London: MacMillan Ltd., 1989), p. 391.

12. Ibid., p. 391, see 7n, letter of August 12, 1960; HMA

13. .H. Basil Robinson, *Diefenbaker's World: A Populist in Foreign Affairs*. (Toronto: U of T Press, 1989), p. 125.

14. For an account of the Federation's woes see Franklin Knight's, *The Caribbean*. (New York: Oxford University Press, 1978), p. 204-206; Gordon K. Lewis *The Growth of the Modern West Indies*. (New York: Monthly Review Press, 1968), p. 368-386; and Eric Williams, *History of the People of Trinidad and Tobago*. (London: Andre Deutsch Ltd., 1982), p. 242-277.

15. John G. Diefenbaker, *One Canada: Memoirs of the Right Honourable John Diefenbaker: The Years of Achievement 1957-1962*. (Toronto: MacMillan of Canada, 1976), p. 194-195.

16. F.A. Hoyas, *Grantley Adams and the Social Revolution*. (London: Macmillan Pub., Ltd., 1974), p. 212.

17. For an account of the growing political tensions in the West Indies Federation see Elisabeth Wallace, *The British Caribbean: From the decline of Colonialism to the end of the Federation* (Toronto: U of T Press, 1977), Chapter 7, pp 164-191.

18. Ibid

19. Ibid.

20. Freda Hawkins, *Canada and Immigration: Public Policy and Public Concern* (Montreal: McGill-Queens Press, 1988) pp. 125-127

21. Letter from Roy Balke, Canadian Trade Commissioner, to D.A. Reid, Chief Operations, Immigration Branch, February 8, 1962. PAC, RG 76, vol. 830, File 552-1-644.

22. "Toronto's Jamaicans Celebrate Freedom." *Globe and Mail*, August 7, 1962, p. 5.

23. Ibid.

24. *Minutes of the First Executive Meeting of the Jamaican-Canadian Association at the YMCA, College Street, September 23, 1962.*

25. *Draft of New Constitution to Be Presented for Approval.* See its preamble.

26. Minutes of the JCA's General Purposes Meeting, November 18, 1962.

27. Wilson Head, *A Life on the Edge: Experiences in "Black and White" in North America.* Toronto: U of T Press, 1995.

28. *Toronto Star*, October 12, 1963

29. "Deny Jamaican Girls Get Immigration Sex Quiz." *Toronto Star*, October 7, 1963

30. Memo from the director of the Immigration Branch to A/Chief, Administration Division October 25, 1955. NAC, RG 25 vol. 830, File 552-1-644.

31. Locksley G. E. Edmondson, "Canada and the West Indies: trends and Prospects." *International Journal*, vol. 19, no. 2 (Spring 1964), 196.

32. Louis Parai, "Canada's Immigration Policy." *International Migration Review*, vol. 9 no. 4 (Winter 1975), p. 457

CHAPTER 8

Years of Tears and Turmoil

War and peace remained pressing issues for many North Americans as the turbulent decade of the 1960s ended, and the new decade of the 1970s began. In the US the Vietnam War, women's rights' issues, the so-called generation gap, and attempts by African Americans to peacefully achieve their civil rights objectives were being transformed in the early 1970s by the more vitriolic Black Power Movement. No matter what the means were to arrive at equality, Blacks in Canada and the US were engaged in a revolution that transformed the postwar period. Indeed, from the 1950s onward, the universal Black struggle for equality against the colonial, imperial and international economic forces allowed other subjugated peoples to walk on the same road toward their own liberation. Looking at life from the bottom up, coupled with our actions that were bent on eliminating the old ways of disenfranchisement of the working poor consumed my daily life.

Many Canadians were becoming increasingly emotionally involved in the great divide in Canada: that of the centuries' old tensions between the English and French majorities. These matters were of historic proportions, and had always lurked on the surface. In fact, issues of race, gender and ethnicity were topping the 1960s agenda items in Canada. French Canadians with new vigor, an expanding intellectual class, and aided by the ensuing universal struggle by subjugated peoples were adamant that their voices be heard in a country that had long been theirs before the arrival of the English. Writer Pierre Vallieres in his commentary on how French Canadians have been treated in Canada, went as far as to describe them as the "White Niggers of America." Even before the arrival of the decade of the 1970s, it was becoming apparent to Canadians that many French Canadians were tired of the unbridled English domination in every aspect of their daily lives. They were demanding a role in how Canada was to be governed. When Pierre Elliot Trudeau became Prime Minister in 1968, some Canadians thought that this would placate the radical elements among the Quebecois. It did not. Not long after moving to the Prime Minister's home on Sussex Drive in Ottawa, Trudeau found it necessary in 1970 to enforce the War Measures Act. In doing so, he referred to this period in Canadian history, as "a moment of grave crisis."[1]

By the time the Prime Minister addressed the country in October 1970, social unrest, kidnappings, even murder and bombings had become manifestations of the seething anger some French Canadians felt for Canada's English ruling class. I was deeply saddened by these events that I saw unfolding in the country in which I had now lived in for more than two decades. This sorrow was in no way an expression of a lack of sympathy for the deluge Francophone Canadians had suffered. Having followed the struggles of French Canadians I knew that like the ills that had befallen Black people, they too, had suffered. For three decades after the end of the Second World War, they had not really become part of Canada's economic prosperity. I had visited Montreal for the first time to attend a Canadian Congress of Labour conference in the early 1950s. On that occasion, I could not help but feel that the

English colonizers were still in full control of what was Canada's distinctively Francophone city. My growing disillusionment in the latter part of the 1960s had to do with how many of us had felt that we were making some headway in our attempts to make our world a better place and how the promise was dashed. The assassinations of President John F. Kennedy in 1963, Malcolm X in 1965, and Dr. Martin Luther King Jr., and Robert F. Kennedy in 1968 seemed to me to indicate that the powerful, those in control, were not listening to our calls for real change. It was as if the world I lived in was spinning out of control. I also found the violence that had erupted on the streets of Chicago during the 1968 Democratic convention, and even the trashing of the computer room in 1969 by radical students at Montreal's Sir George Williams University, troubling. As a follower of the teachings of both Mahatma Ghandi and King, I believe that subscribing to violence is not a solution to the ills that we suffer as poor and downtrodden people.

Living through the turbulence of the late sixties and early seventies was quite an experience. My activism was conducted on a voluntary basis so I had had to earn a living. I continued to earn my daily bread in the insurance industry, although by 1970, I had already left Co-operators Insurance and branched out on my own. My years at Co-operators were ones that allowed me to expand my knowledge and develop a keen sense of how Canadian business enterprise functioned. In a nutshell, it is operated from start to finish by the so-called "Old Boys" network. I am not referring here to a democratic model of sharing and encouraging wealth and opportunities for a large group of people. Instead, I am making reference to a small group of individuals who have control of, as Francis Henry and Effie Ginsberg noted: "Who gets the Work?" The

Old Boys represent status quo Canadian money, and they have attended the right schools, including universities. If they are immigrants, they hail from the Old British Dominions, and there is no room for hard working people with backgrounds like mine. The Old Boys form a clique of political and economic interests in Canada, to the extent that a University of Toronto professor acknowledged their influence in his book entitled, *The Vertical Mosaic*, (Toronto: U of T, 1965).

In his publication, Porter left no room for doubt that only certain persons could successfully climb that ladder of success. The further up one progressed, the closer one was to power and influence. My ability to work hard and earn a decent living when I worked at Co-operators was oftentimes met by my colleagues' willingness to complain to my area supervisor that I was getting too much business. My area would then be taken away and given to someone else. This happened repeatedly to me while I worked as a captive agent at Co-operators. I developed an area by relying on my trade union contacts and my willingness to make cold calls. When some benefits were being realized, and my volume of insurance policies grew, some less-hard working soul would complain. I remembered these times at a later date when I was involved in the fight for the implementation of employment equity in Ontario. I looked at those who argued that it was nothing more than a quota system for Blacks and others who were unwilling to earn their success the hard way. Well, I can state here that I have been part of a system in which I worked and others got the gains, and their right to the spoils was based on their skin colour rather than their brain power. Over the years I have realized that jobs in Canada are inherently political: to the influential goes the cream.

While at Co-operators, I met Sid Forbes, a talented Black Canadian who worked in the office, and received little in the way of recognition for his abilities. Eventually he left for the US, and was able in what is supposed to be a racist country to do well for himself. But this is the way it was and still is. For many years it was difficult for Blacks and Jews to purchase insurance, and then most of them could only do so at a premium of an extra $3.00 per $1000.00 coverage. It was common practice in the industry to penalize those Jews who were purchasing property insurance. The insurance industry held steadfast to the belief that they were a liability because some Jews, it claimed, wilfully burned down their own properties.

At our weekly meetings where we reported on our progress, my colleagues usually queried how I managed to write so many policies. Within the first six months at Co-operators, I became the company's second highest earning sales representative in Toronto. Yet I languished on the sidelines as the company gave everyone else but me, a raise. New in the business, and without anyone to provide guidance and mentoring, I was unaware of how this particular industry functioned. Frustrated, eventually I went to see the general manager and told him I was going to quit. He took me to lunch and we discussed the problem. I told him I knew that raises were given not on seniority, but on ability, and that I was now the second highest producer in the company. After listening attentively to my remonstrations, he advised me that the insurance business was not one based on short-term performance, but on a person's ability to maintain production over time. "Do not quit," he cautioned me, and he indicated that if my performance kept its present pace I would be rewarded. Six months later, I was the company's highest producer, I got a raise, and my colleagues complained that I was working too hard.

I set my sights on becoming a broker so that I could go into business for myself. For two days each week I took courses, and yet I continued to meet my sales quota. Astonished, the personnel manager called me in and said he could not believe that I was still producing more than anyone else was. He told me that other sales representatives had refused to take the courses because, they claimed not to have the time. I had already put my plan in place. It was nearing my time to leave what had long become an inhospitable and predatory working environment. My colleagues were envious of me because many of them had difficulty equating success and a good work ethic with my Black skin. Furthermore, many of my colleagues harboured the attitude that their skin colour was a form of entitlement that allowed them to plunder my hard-earned gains. What also galled these insurance representatives was that quite often in their attempts to raid my clients, some honest Whites refused to do business with them. In such an atmosphere, and with no one in the company to protect my back, I waited for the appropriate time to get out and go it alone.

When I completed the required courses, I approached a number of insurance companies and offered to write policies for them. After nearly nine years as a captive agent at Co-operators, in the summer of 1969, I politely gave my manager the customary two weeks notice. This was no small gamble. Ironically, I set up shop in my mother's house at 244 Gamble Avenue in Toronto. It took some doing but, both Aetna Insurance and Canada General Assurance companies agreed to let me write policies for them. Phoenix Life of London also came on board, and agreed that I could write life insurance polices for it. Within months of starting, a surge in business caused me to lease office space on O'Connor Drive. Growing success as a broker forced me to move office premises several times. This was aided by my landlords' belief that I was making a lot of money, and of course increasing the rent was their way of claiming a share. Eventually, I bought a property from a barber on O'Connor Drive whom, because of the era of long hair was not doing well. Operating from this location I continued as a broker until 1977 when I was forced out of the insurance business.

When I speak to young people today, they often want to know what has sustained me? What has kept the fire burning inside me while I remained determined to live in what seems frequently to be an unfriendly society. To be sure, those who in Martin Luther King Jr.'s words have sought not to judge me on the basis of my abilities or the content of my character, but instead see only my colour have not made my survival easy. I tell young people, repeatedly that they must have a plan in place. I marvel of how careful some Black parents are to remind their children not to cross the street when the traffic light is red, but are less cautious in getting them prepared for a world that is filled with amber and red lights. At an early age my parents taught us never to act in haste, and in moments of anger, it is always important to recount one's steps. I learned as an adult of how important it is to develop coping strategies, and how staying alive is dependent on an arsenal of problem-solving skills. As I learned at Co-operators, in Canada we live in a country where survival of the fittest counts, and therefore, some people are constantly trying to take away your livelihood. Rather than using the negative deeds of others to justify my failure, I realized early enough in the game that sometimes, it has been necessary to be what Jamaicans call "tallawa." In other words to act with courage and determination. It is such characteristics that have kept me in the driver's seat.

Some of the people that I had sold insurance policies while I was at Co-operators encouraged me when they continued to have me write their policies after I went on my own. In the early period, this was very important because their dedication helped my business to grow. Another added factor was that by 1970, immigration from the Caribbean, and Black immigrants who had previously left the Caribbean for Britain were now arriving in Canada in increasing numbers. Steady sales allowed me to put a realistic business plan in place, and set growth projections for the business to allow me to meet overhead expenditures, and maintain a decent standard of living. My wife Marlene, and I, worked tirelessly to ensure the company stayed afloat. She typed over 150 letters each night, and it is to be remembered that we were operating in a period before word processing and desktop computers. To help make insurance issues important to Blacks, in 1970, I began writing a newspaper article, chronicling insurance matters under a pen name for *Contrast*, Toronto's Black community newspaper.

The eyes of the insurance industry were kept focused on me. My every move was scrutinized. No wonder I ran into difficulty in 1976 with the insurance industry. Many of the companies that I wrote policies for began refusing to do business with me. They claimed that I had too many ethnics buying insurance and where auto insurance was concerned, my clients were having too many accidents. The first step was to reduce my commission rate; next, I was given an ultimatum. Which in this case meant get out of town by sundown. What I was being allowed to earn on a commission basis for each policy I wrote could no longer keep the company viable, and support my family at the same time. It was a conspiracy, or as would be said in polite circles, " a squeeze play" to have me get out of the insurance business. That is how things are done in Canada. In the end, it is all about appearance. Someone is at the other end of the phone claiming to feel your pain, telling you they just wish they could do more for you, and while you are running on empty, you are being made to feel that you should have no hard feelings. Today's Black youth are amazed that their community has not advanced beyond prototype businesses. We as Black community members share some of the blame for this dilemma. However, in Canada, Black entrepreneurs are usually not allowed to operate on the so-called "level playing field." The majority of the financiers, regulators and other gatekeepers with linkages to commerce and little-known networks do not want to see Black folks succeed.

In the spring of 1977, my insurance business was worth approximately $125,000, and within weeks it was worth naught. Seeking help, I turned to the superintendent of insurance in Ontario, and he verified that I had an unblemished record. I met him and the president of the Insurance Brokers of Canada, of which I was a member. They both agreed that insurance companies should be pleased to have me writing policies for them. It seemed as if every effort would be made to intervene on my behalf and have me stay in business. Later, I met with the president of the Insurance Brokers of Canada in his office to finalize what I thought were arrangements for me to write policies for several companies. Circumstances, however, suddenly went from bad to worse. I realized that I was being given the old polite Canadian song and dance. After making a phone call, the president told me that for many years the association had had difficulty with ethnics, and now me. He indicated that they were trying to come into the business, and the insurance companies did not want to establish relationships with them. Furthermore, "although it was nothing personal, because I was Black, they also did not want to do business with me."

I was told later that, the members of the insurance industry thought that I was too active in the community, and that my name was too frequently linked in the media with controversial issues. As a consequence, they did not want somebody so vocal. I had to pay the price. This meant that everything would be done to make life as difficult as possible for me to be a breadwinner. Some of us in putting ourselves on the line, with the aim of making Canadian society more humane, have oftentimes suffered severe consequences. Loss of jobs, businesses and our dignity can be listed among the prices that we have paid. Were it not for my supportive spouse who gave me her unconditional love, my story would have long been over.

Only a fool could not understand why the screws were being put to me. I was elected president of the JCA in 1970, in a period of upheaval and ongoing Black community response to Canadian racism. In 1973, I began publishing the *Islander* newspaper and it flourished until 1977 after my insurance business closed. It started as a cooperative venture with nine other people, but before the first issue was put to bed, the nine others left me holding the bag. Initially, the paper was published on a biweekly basis but because of its popularity, within several months the *Islander* became a weekly organ. It chronicled events affecting the various solitudes making up Canada's 1970s' Black community. Although it was published from my offices on O'Connor Drive, the paper was actually printed in Shelbourne, Ontario where the cheapest tender for printing the paper was found. In the winter, the printer would meet us half way on his snowmobile on which he carried the newspapers. Marlene and I would trudge through the snow in our car and judging from its performance the old thunderbird seemed to suggest to us that it preferred the less treacherous conditions of the city. I am indebted to three of the people who served as editors of the paper. Top students at Ryerson Polytechical Institute,[2] Carl Jackson won the gold medal for journalism when he graduated, Russel Keith was from Jamaica and Jo Jo Chintoh who is now a veteran television journalist with CITY-TV (Toronto).

Many individuals in need of my help and support also visited my offices and even members of the Toronto, Ontario Provincial and Royal Canadian Mounted Polices Forces came to see me when the need arose. I was very visible, and when necessary, I spoke out, and the conservatively managed Canadian insurance industry had among its membership those in the status quo that I actively fought against. Having me fold up my business was an act of payback. I did not like it, and when I turned to friends in the political community, they shied away from helping me. Having no other recourse I closed the doors of my business, and with a family to support, I decided to press on!

The JCA continued to flourish in the early 1970s. In my capacity as president, I had seen how growing numbers of immigrants from Jamaica and other parts of the Caribbean had served to positively reinforce growth and development in Toronto's Black community. For a period of time in the 1960s, the JCA rented an office in downtown Toronto, later we shared space with a group of African students on Colbourne Street. However, more space was required as the organization's membership grew, and more activities were implemented to meet the Toronto Jamaican-Canadian community's needs. In 1971, a building was purchased at 65 Dawes Road, but unfortunately, it was destroyed by fire in 1972. For a period of time the JCA operated out of my office, at 200 O'Connor Drive. It was not until 1985 that the JCA would once again obtain suitable premises at 1621 Dupont Avenue.

The decade of the 1970s was a period of mushrooming community organizational development. For example the Black Investment Group was started by a group of women in domestic service. They were pooling their funds, and turning the money over to Eric and Ethel Lyons, owners of two furniture stores in Toronto to put into the bank for them. Ethel asked for my assistance in setting up a cooperative for these women. I advised her against such a financial model because most cooperatives as I remembered from my trade union days did not do very well. I suggested that the route to go was to set up an investment club. In the hope of making the enterprise more viable, I invited Charlie Roach who is a lawyer, and some other people I knew in the community to join with us in this new venture. Meetings were held at the Lyons' furniture store at 934 Bathurst Street, but our efforts to register the company under Black Investment Group were rejected. The Ontario government would not issue a registration for a company entitled Black Investment Group. We could only use the acronym and in 1972, BIG Limited was established. In its first major undertaking, BIG Limited bought a building in Guelph, Ontario in proximity to the University of Guelph. It was then rented out to students, and for a period of time the investment club seemed to flourish. Money was being lent to borrowers in need of mortgages. Our ability to successfully manage the enterprise gave way to declining relationships among the members in the investment group, and BIG was absorbed by a larger investment group.

In this period the political arena was facing some major changes. Acceptance of the Royal Commission on Bilingual and Biculturalism recommendations by the Trudeau government led to Ottawa's introduction of a policy based on ethnic pluralism. In other words, Canada was now being recognized in 1971 as a multicultural country. In Trudeau's words: "...[T]here cannot be one cultural policy for Canadians of British and French origin, another for the original peoples and yet a third for all others."[3] Seeing that I fit into the category of "all others, I was impressed with the Prime Minister's actions. In part, my civil and human rights activities after arriving in Canada embodied what Trudeau acknowledged. In essence to ensure that: "in Canada, there is no official culture, nor does any ethnic group take precedence over another."[4] I was not that naive to believe that when the Prime Minister made such a public pronouncement all was well. Far from it! As I discovered in the 1970s when my insurance business was shut down, Canada had miles to travel before becoming a country in which privilege based on cultural preference no longer played a role. But the 1971 announcement by Pierre Elliot Trudeau suggested that we were continuing to make some nominal progress. This policy of multiculturalism set Canada on a new course. For the next two decades programs and public polices in some of Canada's provinces, and at the federal level, were influenced by this recognition of Canada as a plural society. Ultimately, it would also lead to a serious political backlash. Twenty years later, in the 1990s the White angry males in responding to what they perceived as preferences on the basis of race, gender, and ethnicity, elected Mike Harris and his Conservatives in Canada's largest province, Ontario.

The Ontario Multicultural Advisory Council was initiated by the government of Ontario for the purpose of encouraging dialogue between the province's different ethnic groups. It was administered by the minister of Citizenship. As one of twenty-six representatives, in 1972, I sat on this provincially appointed body. In this capacity, I repeatedly pushed for changes in the area of human rights. There were other members representing a variety of ethnic groups, along with a delegate from the First Nations. One of our definitive tasks was to define what multiculturalism was, and what culture represented within a Canadian context. It is a task that took us almost three years to complete. I was on the citizenship committee that dealt with human rights and citizenship issues. I learned a lot during my tenure, and was fortunate to meet many knowledgeable persons. The Italian community had a lawyer and businessperson as its representative. A professor from the University of Windsor represented the German community, and a dentist represented the Estonian community. The Greek community had the chair of the Sudbury school board as its representative. Many of these ethnic groups sent professionals to sit on the advisory council and articulate their respective community's points of view. Unfortunately, most Black community professionals remained aloof and they were usually uninterested in making similar contributions and giving their community an amplified voice.

We met each month to discuss issues affecting the multicultural make up of Ontario. As a result of meeting Omar Peters, the First Nations' representative on the committee, I grew increasingly familiar with Aboriginal matters. He and I talked about, *Bended Elbow*. It is a book that was written by a nurse detailing the life of the so-called Indians from Kenora. It supposedly told the true story of how many First Nations' people were drunks, and in so doing, described their antisocial behaviour. *Bended Elbow* upset me immensely, and when I returned it to Peters, he cautioned that he wanted me to know that much of what the author chronicled on its pages was true. Peters advised me not to become overly disturbed by its contents. He suggested that I needed to pay closer attention, not only to the contemporary events shaping the behaviour of Aboriginal people, but the roots of the problem. "Many people in my community could not get jobs," Peters said. Of the three Reservations located on the outskirts of Kenora, the closest was more than twelve miles from the city. With no transportation to take them to and from the Reservation, welfare was relied on as the primary source of income for most Native people. Liquor was not sold on the Reservations, but the overstocked shelves in the liquor store in Kenora acted as a magnet. It was there that they would drink excessively, and when they were drunk, the police picked them up and put them in jail. This process began a slippery slope to hell for many of them. Appearing before the court, the judge in finding those Aboriginals accused of antisocial behaviour found them guilty and would have them incarcerated for sixty days. They were then put into a rehabilitation program, and sent to a place where they learned woodworking, and were taught how to make canoes and paddles.

After I left the Ontario Multicultural Advisory Council, and received an appointment in 1976 at the Ontario Human Rights Commission where I worked as the liaison for the minority community and the police. I visited Kenora as soon as I could. Everywhere I went, I was told about these so-called "drunking Indians." I got sick to my stomach when I heard such comments. Because in the same breath, others have referred to those of my community as "these Niggers." I was provoked to speak out about how I saw members of Canada's First Nations' Peoples being poorly treated. I did so because I wondered why others who were more fortunate were not trying to help them to help themselves.

When I met the Kenora deputy chief of police who was Ukrainian, he tried to convince me that there was no discrimination in his city. He took me on a trip, about six miles up the railroad tracks to show me all the Native people, he claimed that would be drunk and lying in the bush. We found no one. He finally said to me on the way back: "Bromley, I have been out with you all morning and I have tried unsuccessfully to convince you of my experience with the Indians." I said, "no, you have not convinced me because you have not shown me any evidence to support your claims of how these poor and unfortunate people live." He then took me to a new detoxification centre that had recently been built with federal government money. It housed only two patients, a White man from Winnipeg and a Native woman. This further added to Walter's angst.

On another occasion, I asked the deputy chief for the number of Native people who were gainfully employed in Kenora. He became very angry, and asked, "What the hell do you want from us?" I told him, some sense of justice for the Native people who have been here longer than you have. He was scheduled to speak at the local service club about raising money for relief in India and Africa. "Since you are scheduled to speak," I told him, "why not ask for money to assist the local Kenora program initiatives for its Native population." He told me that they had tried to hire people from the Reserves, but when a hairdressing parlour hired a Native woman, no one would let her wash his or her hair, even after six weeks, solely because she was an Indian. "What about getting a Native person to work selling stamps in the post office, and one person for the liquor store," I asked. I told the deputy chief, people in Kenora needed to gradually break down the barriers. Because, if someone needed stamps for a letter, why should he or she care who is taking care of the order behind the counter. And if you need booze to drink, why should anyone care who is selling it to him or her? "Oh no!" he said, "you don't understand." Finally, he admitted, "Bromley, I know what you are talking about. Because I am not an Anglo Saxon, I will never become Kenora's chief of police."

My visits to Kenora as a roving commissioner for the Ontario Human Rights Commission allowed me to gain a vast amount of experience about many ethnic groups and our

Native people in Ontario. Although I was perceived by many in Kenora as that radical from Toronto, I made many friends. Of course for four years, the chief of police refused to speak with me. But my trips did allow me to establish a relationship with his deputy. Police brutality was a big issue among Kenora's Native community. When anyone from the Reservations was picked up for drunk and disorderly conduct, in trying to put him or her in the police car, the arresting officer would at times, allegedly by accident close the door on some part of the person's body. I discovered that the Kenora police department did not have patrol wagons, or vans of any kind. In my conversations with the deputy chief, I made the suggestion that, the chief of police should be asked to requisition the purchase of a wagon and a stretcher. This would make it easier therefore, to arrest a person who was intoxicated. If the person is drunk and lying on the ground, the stretcher could be placed along side the individual, and then two police officers could pick him or her up and place the person on to the stretcher and then into the van. My suggestion was implemented. A few years later when I saw the deputy chief in Kenora, he took me to see the chief of police. He admitted that my suggestion saved him a lot of time, and that his officers were no longer away from work because of receiving injuries while attempting to place intoxicated persons in their cruisers.

    In the 1970s, there were mounting concerns in several communities about the lack of response by the police for a growing number of attacks against Blacks and South Asians in Toronto. This concern led a small group of people including Dr. Wilson Head, Bev Salmon, and other individuals including representatives from the Social Planning Council of Metropolitan Toronto and myself to begin meeting informally. We met and talked about what we felt might be done in the areas of, multiracial, multiethnic, and multicultural and equity and access issues. A series of such consultations led to the creation of the Urban Alliance on Race Relations.

In 1976, under the joint sponsorship of the Urban Alliance on Race Relations and the Social Planning Council of Metropolitan Toronto a conference was organized. Dr. Dan Hill, chair of the Ontario Human Rights Commission was the guest speaker. Seizing the occasion, he proposed that initiatives be undertaken that would foster improved police community relations. He also suggested to Judge C.O. Bick, who was then the chair of the police commission that we establish pilot projects in four police divisions. Members of the Urban Alliance on Race Relations undertook what may be described as a number of cutting edge projects to also encourage better relations between the peoples of the City of Toronto. It was not an easy undertaking, especially since many politicians were wary of taking risks for initiatives with the term "race relations" attached. Under closer scrutiny the claim by the pretenders of how good existing relations between the peoples of Toronto could not be reconciled with the realities of incidents of racism and religious intolerance. In 1975, Toronto police chief, Harold Adamson accounted for the clashes between Black and White youth in an Etobicoke housing project as economically motivated. When the *Toronto Star* interviewed me in my capacity as publisher of the *Islander* newspaper, I countered that it was a racial situation, one that was on the increase at the time. Of course, it was less dramatic than if it had been the reverse, and Black youth were being beaten by White youth.[5]

Working diligently, a number of people affiliated with the Ontario Human Rights Commission, including Mark Nakamura were able to help establish the first North York race relations committee. In the mid to late 1970s, there were a series of incidents where members of White gangs were attacking members of the South Asian community. These actions ranged from slurs, to assaults in the subway system and on Toronto streets. In one such case, while being held down, a cigarette was pushed in the mouth of a Hindu religious leader and he was made to puff. South Asian leaders in Toronto were sufficiently concerned that they put together a brief, authored by Dr. Bhausaheb Ubale, entitled, *Equal Opportunity and Public Policy*. It was presented to the Ontario Attorney General in October 1977. By that date many other racial incidents had been reported in Toronto papers. A week after I was appointed as an Ontario Human Rights Commissioner, in March 1975, two rocks were thrown through the window of my office on O'Connor Drive. One of the rocks was tied to "a ticket to Africa message. To Nigger Rights Commission from White Peoples Vigilantes." The mock ticket had a caption, "Boat ticket to Africa."[6] On another occasion, my wife Marlene and I went to the office to work on the *Islander*, and I found an envelope on the floor. It was painted red to resemble blood. "Prepare to die" its contents said.[7] In August 1975, I found a package in my office with a stick of dynamite and a "watch your step nigger message" attached to it. It was signed by the White Nationalist Revolutionary Society.[8]

Such incidents and attacks were usually not seriously addressed by the police. On another occasion, a late tavern leaver in search of a place to urinate pushed open the front door to our O'Connor Drive offices. When he relieved himself, the evidence seeped into the basement where we were assembling the pages of the *Islander*. Fearing the worst, we were constantly on guard for the faintest sounds, stirrings and possible threats to our safety. Racial intimidation and harassment became a part of everyday survival for Blacks and South Asians and others in Toronto. Concerns for their safety caused some South Asian community leaders to invite Dr. Ubale who later became a human rights commissioner and myself to go with them to police headquarters to see the deputy chief of police, Jack Ackroyd. He listened, but felt no need to assuage the concerns that were being expressed to him about the lack of support his officers displayed when South Asians were being attacked by thugs. I was appalled and was very vociferous during the meeting. The same could not be said about Ubale. After the meeting members of the South Asian community, of which he was a member, let him know that he did not adequately represent their interests the way I had. His response was to tell them that this was my portfolio.

After the group disbanded, Ubale and I had lunch, and then we travelled to a meeting in progress at the North York City Hall. The purpose of the 1979 meeting was to try and convince the mayor of North York, Mel Lastman, of the need to establish a race relations committee for his borough. On arrival, we noticed the frustration on the faces of those in attendance. This process was part of an Ontario Human Rights Commission initiative undertaken by Mark Nakamura, manager of the Community Race and Ethnic Relations Division. He and Rabbi Gunther Plaut were also in attendance. When John Sewell was mayor of Toronto he had promised to establish a race relations committee, but after he was defeated and Art Eggleton took his place, there was little in the way of movement to institute such a body. It is for this reason that we turned our attention to North York at a time when Joyce Burpee had completed the Ontario Human Rights Commission report on racism. In the report's recommendations Burpee had called for some decisive steps to be taken to address racial intolerance in North York. To many of us in the room, a race relations committee was the way to go. But Lastman acting on the advice of a number of his bureaucrats remained resistant, because he could see no political merit in the idea.

It was no secret that racism was ripe and rampant in North York. There he was, the mayor of one of Canada's fastest growing diverse areas, puffing on his big cigar. I will never forget how his look of disinterest changed when I said to him: "Mr. Mayor, I can see from the discussion that you are not interested in establishing this race relations committee. However, you know we brought to you something that will put you in the Canadian history books. Accepting this proposal means that you are going to be the first mayor's committee on race relations and here you are throwing it down the drain because of what your advisors are telling you." Lastman thought for a while, then looking at me, he said, "you have something there." Turning to his advisors, the mayor said: "I think we should consider this thing." We walked out of the meeting feeling empowered, For we had gotten what we came for! On the way out Rabbi Gunther Plaut, an associate of Lastman's says: "Bromley I have never seen anything like this, let me tell you something, the mayor was shooting us down, every idea that we gave him, he blew it out of the water. You came in and you sold him on the committee, and he comes to my synagogue, and I could not convince him."[9]

What was very interesting about the 1970s and beyond was that although we had to fight repeatedly to effect change, from time to time those of us involved in human and civil rights issues made some progress. But we had to take a lot of flack from those persons who felt that our gain was their loss. I remember attending a conference on race relations in Oshawa in the late 1980s. Sitting on, and leading a panel discussion before mine was Trevor Wilson, special advisor to the premier of Ontario, David Peterson. During the course of events, a local politician became rather impatient with the discussion about racism. She chose to refer to those of us in the room who did not look like her, as "you people." I found both her tone and comments to be offensive, and later, when I took my seat among my panel members, I said so. Our task at the conference was to speak about race relations and human rights. Before doing so, I told the audience, I would like to address the "you people remarks" which were spoken earlier. The speaker had referred to us as "you people" which I did not appreciate. To begin with, I do not want to be counted among the so-called "you people," I am one of the "us people." You could have heard a pin drop in the room. I said: "This is what the whole problem is about. Some people perceive those of us that have any colour as 'you people,' as outsiders. But I want to make it clear that I am a citizen of Canada. As such, I do not fall into the 'you people' category. I also want you to understand that the so-called 'you people' come in many colours and complexions. If we are going to make any progress, we have to forget about who are the 'you people' and who are the 'us people,' instead, we have to be all, one people."

I then proceeded with my speech. When the session was over many delegates and individuals from the Oshawa city council where the speaker to whom I responded was a member, came up to me and indicated that, they had never heard anybody address the problem the way I did. In the audience that day was Gerry Phillips, the Ontario minister of Citizenship. He too, approached me and thanked me for responding the way I did. Later, I attended a function at Queen's Park where Phillips announced an amount of $700,000 for race relations and many millions more for multiculturalism initiatives in the province. At the reception, he included the "you people" versus "us people" in his remarks. Looking out into the audience, our eyes made four. He stopped, and acknowledged to those gathered, that it was I, who had spoken about the aforementioned, at a conference he attended.

I have always taken my appointments to official bodies and agencies, my invitations to address audiences, my participation in round table discussions and my discussions with students very seriously. As a human rights commissioner, I was one of eight private citizens that served the public interests of all Ontarians. In an address before the Windsor and District Labour Council in 1977, I reminded its members that in Ontario: "We needed the tools to ensure that the rights of native people, women, the handicapped, that all peoples' rights are protected."[10] At another occasion, when I was speaking for the Ontario minister of Social Services at a conference for the disabled in Barrie, Ontario, I got myself into hot water because of comments I made. At the hotel where the United Handicapped Groups of Ontario were having this conference, many disabled delegates could not get into the hotel because it was not wheelchair accessible. The disabled delegates had to be wheeled into the freight elevator at the back of the hotel to gain access to rooms where the conference was being convened. I have never seen an event planned so poorly.

Many disabled persons could not get a cup of coffee because the conference organizers had chosen a location where it was difficult for wheelchairs to gain access to the hotel's restaurant. A disabled man came to the conference on his bed, he had been brought from the hospital, and after being brought up in the freight elevator, there he was lying on a bed at the front of the conference room. I just could not believe it! I was there to represent the minister, however, forgetting about political decorum, I said: "If I were a disabled person at this convention and my leaders had put me in a hotel like this, I would vote every single one of them out of office." Having said these words, I discarded my speech. My sensitivity to being misquoted in the media had caused me to tape some of my speeches. I turned on my tape recorder, and looking at the audience, said: "I would like to tell you that the Ontario Human Rights Commission delivered to the government of Ontario, in 1977 a report called, *Life Together*. Included in it are a total of 97 recommendations dealing with human rights issues. Amongst them was, a suggestion for official recognition that disabled persons have the right to be treated equally under the law. The report has a total of nine recommendations addressing issues relating to disabled persons. After ten months, it was subsequently tabled, but on the night that it was to be discussed in the provincial legislature, there was a hockey playoff game between the Montreal Canadians and the Toronto Maple Leafs." Looking directly at the delegates, I continued, "then you know what you can say to me: "Human Rights has been defeated by hockey night in Canada." This became the caption in the *Barrie Examiner's* coverage of the conference.

When I returned to Toronto, Dorothea Crittenden, the Ontario Human Rights Commission chairperson called me. She indicated that I had criticized the minister and the government. "You can't do that," she said to me. I responded, "yes I can, because the government is not doing what it is supposed to do." She went on to tell me that I was a commissioner, and that the government had appointed me. I had had enough, and I let her know it. She responded to me by turning over a copy of my taped remarks that I made before the United Handicapped Groups of Ontario to her executive assistant Naison Mawande. After it was transcribed, Mawande reviewed my comments and reported his findings to his boss. "Madam chair," he told her, "I think Mr. Armstrong is right, and I wish other commissioners would do the same thing he did, because, it is only when Mr. Armstrong goes out and speaks, that people hear about the good work of the commission."

Before, the Buddy Evans shooting, some police officers allegedly would abuse and brutalize minorities and First Nations' peoples. However, in such instances care seemed to have been taken by those police officers to ensure that their somewhat racially motivated actions were not fatal. This was not the case with the 1950s Belfon shooting. James Belfon was a barber with a business located near Huron and Dundas Streets in Toronto.[11] His son Garfield was shot as it is alleged, when he and a number of other youths were caught in the act of breaking and entering a dental warehouse in Toronto. The next fatal police shooting of a Black person in Toronto occurred on August 9, 1978 when after a struggle, police constable John Clark, assigned to the Metropolitan Toronto Police Force, shot and killed the Nova Scotia-born Buddy Evans at the Flying Disco Tavern. This incident proved to be a watershed in terms of Black community-police relations. Unfortunately, the Evans shooting became one in a series of questionable shootings of Black people by the Metropolitan Toronto police. Questions about the propensity on the part of the police to use excessive force in their dealings with Toronto Black community members remained a hotly debated topic for the remainder of the century. Apparently, in defence of his younger brother, Preston, Buddy Evans had an altercation with a bouncer at a club on King Street West near Spadina Avenue. Dissatisfied with the bouncer's response, it is alleged that the older Evans bought a machete and told others publicly of his intentions to use it on the bouncer; the police were notified. Buddy Evans, aged 24 was confronted at the club where the bouncer worked. Their attempts to physically subdue him failed, and Clark a police officer aged 24 then shot him.

After this shooting, I was invited to a meeting at the Four Brothers Community Centre located on Spadina Avenue near College Street. I met with approximately three hundred, mainly young Nova Scotian Blacks. Riled up by the shooting, they were angry and threatened to show their displeasure by rioting over what they considered to be unnecessary police force. As an Ontario human rights commissioner, it was my duty to listen to their points of view. I sat and listened, and became concerned that they were not just in a mood to talk. Many of these young people seemed ready to do some physical damage to public and private property. Frustration was expressed by some that there was no one to lead them into action. This was followed by a loud voice: "Mr. Armstrong is here! He is a human rights commissioner, lets hear what he has to say!" I had to rely on my years of experience to guide me through what I found to be a trying situation. The fatal shooting of Buddy Evans troubled me and I was also very concerned that any unruly action on the part of these Black youth would give the police cause to shoot more of them. Hoping to quell the situation, I responded:

> I am here with you! I know you are frustrated and I know that you are not happy with the turn of events. But I must say to you, if you want to do something legally, I am willing to stand at your side. If you want to go on a rampage, smashing up cars on the street, getting yourselves in trouble, count me out.
> If you want to burn down city hall, that's your business. I am not a supporter of that kind of action. But I can tell you, if you want me to help, I will help. Go home and meet me tomorrow morning at city hall, where we will demonstrate peacefully.

They agreed, and I advised those assembled to make signs, and bring them to city hall for the peaceful demonstration. Adding fuel to the fire was the fact that Buddy Evans' brother Preston was also arrested at the club. To those assembled, the charges against him were without foundation.

I arrived at the Toronto city hall at 9.00 a.m. along with *Contrast* newspaper publisher, Al Hamilton, entrepreneur Denham Jolly, and a few others. We joined those who had assembled. They were mostly young people, and together we marched around city hall. When municipal officials caught their breath, they obviously called my boss at the Ontario Human Rights Commission. I realized this because Mark Nakamura appeared on the scene with a note asking me to come to the office for an urgent meeting. I refused to go. Instead, after the demonstration I headed to the courthouse to lend my support for the Preston Evans' bail hearing. It was closed to everyone except the Evans family, but I went to the door where I saw a police officer, showed him my commission identification, and told him that I wanted to observe what was going on in the court. Denham Jolly and myself were finally let in.

It was apparent that they were going to let Preston out on bail, but with stringent restrictions. He would not be allowed to travel downtown, or associate with anyone except family members. While I was seated in the courtroom I heard noises, and when I looked up, there was a Black man, obviously standing on someone else's shoulder, in the judge's view, looking into the courtroom through a paned glass window. I went outside and here is this person interrupting the proceedings and cursing a police officer who was assigned to guard the gate. The small crowd assembled outside the courthouse was in no mood to be hospitable. An unidentified individual walked up to me, and asked, "what is going on in there, and why are you in there?

Are you a relative?" "No!" I said, "nor do you employ me. I am not giving you any information. Furthermore, stop cursing this policeman. He is only doing his job, and is only here to guard the door. Why are you cursing him? Why are you behaving in this way, because it is surely not helping the situation." They finally quieted down. Before Preston Evans was let out on bail, it was necessary to satisfy the court that until his case was heard, he would not be a nuisance to society. Al Hamilton, Denham Jolly and myself formed the Committee for Due Process, and were instrumental in getting him a job at the Black Resource Information Centre (BRIC), located on Bloor Street West. The court had ordered that Preston Evans be kept out of the downtown area. At the end of his workday, he returned to his aunt's home in Don Mills. Since he had not broken any laws in the first place, the charges soon amounted to nothing.

The Ontario Human Rights Commission did not like my front and centre position on the Buddy Evans shooting. No one at the commission wanted to understand that this Ontario government agency had a vital role to play in such an incident. The chair, Dorthea Crittenden, called an emergency meeting and invited Roy McMurtry, who was then, both the solicitor general, and attorney general for the province of Ontario. It was unusual to have a minister of the provincial cabinet at such a meeting. Heretofore, such invitations were only extended to politicians and bureaucrats to visit after agenda items had been completed. When I asked why the meeting was being held, I was given the flimsy excuse that it was an opportunity to discover what was going on with the Buddy Evans case. I was in no mood to play the bureaucratic, pin the tail on the donkey, so I got to the point. Looking at Mr. McMurtry, I asked, "Do you want me to resign?" "Oh! No! No!" was his response. To put me at ease, the chair stated that, the minister was in attendance so that "we could touch bases with him." They were all caught at their own game, and nothing decisive was done. No one wanted to take responsibility for belling the cat that was supposed to be me. I got the message, for it was a shakedown. The chair was unhappy with my role in the Evans case, but for appearance sake, so that I could not charge racism, every step was taken by the commission to tip toe around on eggshells.

Another meeting was called, and this time, the location chosen was Ottawa. While in Ottawa our chair asked the federal human rights commissioners to meet with us, and just by chance, the topic was: "Whether commissioners should be involved in community activism?" One of the Ontario commission members was, the now, Madame Justice Rosalie Abella. Seizing the occasion, she cut to the chase. "If you are going to discuss what Bromley Armstrong is doing, I should tell you that I support him, one hundred percent. Because, if this was the Jewish community, and I did not take any action, my community would want to know, what's going on? What am I doing on this commission?" Chief Dan George's granddaughter, Gloria George was also a federal commissioner, and she too, chose to speak out: "I do not know what you people are discussing, because I think [Bromley] is doing exactly what he is supposed to do. If this were my community, I would be expected to be involved. The chair of the Ontario Human Rights Commission was unable to obtain a consensus from commissioners at either the federal or provincial levels. Finally, I was told that they really did not mind me being involved in community action, it is just that I should slow it down a little.

Anger surrounding the fatal shooting of Buddy Evans remained strong. It was a hair-raising experience for many of us, and on reflection, we felt that something had to be done.

With the Evans incident, as a community we were all witnessing the results of raw police power, and on a daily basis, I received calls from many Black community residents who themselves were afraid to publicly add their voices to ours. They would however, ask that more be done to protect members of the community from this sort of police action. I did agree that we needed to show the city powers, including the police that their actions were not going to be taken lightly. Of course, I was also mindful of how behind the scenes attempts were made to intimidate me. The actions of my employer, the Ontario Human Rights Commission represents a case in point. Not to be stopped, I carried on, and so did Al Hamilton and Denham Jolly.

A big demonstration was planned to take place at Queen's Park, the heart of Ontario provincial power. On the day of the demonstration McMurtry agreed to meet a delegation of seven of us. The demonstration continued while six individuals and myself were let through the barriers to meet with him in his Queen's Park office. The attorney and solicitor general said to me in his usually sedate voice: "Bromley why are you doing this? We are friends, why did you not come and talk to me?" I told him that I could not come to him as a friend and talk to him about this troublesome matter. This is a community problem, and it was up to the community to decide what appropriate action was required. He agreed that something had to be done and after some deliberation he said that some money would be made available to us to pay an investigator to determine the facts of the Buddy Evans case. Twenty-four hours after hiring a Black private investigator he disappeared from the case. Apparently someone had told him to back off. For us the question was who?

It took me almost eighteen months before I found out why the private investigator left the case so suddenly. After speaking at Holy Blossom Temple, a sergeant with the Metropolitan Toronto Police whose brother was once deputy chief offered to give me a ride home. During the course of our discussion, he called the name of the private investigator, and asked me if I knew him. I said, "you mean the private investigator we had hired to investigate the facts of the Buddy Evans case." He said, "yes." Then the sergeant told me that it was with the police's assistance that he had obtained his investigator's licence. When the police learned that he was involved in the Buddy Evans case, the private investigator was told that if he continued his involvement, when his licence was up for renewal, he would be finished. The hidden hands were having a great deal of difficulty in their attempts to stop us. Refusing to let the matter fade from the public eye, we had a third demonstration that led to Roy McMurtry's King Street West office and in our meeting with him, he heard from a broader cross section of community members. I however, remained unsatisfied with how events were unfolding. Unfortunately, it was Toronto in which we were demanding justice, a place where the rich, the powerful and those who dispense justice are one in the same. Yet we had to satisfy ourselves that everything was done, that could have been done for Buddy Evans. No one said, that Evans was a saint, but it was not for the police to decide his punishment. That was for the courts to determine.

    I decided to go to Halifax, Nova Scotia to talk to Evans' parents and I bought a plane ticket and booked myself into Holiday Inn just outside Halifax. The meeting with them and their lawyer, Anthony Ross was cordial, but as parents who had suffered a loss, they were grieved. Our, Committee for Due Process wanted to hire Jack Pinkofsky to manage the details of the inquest for our side. For a period of time Vibert Rosemay had acted as counsel for the Evans family in Toronto. But approval to bring Pinkofsky on board was needed from the parents, especially since they had already hired their own lawyer in Nova Scotia. I returned to Toronto with a power of attorney to represent the interest of the Evans family in Ontario. Journalists at the *Toronto Sun* newspaper found out that I went to Nova Scotia and it is alleged that someone at the newspaper began investigating my moves. The feeling was that since I was a human rights commissioner, I had somehow passed on my incurred travel expenses for my Nova Scotia trip to the Ontario taxpayers. The person who supposedly did the investigation to dig up the dirt on me thought that he had me on the ropes. He believed that I was going to be mired in a big scandal and that somehow I was done for. I had nothing to hide. I received a tip from a *Toronto Sun* editor who told me that I was being investigated, and that the journalist assigned to do the digging was meticulously checking me out. This editor said to me, "he knows everything that you do." I found out that inquiries were made through the Ontario Human Rights Commission to see if my Nova Scotia trip to visit the Evans family was expensed. They found nothing!

One of the outcomes of the Buddy Evans case was that sectors of Toronto's Black community were galvanized, and some Blacks developed a better understanding of how the system can work for or against people of colour in Canada. They were also made aware that their collective actions could summon the attention of more powerful interests. I was however disheartened because the community support was not as forthcoming as it should have been. Buddy Evans was not a West Indian or a Jamaican in particular. Accordingly, some people in the Toronto Black community were unwilling to throw their support behind our efforts. By the time the inquest started in July 1977, the trail was already cold, and the city and provincial power brokers were aware that Toronto Black community interest in the case had waned. Even some of the staunchest supporters of the Evans case who wished to see justice prevail had already moved on to other matters. They had families to feed, and courses to attend at school so that they could get on with their lives.

How could Toronto's Black community, one of the poorest communities economically, fight the State's resolve to do as it pleased? In years to come, it would be a strategy that the police and their supporters employed repeatedly. With the passage of time, the anger in the community will dissipate, and everything will be back to normal. Eleven weeks, 106 witnesses later, the jury at the Coroner's inquest found Constable John Clark, to be blameless. He was just doing his job, and racism played no part in the fatal shooting. Clark, the jurors found, acted with professional restraint.[12] More than any other finding, what is mentioned here portended future actions of the police in their encounters with Black people in Canada. Since the Buddy Evans police shooting, police contact with the Black community in Toronto, no matter how abominable, has met with widespread support from the public and media. Unfortunately, we continue to live in a "you" versus "us society."

Chapter 8 – Notes

1. Notes for National Broadcast by The Prime Minister Pierre Elliot Trudeau, Friday, October 16, 1970

2. It is now Ryerson University.

3. Pierre Elliot Trudeau, Multiculturalism. Government Response to the House of Commons, October 8, 1971 to Volume 4 of the report of the Royal Commission on Bilingualism and Biculturalism

4. Ibid.

5. Pat McNenly, "Racism cause of violence Metro Black leaders say." *Toronto Star*, August 1975

6. Racist attack on black civil rights worker." Toronto Star, March 1975.

7. Lionel Gayle, "Human rights activist continues fight." Toronto Star, July 8, 1986.

8. Ibid.

9. Rabbi Gunther Plaut refers to this meeting in his book, *Unfinished Business: An Autobiography*. (Toronto: Lester and Orphen Dennys, 1981), see 239 footnote. He does so again n his book, *More Unfinished Business*. (Toronto: U of T Press, 1997), see p. 41 and corresponding footnote, 13 on p. 237. Rabbi Plaut does not mention my presence at the 1979 meeting. His recollection differs with mine in terms of how the Mayor, Mel Lastman was persuaded to accept the idea of forming what was soon called, The Mayor's Committee on Ethnic, Community and Race Relations.

10. "Rights commissioner outlines race relations problem, The *Windsor Star*, April 13, 1977, p. 4.

11. I would like to thank Arthur Kirkwood and Arthur Downes for sharing their research on this matter. The authors would also like to express their thanks to Doug Richardson, Howard Matthews, Vincent Carrington and Cecil Richardson.

12. "Inquest proved its worth." Toronto Star editorial, October 05, 1979, p. 5.

CHAPTER 9

Searching for a Brighter Tomorrow

Immigration was good for Canada. In a 1979 appearance before the Toronto representatives of the ethnic media, Ron Atkey, the minister of Employment and Immigration stated that Canada, "needed more immigrants."[1] Inherent in Atkey's comments was his tacit admittance that Canadians had benefited from Ottawa's movement away from an unbridled discriminatory immigration policy. The increasing numbers of immigrants arriving from different countries of origin allowed more people to find work in the Canadian labour force. Which in effect meant that those persons who were here before usually benefited from such a consumer oriented economy, one that was based on the economic cycles of boom and bust. Economic growth in Canada for the two decades after the introduction of the points system in 1967 was in part linked to the arrival of many newcomers. This development led Canada's major cities to undergo a rapid expansion of their infrastructures. Highways, transit systems, telecommunications, hydro and sewage, and services at the federal, provincial, and municipal levels were transformed by unprecedented development. On arrival, all immigrants require food, housing, clothing, access to transportation, and telephones. In turn these demands had spillover effects on the economy. The growth in population influenced some Canadian institutions to address the needs brought about by a more diverse population. The Toronto

School system, for example, responded in 1979 to an increasing Black student population by implementing a Black Heritage Program.[2] Toronto's mushrooming Black population allowed two community newspapers to flourish for a while.[3] And in their pages, the growing impact of that city's Black community population was obvious from the solicitations of a cross section of businesses.

Food, furniture, clothing, movies, and the services of palm readers were regularly advertised in *Contrast* and *Share* newspapers. For those persons who were longing to take a vacation, Air Jamaica provided non-stop flights from Toronto to Kingston, Jamaica. Some Blacks were also entering untraditional spheres of entrepreneurial ventures. In 1976, Denham Jolly expanded his Toronto-based Tyndall Nursing Home and moved it to Mississauga, Ontario to accommodate 180 patients.[4] Torontonians boasted one of North America's largest and prestigious Black restaurants. The Underground Railroad Restaurant was a place where both Blacks and Whites gathered, and socialized. This soul food eatery had an international reputation and frequently, local residents had to book their reservations early at its King Street East location before American visitors started queuing up on weekends. Third World Books and Crafts was another Toronto hangout. Its literary selections featured a variety of titles that triggered awareness amongst Canadians about the richness of Black literature and Black history. In the process, its existence aided the efforts of those teachers and academics who had called on the Toronto Education system to introduce Black learning materials into its classrooms.

Diversity in Canada's labour force meant that more Blacks were leaving the traditional service sector occupations. However, many employers were still hesitant to hire Black post-secondary graduates from Canadian educational institutions. At the start of the 1980s, there were too many Black men and women in Canada with undergraduate and graduate degrees who were unable to find gainful employment in their chosen occupations. The situation was even more dreadful for those immigrants who obtained their qualifications in other than the so-called metropolitan countries. Some Blacks graduating from Canadian institutions who were unable to find work in Canadian companies opted to go to the US. Others began a pattern of return migration to their countries of origin in Africa and the Caribbean.[5] By the early 1980s, the African continent became a major source of Black refugees and immigrants, arriving in Canada.

My struggles as a human rights commissioner continued, and I found it increasingly difficult to convince some of the other commissioners that my efforts were in concert with theirs. The problem was my refusal to conform. In other words, I refused to shut up. My reading of the situation was that my life would be made easier, if only I looked the other way. This I refused to do. In anticipation of the possibility that the Ontario government would not reappoint me to the Commission, in 1979 I enrolled in the Ontario Mortgage Brokers education course. Passing the examination allowed me to apply for a licence at the Business Practices Division of the Ministry of Consumer and Commercial Relations. Thereafter, I was able to loan money for mortgages and as a means of testing the waters I established a small brokerage company.

Someone whom I knew came in desperation and asked for me to assist him in getting a loan. He was supposedly a friend of mine, and was therefore, aware of my tenuous situation on the Commission and of the possibility that I would need to find an alternative livelihood. He took the first loan from my mortgage brokerage solely in his name. Then as I later learned, he found someone to apply for another loan and agreed to co-sign for that party. Furthermore, in what I thought were referrals to my business, my friend got someone else to apply for a third loan. I soon realized that this was nothing more than a scheme and that all parties involved had no intention of repaying any of the money they had borrowed. Any cheques that I received were returned because of insufficient funds. The second person that he co-signed for went missing. Finally, I had to hire a lawyer, and go to court to try and recover my money, and even with the court's judgement, I never received a dime in payment. It is a simple case of being in the public's eye, and people assuming that you are making a lot of money, and so they find ways of taking it away from you. A number of other similar incidents occurred, and unfortunately when you are in the mortgage business, you have to take risks.

The clients who come to you are usually financially unstable to begin with; or else they would obtain the needed funds from a major financial institution. Another so-called friend of mine who was in the real estate business borrowed $12,000 from my brokerage company. His lawyer went to the bank with me, and got the cheque certified. All things considered, I thought that this transaction was going to be above board. It was not. The funds were for a second mortgage, but the borrower had plans to eventually leave Canada for Florida. In the mean time he purchased a house and moved in. No repayments were ever made to my company and a year later the company holding the first mortgage advised me of its intention to foreclose. Eager to protect my money, I went to the house where the grass and shrubbery on the lawn indicated that no one had lived there for quite sometime. Until the house could be sold, I had to maintain the lawn. On my lawyer's instructions

I arranged for a locksmith to open the door and I inspected the premises. To protect my investment, I brought the first mortgage up to date, but eventually when the house was sold I ended up losing $15,000 on the deal. My latest business venture had become too adventurous for my liking.

By 1980, I had lived in Canada for thirty-three years, and through both good and bad times, it was my credibility that had sustained me. I was set in my ways, and metaphorically speaking, after being in the trenches for so long, and giving hope to others and earning the respect of so many, I could not in good conscience give any less than was expected of me. Tough times lay ahead, but I believed that in the end, I would prevail. I was well aware of how some Canadians responded when I spoke out about social injustices in our midst. An irate man sent a letter to me in 1976 in which he reminded me that: "I was always crying out racial discrimination." He went on to point out that in the CTV inquiry, *Two's Company, Three's A Crowd*, eighty-five percent of the Canadian people did not want to turn Canada into a [so called] 'third world' state," and did not want me too either.[6] Oddly enough, there were many others who resisted calls like mine for a more equitable Canadian society. They were not only uncomfortable with the message, but also the messenger. Furthermore, my comments were not limited only to Black community concerns. When the need arose, I added my voice to those that were speaking about injustices in other ethnic communities to include also the gay and handicapped communities. Some government bureaucrats disliked the fact that sometimes when I was quoted in the media, accompanying my name was the title, member of the Ontario Human Rights Commission.

I had no apprehension doing what I saw as my job. I therefore took it to heart that whenever I spoke out against racism and discrimination that I was doing the commission's work. I repeatedly reminded members from a variety of ethnic backgrounds about the importance of the human rights code. "We have got to stop playing politics with people's lives and livelihoods. All parties should understand that human rights cover all parts of [Ontario], and all parties should support that idea equally." These words were part of a speech made before the Ottawa chapter of the National Association of Canadians of origins in India. I also told them that: "Lip service is what we've been getting for 200 years. And lip service is what we will get until we become part of the system so we can make the laws."[7] When I learned, therefore, that my term on the commission was not to be renewed, though not pleased, quite frankly, it did not come as a surprise.

In my capacity as a commissioner many individuals called me personally and complained about the lack of attention that the Ontario Human Rights Commission paid to their problems. They were right. For there were just too many cases that went unattended. In my capacity as the community and police liaison for the commission, I saw a creeping ineffectiveness in its day to day operations. To be fair, when the commission was established in 1962, Ontario's non-White population was relatively small. In the aftermath of a more liberal immigration policy, significant numbers of visible minorities, and members of ethnic groups most likely to need the commission's services, entered Canada, and Ontario in particular. By 1980, the commission had been under staffed for quite sometime, and this human resource shortage impeded its ability to deal adequately with the mounting number of cases that were received annually. Commenting on the backlog, Naison Mawande, the commission's director of Conciliation and Compliance indicated that due to the staff shortage, it was difficult to prosecute the more than 1,500 cases that were received each year.[8] I came to the commission with some knowledge of how members of certain communities felt about its ineffectiveness. It is for this reason that I tried to pay close attention to their concerns. While I was a member of the commission, I tried to ensure that the visible minority members I came in contact with understood its role. While it is true that some of them felt it was not necessarily addressing their concerns, others believed that a commissioner with my advocacy background demonstrated sympathies for their problems. In some small measure, I do believe that my efforts helped to dispel rumours that by the late 1970s the commission was fast becoming nothing more than a paper tiger.

Towing the line is what the Ontario government expected me to do. On the other hand, many persons from diverse groups at the community level called on me as a last resort to assist them in finding solutions for their problems. Over the years, I have sometimes encountered a great deal of difficulty when I have tried to explain the societal costs of racism and discrimination. When someone calls me and claims not to have been hired or to have been fired because of some form of bias or prejudice, that individual is not just speaking about an abstract action. Apart from the psychological dimension, racism also has severe economic costs. Frequently, those persons that are experiencing discrimination are not in a sound enough economic position to acquire effective legal counsel. Even if they have the means to pay the legal costs, their families are still required to bear some economic burdens. Hearing of someone like myself on the commission meant that literally many people sought my help. In doing so, they were also putting their trust in me. It is a responsibility that I never forgot, and to the end, never betrayed. The political and bureaucratic authorities at Queen's Park were not happy with me. This animosity in part was exasperated by my role in the Buddy Evans case, and was further compounded when I refused to take a back seat when Albert Johnson was fatally shot by an officer on the Metropolitan Toronto police.

Albert Johnson was an eccentric man. On a number of occasions, the police had arrested him and judging him from his demeanour, some of his neighbours thought that he was troubled. Johnson lived in Toronto's west-end near Ossington Avenue and Davenport Road. Media accounts indicated that the police were familiar with Johnson. He had been repeatedly arrested because of his alleged propensity to disturb the peace by preaching in Toronto's High Park. He was also known to preach and read his Bible from the roof of his home. Prior to his fatal encounter with the police, they had on one occasion chased him while he rode his bicycle. Staying ahead of them, he managed to get back to his home where he bolted the door. In the process of the police's attempts to gain entry to Johnson's house, his arm was cut by broken glass. Johnson's doctor gave him a cane to help relieve the muscle tension in his arm and advance the healing of the wound.

Again in High Park after the incident, Johnson was reading his Bible and the police charged him with possessing a dangerous weapon which in this case was supposedly the cane his doctor had prescribed. He was also charged with creating a disturbance and being a public nuisance. These latter charges were subsequently dismissed in court, and Johnson then filed a complaint with the Human Rights Commission. His encounters with the police were documented by an investigations officer and then passed on to me. This investigator left for vacation on Friday August 24, 1979, and Albert Johnson, an immigrant from Jamaica, was fatally shot by police officer

William Inglis on Sunday August 26, 1979. Apparently, after running into Johnson, Inglis and his partner Walter Cargnelli asked him why he had not as yet returned to Jamaica. Johnson left the scene as quickly as possible, and he returned home with the police officers in pursuit. Again, Johnson barred the door to his home. According to police reports, officers Inglis and Cargnelli supposedly fearing for the lives of Johnson's four young children and his sister-in-law who were in the house broke down the door and entered the Johnson premises. Albert Johnson allegedly reached for something under his bed that the police said "looked like an axe." With Johnson in a rage, seeming to go berserk and appearing dangerous, a shot was fired that entered Albert Johnson's abdomen. The incident occurred in front of one of Johnson's daughters. It turned out that he was reaching for a garden hoe.

Once again, the community did not adequately respond to this incident to ensure that the police were held accountable for their actions. It was not a question of only who was right and who was wrong. In a democracy like ours, the use of force needs to be held in check by civilian authorities. The police at all times must be able to demonstrate that the calculated actions they take are justified. Since the force used by the police caused Johnson to die, it was important for all of the facts to be brought to the public's attention. Most members of Toronto's Black community stood on the sidelines. This was an inappropriate position for us to be in, especially since this was the second fatal police shooting of a Black person in just over a one-year period. To the community's credit, Dudley Laws, Charles Roach, Denham Jolly and a number of us got together and started a series of demonstrations and demanded that an investigation take place. Al Hamilton, the publisher of *Contrast* newspaper took an interest in the Johnson shooting. We really appreciated his involvement, because similar to the shooting of Buddy Evans in 1978, Hamilton was relentless in his efforts to bring the facts to the public's attention. Johnson was an eccentric Black man who was not a member of the small but visibly connected Toronto Black middle-class. Not very much attention was paid therefore, to our calls for a proper investigation and to determine if the actions of the police were justified.

The Albert Johnson shooting was an issue that divided his family and sectors of Toronto's Black community. In the end, an out of court settlement was reached with Johnson's widow who received a yet to be revealed undisclosed sum of money. From the beginning of the investigation, a number of issues relating to the Johnson case were rather secretive. Under the circumstances, a few of us did what we could to remind authorities that their actions were being closely scrutinized. I stated publicly that it appeared as if Albert Johnson had been beaten, and that the police were harassing him. I went further and called for a police investigation of Division 14 where the two police officers were stationed. I remained resolute that my role as a commissioner did not "take away my rights as an individual to speak on matters concerning the Black community."[9] Realizing that when people are unwilling to learn from their history, they are bound to repeat it, I walked away in disgust from the Johnson matter.

Like others who were initially involved in the aftermath of the fatal police shooting of Johnson, I have a story to tell. But I too, will remain silent. This police shooting was followed by a number of others, including that of Lester Donaldson. But the regular response to these tragedies is for some members of my community to willingly, step and shuffle. Accordingly, when Dudley Laws and other members of the Toronto-based Black Action Defence Committee (BADC) speak out against the use of unbridled force by some Toronto police officers, their comments are usually labelled as controversial. Some reporters in the media are able to find someone in our midst that is only too willing to proclaim that: "Dudley Laws and BADC members do not speak for us." Whether they do or not is irrelevant. Laws and BADC have their constituents in Toronto's Black community. I may not always agree with everything they do, but were it not for their clarion calls, many more of us would choose to turn our backs and walk away.

It is my belief that my involvement in the Evans and Johnson cases hastened my departure from the Ontario Human Rights Commission. Additionally, I have no doubt in my mind that when I also spoke out on behalf of other communities, Queen's Park took note. When members of Toronto's Chinese community invited me to respond publicly with them to a television program that was aired on the Canadian television network CTV's program "W5" in 1979, I did so without hesitation. This "W5" segment referred to the supposedly dramatic increase in the number of Chinese students enrolled in the U of T's medical school. The program suggested that they were displacing Canadian students; meaning White Canadians. The manner in which the show was presented led viewers to believe that the presence of so many Chinese medical students at U of T was somehow detrimental since they were not Canadians. It turned out that the producers of the "W5" program were wrong. When the Council of Chinese Canadians in Ontario called on me to publicly support their outrage of the CTV program, I was only too glad to do so. This was a classic case of systemic racism. Had this incident gone unchallenged the status of all qualified visible minority students wishing to enrol at the U of T medical school would have been put in jeopardy.

Due to the expectations at the community and bureaucratic levels I was under a lot of pressure. Furthermore, my ability to earn a livelihood appeared to be at risk in January 1980. Were it not for the kindness of a bureaucrat, I would not have had anywhere to go after my term on the commission ended. The higher-ups in the Ontario government had debated for sometime what should be done with me. At one point, a recommendation seems to have been made to put me out to pasture by appointing me to a do-nothing position. There were strong objections to this approach. Fortunately, I met Tim Armstrong, the deputy minister in the Ministry of Labour at a function, and he told me of the decision that had been made to not reappoint me for another term as a commissioner. During the course of our conversation he offered to arrange for me to have an interview with the Ontario Labour Relations Board (OLRB) chairperson. With the help of Ontario premier, William Davis, Tim Armstrong and my friend Dennis McDermott, I was appointed to that Board for a three-year term, effective February 19, 1980. Of course there was speculation in the media about my departure from the commission. I refused to comment on the matter. But when Davis' press secretary, Vince Devitt was asked "whether my new appointment was meant to cover my "removal from the human rights commission," his reply to the reporter was: "You are going to have to make those assumptions. You won't get anyone around here to say it. He has a good solid background in labour relations."[10]

But as everyone knew it was a way of keeping me quiet. My role as a commissioner was a hot potato for both the government and for the commission. The climate in Toronto in the late 1970s and early 1980s was one in which racism, discrimination and the use of questionable force by some police officers were on the rise. I had become the wrong person for the job, and because human and civil rights issues had been my forte since arriving in Canada, looking the other way, for me, was unthinkable. When the issue about the reasons I was shifted from the human rights commission to the Ontario Labour Relations Board refused to go away, Labour minister, Robert Elgie was asked to comment. He denied the charges that I was forced out, and told the media that I had indicated before my term was up that I was interested in some other public post. I was happy when my community honoured me with a testimonial dinner in April 1980. It provided me with the platform to assure those who looked to me for leadership and guidance that although I was not unscathed, I had survived the ordeal by fire. In my speech to the 500 guests gathered in my honour, I reminded them that, "we have to be ready and prepared to stand in the line of battle over civil rights."[11] It was my message to those who thought that they could suppress my efforts in the area of human rights. I assured everyone that despite the pitfalls, I intended to continue to be their tireless champion for just causes.

George Adams was the chair of the OLRB when I was first appointed to that body as one of six people representing the union sector in 1980. Before moving on to become a justice in the Ontario court system, he was instrumental in providing me with support and guidance in my early days as a novice on the board. I served with four other chairs. In addition to Adams: Rosalie Abella, who is now a Madame Justice with the Ontario Court of Appeals; Mort Mitchnic; Judith McCormack and Richard MacDowell. The OLRB is a tripartite body made up of representatives from the corporate sector, labour, namely: the Ontario Federation of Labour, with its representatives from the industrial and construction unions. There is also a board chair and a number of vice-chairs. Aggrieved union members file complaints that are addressed by the OLRB under the jurisdiction of the Ontario Labour Relations Act. A panel of three members listens to complaints and renders a decision in conjunction with the OLRB.

I learned to ably manage my mandate, which included hearing union member grievances pertaining to wrongful dismissals, strikes, lockouts and other workplace problems. Our tasks included the certification and the decertification of unions. Over a sixteen-year period I developed a keen sensibility of how the Ontario Labour Relations Act should be used as an instrument to adjudicate troublesome issues relating to the aforementioned. During my OLRB tenure, I had a bird's eye view of how the Ontario wheels of justice turn and this also helped to determine the outcome of thousands of cases. As a consequence, I met good, not so good and rather bad lawyers who appeared before the panels that I was part of. However, I enjoyed my nearly six terms of office at the OLRB. Additionally, I benefited from the relationships that were established with my full-time and part-time colleagues from a variety of labour unions in Ontario. This included most of the management representatives, the vice chairs and the support staff. In this regard, Ontario, drawing on its pool of workers with their diversified talents is blessed, moreso than any other province in Canada.

There were many vexing problems brought to the OLRB that convention prohibits me from repeating here. However, I recall an issue in the 1980s that was played out in the public arena when Grace Hartman, national president of the Canadian Union of Public Employees (CUPE), supported an illegal hospital workers' strike. The union's national president knew hospital workers were designated as essential, and they were therefore not allowed to take strike action. The OLRB was called on to determine the legality of the CUPE strike, and I sat on the panel that heard the evidence. The industrial action was found to be illegal. Hartman refused to back down and after the OLRB had rendered its decision she made public statements in support of her union members. The matter was taken to the courts and the CUPE national president was found in contempt of our decision and incarcerated for thirty days.

Throughout my years as a change agent, I have learned that a handful of people responding to questionable actions by the State is an ineffective means of commanding attention from the policy-makers and members of the society at large. The days of the Sixties had long been over. If members of any group wished their grievances to be taken seriously, they had to find ways of getting the attention of the often distracted, electorate-sensitive, and public-opinion-centric politicians and their minions. Running around with ten or fifteen people holding up placards is an impotent means of delivering one's message. Members of the Toronto Chinese community underscored this point with their massive well-coordinated public and private responses to the CTV attempt to scapegoat Chinese medical students at the U of T medical school.

As the decade of the 1980s progressed, the State became more adept at subtly turning back the clock on some of the civil and human rights gains that benefited Canada. In this regard, the Human Rights Commission was no longer adequately supported financially by the Ontario government. Hence staff shortages, and an inability to address many of the concerns of an increasingly diverse Ontario population. It would be the power of the purse that would prove to be our undoing by the end of the decade of the 1980s. Many community organizations and social action groups had become dependent on government grants. In the case of Canada's Black community such a dependency courted disaster. For if you are not able to pay the piper, then you cannot name the tune. In his 1978 report to the National Black Coalition of Canada, Wilson Head pointed out how that organization had survived and progressed solely on the strength of funding from the federal government. Sadly, Head concluded that by the late 1970s, Black people in Canada were still unwilling to finance a national body on their own. "Outside the Black church, Black people [in Canada] simply have not on a large scale financed many national Black organizations."[12] Head's remarks foretold the demise of the National Black Coalition of Canada, and ironically, other groups have used this organizational model to establish their own national bodies. In the early 1980s, business interests in Canada were no longer that concerned with the upheaval and social conflict of the 1960s.

Into the 1980s, the popular television program in North America was *Dallas*, in which the only concern of one of the main characters J. R. Ewing, was about making more petro dollars for his company. In Canada, the politicians were turning their attention less so to social issues and concentrating on what American president George Bush would later describe as the "new-world order." Toronto's Yorkville became one of the embodiments of the new Canadian economy. What used to be the city's epicentre in the 1960s and early 1970s, of free love, hippie power, and the counter culture had been rebuilt as a symbol of the "can do" attitude of capitalism. Expensive stores, hotels and restaurants in Yorkville, and the newly built Eaton Centre came to symbolize the business as usual attitudes of capitalism.

In response to the calls by a variety of representatives of ethnic groups and women's organizations for more equitable employment legislation, and pay equity legislation, the Right and the Old Boys network chose instead to label these efforts as reverse discrimination. Powerful business interests in Ontario had had enough of our requests for a revamping of the Ontario Human Rights Commission, and fairer access to trades and professions for immigrants arriving in Canada with suitable qualifications. We were also agitating for a more equitable selections' process for members of minorities who wished to seek employment in the fire departments and police forces in Ontario. But by then the Bay Street lobbyists representing commercial and business interests had already reinforced and set higher the walls of exclusion. Speaking at a seminar on racism in the workplace, I pointed out that threats from more powerful interests influenced the Ontario government to adopt a watered-down version of the Act to revise and extend protection of human rights in Ontario.[13] What was called Bill 7 did little to remove the barriers we had fought so long and hard to eradicate. Labour Minister Robert Elgie proposed changes to the human rights code as a response in part by the premier Bill Davis government to stem the rapidly declining relationship between Toronto's East and West Indian communities and the status quo. Bill 7 was approved by the Ontario legislature in December 1981. However members of the business community and many other Ontarians were outraged by what they perceived as a growing influence of visible minorities in their midst. This was furthest from the truth, but powerful interests banded together and thereafter the Ontario Human Rights Commission fell into disrepair. My frustration was that even when a member of a minority group found employment, limitations were usually placed on his or her ability to advance and receive an equitable wage. Such persons are criticized when they are on welfare and held back when they have a job.

I lived through a personally troublesome period in the early 1980s. Making ends meet and supporting my family required me to rely on politically appointed positions. To those who saw me speaking out on their behalf, I was a hero; Brother Armstrong, someone they were confident if they told their troubles to, would find a suitable solution. But I was stressed, and uncertain of the future and by 1981 I was very introspective. What had I really accomplished since I left Massey Ferguson? And how had any of these accomplishments made a difference in my own life. Reflecting on the past, I could see some concrete results: the brokerage business, establishment of the *Islander* newspaper, appointments as human rights commissioner, service to my community and Canadian society. The question for me was how important were all of the things that I knew I had done to the society, the community I served, and to myself? I considered myself to be a rebel for just causes, but the reality was that in February 1981, I was now fifty-five years old. Many Canadians at this point in their lives had already secured their retirement incomes, and had paid off their mortgages. Indeed some of them were in a position to take early retirement at this age. But I was still struggling, still climbing the mountain and worrying about my family's security and my own future. When I took my early morning walks I tried to find solace in the good everyone told me that I had done. But time appeared not to be on my side. In the words of Martin Luther King Jr., "We may cry out desperately for time to pause in its passage, but time is deaf to every plea and rushes on."[14]

As time rushed on, I had the sense that it was leaving me behind. Was it that I had expected to achieve more by my mid-fifties? When I arrived in Canada in 1947, I was penniless. I wished to attend school, but could only do so on a part-time basis. I learned all that I could about the Canadian trade union movement, the principles of business management, the insurance industry, of how bureaucracies function in Canada, and I maintained a strong commitment to a community-based social action agenda. Each time I walked the Toronto streets or rode on the Toronto Transit system I could see many results of which I believe that I had helped to make possible. There before my very eyes were thousands of people who looked like me, whereas in the 1950s there were few of us. I could watch the industry of my community take shape on Bathurst Street, Eglinton Avenue West, and in many other parts of Ontario and Canada. I would go out of my way to search out young people, and while speaking to them marvel at the numbers of our Black youth who were making it beyond the hall ways of their high schools. This was a fine testament for the sacrifices that Don Moore had envisioned as he spoke with me in front of his dry cleaning business in 1950. All of this I could share in, yet in 1981, I was not yet at peace with myself. As the scriptures ask, "how do you sing the Lord's song in a strange land?" Press on Bromley, press on, were the words I heard from within, and so despite my own personal struggles, I continued to climb the mountain.

For more than twenty years I had maintained a good record with my bank and frequently other financial institutions competed for my business. Before the manager whom I had known for years left the branch where I did my banking, he referred me to the person taking his position. Shortly thereafter, I needed a mortgage in 1981 and in response to my inquiry I was assured that there was no problem. I soon discovered that there was a problem. I went to see the new bank manager and she appeared to go through the motion of making a telephone call, she claimed, to her head office. Then the manager hung the phone up and told me how sorry she was to be unable to approve my mortgage application. However, she offered me a personal bank loan.

The fact that I had served previously as a guarantor for B.I.G, Investments was not helping me at all. Although the investment group had been taken over by another larger entity, it was still registered as an operative company. All of this became apparent to me when I received a demand letter from B.I.G's bank asking that I pay the amount of $17,850 principal, plus accrued interest of $192.47. I had severed ties with B.I.G., Investments, but it seems that I was still being held liable for its indebtedness because of my historic relationship with the company; a fact that served to blemish my credit record. Borrowing money for a mortgage in 1981 required interest payments of twenty percent and approximately twenty-four percent for a personal loan. Having been a mortgage broker, I naturally refused the manager's offer. It was my belief that if I shopped around I would find a more reasonable rate. However other institutions could only give me a portion of the money I needed.

My bank's decision to rescind the original understanding to provide me with the money I required was having a domino effect on my finances. The tenuous financial situation I found myself in seemed perpetual, and all that I had worked for appeared to be going down the drain. My building on O'Connor Drive and another investment property were also part of the hazardous circumstances that seemed to have my life spinning out of control. Both properties were also up for grabs. My bank had also promised me $12,000 so that I could retire a first mortgage on the O'Connor Drive property. It was to be repaid once the deal to sell the building was finalized.

I was away in Kenora doing work for the Ontario Human Rights Commission when my wife Marlene learned with less than a day before the deal was to be closed that my bank had reduced its obligation from $12,000 to $6,000. She was frantic!

Fortunately, her close childhood friend was having lunch with her when a series of calls signalled that there was trouble in the house. Hearing about the difficulty caused Marlene's friend to expeditiously come up with the additional $6,000 that was required, and she helped us out of what was fast becoming, a tenuous situation. Marlene and I were still in a financial abyss. Our home in Pickering, Ontario was nearing completion, the closing date was just around the corner, and we urgently needed a mortgage. Finally, an acquaintance referred me to a financial institution that was willing to give me a mortgage, but with an interest rate of 34 percent, and I was expected to use my properties as collateral. The manager also offered to loan me $5,000 for a three-month period to pay the initial interest on such an exorbitant mortgage. I asked him instead to also include a tent, because I knew that after the three-month period was up, my properties would have to be relinquished, and needing some place to live, a tent is all that I would be in a position to afford.

With only two days before my closing date, I spoke to the builder and asked for a week's extension. "Oh, no," he said, "there is going to be no extension." This meant that my substantial downpayment would be forfeited. Desperate to find a solution, I turned to Robert Elgie, the minister of Consumer and Commercial Relations, and he was kind enough to arrange some appointments for me with a number of different financial institutions. After my visit at another banking institution, the manager walked me to the door and looking at me wondered where he had seen me before. He was obviously referring to the fact that my picture and name appeared frequently in the media. I was not going to take any chances, however, and self identify.

Finally, Elgie called me at work and told me that he thought that he had found someone who would lend me the money. He begged me "not to let him down." I assured him that he had nothing to worry about and that if I got the mortgage every penny of it would be paid on time. I called the trust company as he instructed and eventually spoke to the manager who had already been appraised of my dire financial circumstance. "Mr. Armstrong" she said, "I was told that you are having problems, I know exactly what you are going through, you have a substantial amount of assets, but no cash flow." I went to see her as soon as I could, the paperwork was completed and I received the mortgage.

This is how tenuous my life had become in the early 1980s. But for most Blacks living in Canada, life oftentimes is filled with pitfalls and uncertainty, and depending on one's outlook such challenges may appear insurmountable. I remember meeting my former boss whom I worked for at Commodore Business Machines. During the course of having lunch together we reflected on the past, and he reminded me that I could have been a millionaire. He was right. But following the teachings of Mahatma Ghandi and Martin Luther King Jr., I chose to sacrifice self, power and money. In this regard, I am comforted by the thought that: "there is an invisible book of life that faithfully records our vigilance or our neglect. The moving finger writes and having writ, moves on...."[15] I too, had to move as the 1980s progressed, because, I began seeing a horizon that was beckoning me.

Chapter 9 – Notes

1. Jules Elder, "Canada Needs More Immigrants." *Share*, November 24, 1979, vol. 2. No 34, p. 1

2. Poe Mutuma, Ibid.

3. By the end of 1979, *Contrast* newspaper had been published in Toronto or almost twelve years, and *Share* newspaper had been published for more than two years.

4. "Black businessman opens new nursing home in Mississauga." *Contrast*, February 17, 1977 vol. 9 no 7, p. 1

5. Editorial, *Contrast* newspaper, February 17, 1977, vol. 9 no 12, p. 6

6. Letter to Bromley Armstrong from Louis Horvarth, 1910-10 Edgecliffe Golfway, Don Mills, Ontario

7. "Immigrants urged to fight racism." *Ottawa Journal*, April 5, 1977, p. 60.

8. "Human Rights Commission understaffed." *Contrast* March 24, 177, vol. 9 no. 12

9. David Oved, "Bromley goes into labor." *Toronto Sun*, February 15, 1980.

10. Ibid.

11. "Fight for rights Armstrong tells Metro blacks." *Toronto Star*, April 13, 1980

12. Wilson Head, *Summary of the National Black Coalition of Canada Task Force Report*.

13. Walter Kroboth, "Rights lost to might, seminar told." *Toronto Star*, April 26, 1982.

14. Martin Luther King, Jr. *Where Do We Go from Here: Chaos or Community*. Boston: Beacon Press, 1967, p. 191.

15. Martin Luther King Jr., op cit., p. 191

CHAPTER 10

Legacy

Nelson Mandela's release from prison on Sunday, February 11, 1990 had a profound impact on me. Like millions of people around the world, I sat glued to the television as the South African freedom fighter took his first deliberate steps to freedom. After twenty-seven years of hell in the South African prison, Robben Island, Mandela emerged as a super-hero. Silently, I wondered how he could have survived such an ordeal by fire. Here was a man who stood his ground in the face of adversity, and willingly paid the price for his beliefs. Four months later in Toronto, I attended a dinner in honour of himself and his wife Winnie Mandela. Prime Minister Brian Mulroney hosted the dinner, and some members of Toronto's Black community were among the invited guests. As the future president of South Africa entered the room, I could see from his frail demeanor that apartheid and prison had taken its toll on him. Yet his declining health did not deter him from his ultimate goal. Mandela continued his campaign of ensuring that Black South Africans would some day enjoy the same freedoms and human rights that others did. While in Canada, Mandela invited Canadians to "walk the last mile" with him to the end of apartheid in South Africa.[1] At the dinner, I observed how Winnie and Nelson Mandela were fussed over by everyone.

Among the guests were many of us who had worked unswervingly over the past forty years to improve Canada's human and civil rights climate. None of us would question Ottawa's sincerity in supporting Mandela and the African National Congress's (ANC) quest for freedom for Black South Africans. But as our nation agitated on behalf of the ANC, some of its Native leaders from Ontario and Alberta were boycotting the Mandela State dinner because they had been "muzzled on the subject of Meech Lake."[2]

I later read that while Mandela was in Toronto, he appeared before 1,000 cheering students at Central Technical High School. In his remarks, he told them that in "South Africa, Black students are the victims of a reign of terror by police." He also said that, the type of education presented for Blacks is vastly inferior to that available to Whites."[3] I am not sure if Nelson Mandela's briefing on Canada by South African officials included the circumstances under which many Blacks lived in Canada. But had I been given the opportunity to speak with him, other than in the public setting that leaders of the Black community were afforded, his knowledge of our own struggles would have been expanded. He would have learned that in the early 1950s, Don Moore likened Canada's immigration policy to those of the South African apartheid policies under which Mandela and millions of Black South Africans suffered. Mandela would also have been told that Toronto Blacks had been involved in a series of incidents, some fatal, with the Metropolitan Toronto police. Given the opportunity, I would have admitted that what Toronto Black students faced in their schools is less dramatic than those in his native land are. Nonetheless, the fact was that in 1990, more than half of them were unlikely to graduate and even fewer of them had the opportunity to attend a Canadian college or university.

There might not have been any way for Mandela to know that, as he and his delegation was housed in some of Canada's finest hotels, in parts of Nova Scotia, some Black people were without indoor plumbing and running water. On one hand Mandela, a Black man, received hugs and kisses as he walked along University Avenue, and the Toronto police guarded him in a manner usually reserved for royalty. But the grim realty for a majority of Toronto Blacks as the last decade of the twentieth century unfolded was that they lived in a city where many of its residents cared little for their presence.

A new resolve had taken hold of Canada's largest city. For as Mandela toured not far from its premises, the Royal Ontario Museum (ROM) chose to close. When its officials were asked to explain why, they indicated, "it had nothing to do with the recent controversy over the current exhibition, *Into the Heart of Africa*."[4] In what was the ROM's in-house African exhibition, critics claimed that it: "glorified the brutal treatment of Africans by Europeans."[5] Such a degrading event may not have taken place a decade before. But the changing climate in Canadian society gave license to persons who were willing to reaffirm the lowly position of Blacks on the Canadian totem pole. At one of Canada's premiere cultural institutions, the Royal Ontario Museum, the exhibition, Into the *Heart of Africa*, graphically displayed for school children to see, a White military officer, thrusting a weapon into the body of an African tribes-person who assuredly was defending his freedom. When some members of the Black community protested, some police officers were only too happy to lead the charge against them.

Racial discrimination remained a major concern among many members of Toronto's Black community in the 1990s. In a forum with mayor Art Eggleton in 1990 I told him that "we wanted to see a city where kids can travel the streets without any problem." The mayor was also asked to support our calls for an independent civilian board to investigate police wrong doing.[6] My mood had soured somewhat. As I grew older, the luxury afforded many Whites of my generation was absent from my life. The time had not come as yet where I could turn my attention to a hobby of my choosing, and go with my wife for extended trips overseas. Nor was I given the opportunity to brood about my successes and ask my enemies for forgiveness. Old challenges were still parked at my doorstep, and my frustrations would not abate. To the chagrin of William McCormack, deputy chief of the Metropolitan Police Force, in 1988, I said publicly that Metro police had a license to kill Blacks.[7] Admittedly a harsh statement, but it was one made in response to the repeated willingness of some police officers to use their guns on Black people with impunity. At the time I was sixty-two years old, and the issues of securing a pension and fading away from the public limelight were superceded by a lifelong goal of ensuring that I left Canada a much better place than I found it when I arrived in 1947. The August 9, 1988 police shooting of Lester Donaldson in his Toronto home by Constable David Deviney was vexing. It was more of the same old thing. Even with the status quo's sanctioning of various investigations of police minority relations, including a commission, I remained unconvinced that police relations with the Black community would improve in my lifetime.

Some of my friends in the White community have written their memoirs, which I have read with a great deal of interest. For the most part, their words emanate from the pages of their books in a rather stately manner. In cases where they chronicle their involvement in human and civil rights activities, their recollections are presented in a neutral fashion. The deed is discussed, but with the passage of time, all seems to have been forgiven. Indeed many of those who I fought with in the trenches and who equally shed their blood sweat and tears have been accepted into the status quo. It is an accommodation that few, if any Blacks have been allowed. I now understand why so many of my older Black colleagues simply tied their ships to their moorings and faded away. Unlike my White friends, telling my story is one cast primarily in Black and White. For much of what appears on these pages refer to racism and how Black people have been treated in a country called Canada. In telling my story I have also recognized how First Nations' peoples, the original Canadians have been poorly treated. It was Martin Luther King Jr. who recognized that justice and freedom cannot exist anywhere until injustice and subjugation is eradicated everywhere.

Admittedly, in the 1990s, I was becoming impatient with the pace of change in my adopted country Canada. Even within my beloved trade union movement change was occurring at a snail's pace. For Whites remained tight fisted about their control of Canada's unions. Although we had made it to the shop floor, few of us graduated to the union office. Sadly, I had to publicly admit that, "within the union movement there's no place for people like us."[8] This criticism transcended my friendships with Dennis McDermott, Buzz Hargrove, Gord Wilson and Bob White. Each in his own right had remained union stalwarts, and I could not remember a time when having called on any of them for support that it was not given. But the reality was that I was moving on in years. And I wondered if the next generation of Black leaders would be able to pick up the phone when the need arose and call the successors to McDermott, Hargrove, Wilson and White. Had our efforts amounted to the perpetual forging of linkages and alliances that would ensure the future progress and protection of Canada's working class, its poor and subjugated peoples? I remained unconvinced in the 1990s. Though many political and community leaders acknowledged that the time for the healing of the wounds had come, few seemed ready to walk their talk.

Blacks in 1990s Canada, despite their growing numbers remained in a position of political and economic weakness. On an individual basis, some Blacks were doing well in the education, professional and business fields. More Blacks than ever before were graduating from Canada's colleges and universities. In the 1950s, if you saw a Black person on Bay Street, it was usually with a mop and pail. But in the 1990s, Black people numbering in the thousands were engaged in a variety of business and commercial activities. From my office located on the sixth floor of the Ontario Labour Relations Board, I could see my brothers and sisters walking confidently on University Avenue. Periodically, I encountered young Black lawyers in hearings, and watched as they continued the legacy of B.J. Spencer Pitt who in the late 1940s might have been the only Black lawyer in Toronto. But we have experienced great difficulty harnessing this new energy that is being elicited by Black communities throughout Canada. Our efforts to maintain a national organization have been less than successful. The National Black Coalition of Canada had floundered, and in 1987, as president of the Council of Jamaicans in Ontario, I helped to establish the National Council of Jamaicans and Supportive Organizations in Canada. However, internal rivalries undermined that body, and by 1990 it was no more than a paper tiger.

Young people would ask me about our failure to create stellar business enterprises. They would look at other communities and seeing the great strides some of their entrepreneurs have made in commercial and business enterprises, ask, why not us too? Many of us who were in business usually operated beyond the boundaries of the abstract Black community. As a consequence, our youth had difficulties finding jobs either to support their educational ambitions or to help subsidize their household incomes. If one takes a stroll along Eglinton Avenue, west of the Allen Road in Toronto, one sees many Black-owned businesses operating side by side. Barbershops, beauty supply stores, clothing boutiques and record stores adorn the area for the past twenty-five years. However, without access to capital and technology, most of these ventures have not expanded. For the most part we still rely on others to import our goods and provisions from the Caribbean. Ordering take out food is a frustrating exercise for many of us wishing to support Black-owned restaurants. Even if we are able to find such establishments in the *Yellow Pages*, few if any of them meet the requirements of prompt delivery.

Despite the presence of a significant number of well-qualified Black lawyers in Toronto, some Blacks believe that if their cause is to be well represented, they must employ lawyers from other communities. Ontario's prisons are filled with our young people, and they flounder and languish without any sense of direction and hope. And even with churches numbering in the many hundreds, our souls seem lost. After the hope and the promise we saw in the 1950s and beyond, how did we get here? How is it that smaller and more recently arrived groups have passed us on their way to realizing their dreams in Canada? These are the questions that those of us who were engaged in community building efforts have wrestled with over the past three decades. But answers that will turn our efforts into tangible strategies remain beyond our grasp. In searching for such answers we encounter criticism from some Blacks who argue that our dirty linen should not be washed in public. Who are we fooling? As one of the most studied groups, our status is more widely known in the broader community than in our own.

In 1991, I was among those persons who reaffirmed their commitment to dialogue and non-violence. At the *Social Change and Non-Violence: Ghandi and King* conference held in Toronto, we continued our search for peaceful solutions to the societal ills that were putting a drag on the more uplifting aspects of the human experience. It was an international conference with speakers from different parts of the globe, and each presenter shared ideas that challenged us to continue the struggle. I remember the remarks of Henderson Butcher, a young man who grew up in the much-maligned Jane Finch community. Butcher reminded the conference delegates that when we spoke of the future, it was his generation's lives that we were referring to. Forging a better world for him meant that we would pass on a legacy, one that would be understood and improved upon. I can still hear his words:

> Social action must also be seen as having benefits in the lives of young adults, and must be a liberating force that supports the activism, diversity, radicalism, and solidarity that shape the social awareness of this group. Through this process of perpetual learning, social action predicated on human freedom and rights become the bridge between the gaps created by economic status, intellectual misunderstanding, racist polemics, geographic and political isolation and antagonism.[9]

The promise that Butcher's speech seemed to hold was

important for his generation of leaders. My daughter Lana, sixteen years at the time, was part of this new generation that the torch was being passed on to. Hers, like Butcher's challenges were different than mine when I was a teenager. At age sixteen in 1942, I was caught up in the bread and butter survival in a period in which Jamaica and the rest of the Caribbean were fighting on the side of the allies against the Nazis. My two older brothers were on active duty during the Second World War, and their efforts I have often thought, have contributed to me never having to fight in killing fields in some far off location. Yet, the life I chose was one that was often paralleled with warfare.

Each day that I have survived in Canada, I have fought racism, discrimination and intolerance. In the 1950s, it was commonplace for me to suffer the taunts of politicians who would rather call my actions "communist" than face the fact that their Canadian way of life was one infused with racism and religious intolerance. In the 1960s, the critical path I chose to travel in Canada did not endear me to the powerbrokers that resented those like me who dared to show them Canada's pockmarks. In the 1970s and 1980s, my activism continued, and I suffered financially, because regardless of the pain I had to bear I would not go away. And irrespective of the enticements dangled in my direction, I continued to be a rebel to the bone.[10]

My activism often meant that my family has had to make many sacrifices. Suffering and pain have been part of the daily job description for Black and poor people in Canada. But we have not been deterred. Those of us who lived to see the younger generation survive and live under slightly improved circumstances than we historically faced in Canada are mindful that the vicissitudes of life are caused not only by the powerful and the mighty on earth. There is a higher Force, Who calls us to act, and build a commonweal in the name of all humanity. Sometimes we must physically take up arms and do duty on the battlefield to protect freedom. In peacetime the struggle must go on. For we must continue to struggle against intolerance.

It was time to retire. My wife Marlene wanted nothing more. She had watched me dangle in the wind for too long, and increasingly was calling in her marker. Because I loved the fight and the opportunity to make positive changes in Canada, I continued to be aloof to the mounting pressure asking me to head for my homeport. Yet increasingly, it seemed foolish to continue to try and keep my ship out at sea. Though weakening in my resolve, I held on to the mast and slowly, ever so slowly yielded to those who were asking me to set a more favourable course. But I was not done yet! In 1990, I was one of eight recipients who received an award for excellence in race relations that was presented to us by the Multiculturalism and Citizenship minister, Gerry Weiner. This was part of the recognition ceremonies for the International Day for the Elimination of Racism. I was pleased with the recognition I continued to receive for my many years of community work. In 1992, the Order of Ontario was bestowed on me for my work in the trenches as a community and civil rights worker. I was also fortunate to be among those selected for Canada's 125th Anniversary Medal. Two years earlier the Black Business and Professional Association had given me the Harry Jerome Award.

Such awards are important, not just for the sake of the personal recognition that is bestowed on the recipient. More importantly, awards based on one's service to community and society should help to encourage our youth that voluntarism must become an integral part of their daily activities. But when we needed community activism and a spirit of voluntarism the most, such activities in Toronto's Black community were waning. Receiving awards was not a signal to me that my work had been completed. I continued to do all that I could to contribute to a society that overall was good to me. Despite my uphill climb, I have publicly acknowledged that despite its shortcomings, there is no better place than Canada. When my friend Gerry Weiner established the Canadian Centre for Police Race Relations in 1992,[11] I did everything to support this novel idea. This led me to serve as that body's second chair from 1992 and its mission included: encouraging better relations between police associations, chiefs of police, police services boards, training colleges, the RCMP, visible minority and aboriginal communities.

The 1994 *Show Boat* controversy in Toronto embodied how far we as a society had not come. The old Jerome Kern and Oscar Hammerstein *Show Boat* script was dusted off, somewhat updated, and made ready for performances at the new City of North York's, Ford Centre for the Performing Arts. The play is part of the old genre of musicals in the theatre and on the movie screen that portray Black people in less than a complementary manner. So here it was that Livent theatre mogul, Garth Drabinsky was leading the parade to bring *Show Boat* to Toronto audiences, including school children. Some Blacks felt betrayed and offended, especially because Drabinsky, was a member of the Jewish community. The argument was made that had the issue been the *Merchant of Venice*, for example, such a theatrical production would never have seen the light of day. More importantly for some Blacks was that many members of these two traditional civil and human rights allies, Blacks and Jews drew lines in the sand over the *Show Boat* controversy.

It was a sad affair. For it appeared as if some of our friends in the Jewish community, especially those Jews who over the years had constantly reminded us that they shared our pain, were now abandoning our cause. At some point I said a pox on both our houses. We should have known better. Friends will oftentimes disagree, but if the bonds of friendship are strong enough, then steps are taken to overcome whatever the difficulty that is undermining the relationship. Here we were, the supposedly two stronger links in the human rights struggle, bickering over a commercial venture. Had it been an issue that was assailing both communities because of Aglo Saxon intolerance, we would have known what to do.

Unfortunately, the relationship between both communities has not been the same since. My friend Rabbi Gunther Plaut writes in his book, *More Unfinished Business* that the *Show Boat* controversy "kindled in many Jews a growing disenchantment with Canadian Blacks and, by extension with other minorities."[12] Rabbi Plaut does point to the support for the Black community by the Ontario Branch of the Canadian Jewish Congress.[13] However, it is no secret that relations between Blacks and Jews in Toronto continued to sour in the 1990s. *Show Boat* was an indicator of how far the relationship between both communities had declined. Some Jewish leaders were wary of the perceived budding support among Black youth and young adults for the Nation of Islam. Like these Jewish leaders, I too found the growing appeal among some Toronto Blacks for the supposed Louis Farrakhan-styled Islamic teachings, troubling. Unfortunately, however, what seemed to develop was that the Black community was now being described by some in the Jewish community as being intolerant and insensitive to their circumstances. From where I stood, nothing could be further from the truth. The sadness in all of this is that our enemies stood on the sidelines and joyfully watched as members of both groups destroyed the bridges that had taken a lifetime, and untold sacrifice to build. Increasingly, I charted a course for home.

On February 20, 1994, I received the Canadian Black Achievement Award. In March, along with my friend Dennis McDermott, I received the Ontario Federation of Labour Human Rights Awards, and later that year I was given the Order of Canada. This was followed in 1995 with the prestigious Stanley Knowles Humanitarian Award. As I have always done, I will state here that although these awards bear my name, the honour is bestowed on all my family members.

Over the years we have loved and fought, and there is no doubt that if you have Armstrong blood in your veins you love a good fight. But whether they are relatives who emigrated from Jamaica and settled in Canada or the US, or those who just refused to leave good old Jamaica, so many of them have been there for me. All of my awards are for them. The toils that I have borne in the name of my community have been made easier by my wife Marlene who sometimes vociferously, but usually silently and quietly behind the scenes, contributed to ensure that I did not fail.

When it was time to retire, I remembered both the good and the bad. The malcontents who sent me a stick of dynamite, threw rocks through my window, threatened my life made me fight on more fervently for the causes I believed in. I have never forgotten how I came to Canada in a herringbone coat with a few dollars sewn into its lining. Thus when my ship was nearing its homeport in 1996 as it moved closer to its moorings, I reflected on my life's journey in Canada. Despite the travails, I chose to call my foreign experience "a time of good fortune."

By the early 1990s, Canada's Black leadership had dwindled. Some of its members though vigorous in their desire to see the community move forward, were themselves too elderly to physically take up the challenges the way they did in the old days. Many Blacks, both young and old were leaving

Canada. Return migration to the Caribbean was picking up speed, and some of our more youthful members were heading for destinations in the US.[14] It was history repeating itself. Repeatedly, alienation and a lack of opportunity were lessening the viable Black presence in Canada. Dare I say that it was not by accident? An atmosphere has been created that underscores anti-Black sentiment. Issues of police, community relations and a creeping shift toward right wing politics have compounded such a development. The majority of Canada's Black population would prefer to live and work and play, like most other Canadians without the issues of discrimination and racism. However, this was not to be their reality.

So-called White supremacy was again rearing its ugly head. More troubling was the fact that a growing number of White youth were gravitating to racist supremacist groups in the 1990s. Some Toronto schools became fertile ground where they were being recruited. It seemed that the more things changed, the more they remained the same.

The atmosphere had been poisoned in a period in which Canada's Black leadership was less effective. After two generations of Conservative rule in Ontario, David Peterson and his Liberal party government took the reins of power, and later Bob Rae and a majority New Democratic party were elected to office. Then to the horror of many of us in the civil libertarian field, we witnessed the rise of new kind of conservative political force under the management of Ontario premier Mike Harris. In the 1950s, it was the party of Leslie Frost and the Conservatives that acknowledged the need for a human and civil rights agenda. In the 1990s, Harris and his in-your-face brand of conservative politics were the antithesis to the 1950s Leslie Frost style of conservatism. Doing away with Employment Equity, the Anti-Racism Secretariat and the targeting of mothers on welfare lay at the heart of his political agenda. The destruction of advisory bodies to include those concerned with seniors, women, disabled, and multicultural issues were disbanded, and no semblance of citizen participation remained. All appeared to be lost. For the claim was being made by some analysts, that Harris and his political forces at Queen's Park embodied the so-called White angry male backlash. The status quo clawed back, demanded back and ignored all the progress that had come before their ascendancy to power. In the Ontario civil service, the gains that Blacks had made in terms of moving up the employment ladder were being destroyed. Race relations training in education was discontinued and progressive healthcare, essential components of the safety net appeared to be things of the past. After all, those now running the Harris political ship, unlike the babies whose parents had to wait at hospital emergency rooms for many hours before being served, could go elsewhere to be treated. If this was not bad enough, the poor were told by their Ontario government to relish bologna sandwiches.

Friday February 16, 1996 was my last day as a member of the Ontario Labour Relations Board. Looking onto University Avenue from my sixth floor office I could see people moving back and forth. So many of them looked like me. Fifty years before I had stood in the line on a cold winter's morning hoping to get a job, to begin my foreign experience at Massey Harris. It was a factory with no temperature control, in the winter it was hot and in the summer it was hotter. As workers in the press and forge, we had to take salt pills to give us relief from the heat. Now many Blacks work in offices that are properly heated in winter and fully air-conditioned in summer.

In addition to the many awards I have received, my years of community service were recognized in 1996 with a number of retirement dinners. In this regard, both the trade union movement and members from a variety of mainstream, community and ethnic organizations came together in my honour. On such occasions the person that is being recognized is compelled to listen attentively to all that is said. As I sat at both occasions, I heard from many people that I had worked with over the years of hope and struggle. Madame Justice Rosalie Abella summed up my aims when she said: "Bromley has helped to move us forward to become a society that is more generous, civilized and tolerant." Shaking the many outstretched hands and accepting a multitude of warm embraces at my retirement dinners reminded me, "that I am a part of all that I have met."[15] I have remained thankful for their recognition of my sustained efforts over these many years, and relish their encouragement to me that, "some work of noble note, may yet be done."[16]

The societal ills I discovered in Canada had made a difference in many of our lives. Racism is a travesty of justice, and it has taken its toll on all of us. Those who know better continue to quietly deny its human costs. I will always believe that "out of the experience of an extraordinary human disaster that lasted too long, must be born a society of which all humanity will be proud."[17] If humanity is to endure we need to sow the seeds of justice and tolerance. These gifts should be willed to our children, and they in turn must carry the dream forward. That is why a sunset is so beautiful, not because it signals the end of the day, more importantly, because it holds the promise of a new tomorrow.

Chapter 10 – Notes

1. "Walk last mile, Mandela urges MPs." *Toronto Star*, June 19, 1990

2. "Fueling the dream of Nelson Mandela." *Toronto Star*, June 20, 1990. Meech Lake refers to the terms and conditions arrived at by Canada's first ministers under which Quebec would be allowed to rejoin Canada's constitutional family. Included here was a recognition that the distinctiveness of French Canadians would be recognized. Canada's First Nation's people are without any such arrangement.

3. Walter Stefaniuk and Maureen Murray, "1,000 cheering students 'comforting' to Mandela." *Toronto Star*, June 20, 1990.

4. Op cit. *Toronto Star*, June 19, 1990.

5. Ibid.

6. Tony Wong, "Get tough with police, blacks say." *Toronto Star* May 31, 1990.

7. John Spears and Michael Tenszen, "Police 'Licensed' to kill blacks, activist says." *Toronto Star*, November 26, 1988

8. Leslie Papp, "Minority groups urged to run for union office."
Toronto Star, June 1990.

9. Henderson Butcher, "Martin Luther King Jr. and Mahatma Ghandi." In: *Ghandi and King: Dialogue on Non-Violence*, Ritendra K. Ray (ed.), Toronto, 1993, p. 111.

10. I would like to thank journalist Maureen Murray for this embodiment of my activities in Canada.

11. My tenure was from 1992-1998.

12. W. Gunther Plaut, *More Unfinished Business*. Toronto: U of T Press, 1997.

13. To get the gist of Rabbi Plaut's position on the *Show Boat* controversy, read pages 41-46 in his book cited above.

14. Studies are pending from the usual sources on the topic of return migration to the Caribbean. In the 1790s conditions in Nova Scotia caused a significant dwindling of the black population there. Many Black loyalists who had ventured to Nova Scotia after the American War for Independence left in the 1790s for Sierra Leone. Jamaican Maroons banished to Nova Scotia by the British colonial authorities in 1796, not long after left for Sierra Leone.

15. Quoted from Alfred Lord Tennyson's poem, "Ulysses." (U of T Department of English and U of T Press). As it appears at
http//www.library.utoronto.ca/utel/rp/poems/tennyson8.html

16. Ibid.

17. Nelson Mandela: Inaugural Address, May 10, 1994, www.yoga.com/raw/readings/mandela.html

Afterword

I can now say with a great degree of confidence that retirement is a period in which one may no longer be gainfully employed, but as is my case, giving up the regular mad dash to the office and opting out of the rat race have not reduced my industry. Four years after retiring I am still busy with my lifelong pursuit of making Canada a better place than I found it in 1947. Retirement has allowed me to more ably continue my dream of trying to foster a commonweal, encourage youth to strive for excellence and give counsel to those who repeatedly seek it. Admittedly, there has not been enough time set aside for me to smell the roses. But I see the flowers more clearly now since my daily exercise routine has been reduced to a brisk walk instead of the usual morning jog. It is on such occasions that I have reflected on my life, my reasons for coming to Canada, and my own mortality.

The wisdom of growing older has taught me that life is really an evolutionary process and the passage of time has allowed me to more clearly understand what nature intended for the people who inhabit planet earth. In essence, we are to live in harmony and be mindful that the seasons of our very existence are meant to summon us to greater heights. Dominion over the other living things with which we occupy the same space is a characteristic that we have not been afforded. Ours is a symbiotic relationship. Accordingly, it is our duty to uplift the human spirit and make our own individual contributions to the furtherance of humanity. In this regard, we owe it to future generations of life on our planet to give back as much as we have taken in order that we may sustain ourselves. Without real harmony, humankind is doomed to continue the struggle manifest in wars, poverty, greed, and self-destruction.

In the latter part of the twentieth century we have been rather fortunate in Canada. As Canadians our growth and development have been determined without due consideration to war touching what is for the most part is our friendly soil. This is not to say that unfriendly acts have absent from our daily lives as we marched forward toward the year 2000 and beyond. I have given an account on the preceding pages of some of the ills that have befallen our society. Yet, despite the shortcomings of our society as immigrants, many of us have fared better than we would have done in our countries of origin. It is for this reason that with the exception of the Native peoples, Canada is a land of immigrants. Immigrants who have cherished and participated in the prosperity that they have helped to generate in the postwar period.

In this book, Canada, Ontario and Toronto have been described as rather hierarchical. Ottawa sought to ensure that its Immigration Branch maintained a policy that closed Canada's borders to other than a select group of people from specific geographical areas in the 1950s. But as I also pointed out that the worker profile in the Massey Harris, later Massey Ferguson King Street West plant already revealed in the 1950s a Canada that was increasingly multicultural. This microcosm permeated the general society from the late 1960s, and became rather glaring by the early 1980s. Many of us in the civil and human rights fields have tried to make "our" Canada a reality. However, other forces continue to opt for a Canada delineated along the lines of a separateness entitled, "yours" and "ours". The "yours" is supposedly a Canada for people like myself;

ones who are seen by the high-brows as being different, not of the same pedigree, and more recently arrived. The "ours" is supposed to be the Canada of the old-line families with roots dating back several centuries.

Ironically, I know of some Canadians with eighteenth century roots who are unable to enter this club simply because they are Black. Unfortunately, the colour of ones eyes, skin colour and British antecedents do matter in Canada, but increasingly so too, does ability and education. It is to the latter two that I have chosen to subscribe when I implore young people to do all they can by staying in school and taking advantage of a very good Canadian education system. I am not fool hardy enough to think that Blacks for example will overcome the stumbling blocks of racism and sexism by only subscribing to their upliftment based on higher education. But it is a good starting point. It was a base from which my friend Daniel Hill sprang forth in Toronto in the early 1950s. By 1960 he had earned his doctorate from the University of Toronto, and Hill began a process that would see the *Toronto Star* later refer to him as "the man who has often been called the father of Human Rights in Ontario."[1] As a young man who had left the US and settled in Toronto, he began a process that allowed him to be prominently recognized for his work. Ultimately, he received the insignia of an Officer of the Order of Canada in February 2000.

The successes that I have seen over the years underscore my father's point that, "hard work has never killed anyone." One only has to look at Toronto entrepreneur, Beverly Mascoll, founder of Mascoll Beauty Products, whose Canadian roots date to the late eighteenth century. She remains a successful businessperson in Toronto, and Mascoll continues to make significant philanthropic contributions to Canadian society.

After enrolling at Toronto's York University Mascoll graduated with the class of 2000.

Another success story is that of Jay Hope, Ontario Provincial Police (OPP) Superintendent for the Greater Toronto region. The child of immigrants, Hope has worked his way up the ladder to assume an important position in the chain of command of Ontario's super police force. The message of what success brings is one that I take with me to high schools. I am never more pleased than when the phone rings and it is some one calling from a school asking that I address their student body. I also look forward to the calls I receive from university students. I wish that all parents would develop an understanding of how difficult it usually is for their children to obtain their university credentials. My wife Marlene who is herself a university graduate, and I, learned this fact first hand when our daughter Lana spent fours years in Hamilton, Ontario, at McMaster University. She graduated with her honours undergraduate degree in 1999. But before doing so, Lana always did better when we offered her the necessary support while she pursued her dream.

Following one's dream is the rallying cry of many immigrants of colour who leave their homes for far off lands. Oftentimes, I meet recently arrived members of different ethnic groups, and the expressions on their faces speak volumes. As was the case when I arrived in 1947, they are eager to get on with the process of bettering themselves in what at times is a less than friendly environment. Like many of us, they suffer the slings and arrows of being different. Where are you from? This is a question that many of them are asked even by Whites who can hardly speak English. It is as if, other than White skin, black, brown and yellow skin is akin to foreignness. In this regard, answering that you were born in Canada is met with a look of bewilderment. The other part of the equation is that the person being perceived as not belonging is sometimes made to suffer violently at the hands of those who are intolerant. With hate crimes on the increase in 1999, "visible minorities, especially Blacks, continue to be the target of most hate crimes."[2] It comes as no surprise therefore that professors Scot Wortley of the U of T and Gail Kellough of York University documented that "Blacks in Toronto are routinely treated more harshly by the police and the criminal justice system."[3] However, despite the societal ills and systemic barriers that many of us face in Canada, we must ensure that our youth are left with a sense of hope. They must be shown a positive path and helped to realize that through their own efforts a brighter future can be forged. In the process, parents, family members, guardians, clergy members, teachers and mentors have the responsibility of shaping what are impressionable minds with ideas that their possibilities can become realities if they keep hope alive.

My years of retirement afford me the luxury of continuing my work uninterrupted, with the aim of making a positive difference in a country that I have lived in for more than fifty years. As I explore the ways and means of helping to create a just society, my quest remains one of trying to breakdown the barriers in Canada based on the notions of "yours" and "ours." It is my wish that the day is fast approaching when the land of the maple leaf will be seen as belonging to all of us.

Afterword – Notes

1. "Human rights pioneer honoured." *Toronto Star*, February 09, 2000

2. John Duncanson, "Hate crime in Toronto jumps 28%." *Toronto Star*, February 18, 2000.

3. Elaine Carey, "Police 'bias, hits Blacks, study says." *Toronto Star*, March 23, 2000.

1998 Bahai National Race Unity award winner Bromley Armstrong with Reg Newkirk (left), the organization's executive director, and Chief Justice R. Roy McMurtry, (right).

Index

Abella, Rosalie **199, 243**
Adams, Grantley **153**
Adamson, Harold **188**
African Methodist Episcopal Church (AME) **39**
African National Congress (ANC) **229**
Aitken, Kate **126**
Alexander, Lincoln **73**
Anco, Steve **57-58**
Archer, David **130, 157**
Archibald, Marra **47**
Armstrong, Donna and Sandra **158**
Armstrong, Eric Junior **17, 22, 24**
Armstrong, Eric Vernon **17, 19-20, 23, 32**
Armstrong, Esmine **17**
Armstrong, Everald **18, 22, 32, 49**
Armstrong, George **18, 23, 26, 28, 34, 46, 49**
Armstrong, Lana **236, 248**
Armstrong, Marlene **178, 180, 224-225**
Armstrong, Miriam (nee Heron) **17, 106-107**
Armstrong, Monica **18**
Armstrong, Olive **18**
Armstrong, Tim **216**
Atkey, Ron **205**

Banana Workers **17**
Barbados **36**
Baskerville, W.R. **107**
Belfon James **195**
Belfon, Garfield **195**
Bended Elbow **184**
Bick, C.D. **188**

Black Action Defence Committee (BADC) **214-215**
Black Investment Group (BIG) **181-182, 224**
Black-Jewish relationships **238-239**
Blum, Sid **83, 85, 87**
Bogle, Paul **14**
Braithwaite, Daniel **101, 104**
Braithwaite, John **104**
Braithwaite, Leonard **73**
British Methodist Episcopal Church (BME) **39, 127**
Brooks, Julian **83**
Brotherhood of Sleeping Car Porters (Canada) **72, 108**
Brown, A. H. **113**
Brown, Rosemary **98**
Buck, Tim n.2 **69**
Burke, Mavis **11**
Burnette, Hugh **82, 84**
Burpee, Joyce **190**
Bustamante, Alexander **18, 19, 25,** n.6 **31, 53, 155**
Butcher, Henderson **235**

Canadian Association for the Advancement of Coloured People **133-136, 156, 159**
Canadian Bill of Rights **90, 146-147**
Canadian Centre for Police Race Relations **238**
Canadian Congress of Labour **101, 103, 111**
Canadian Pacific Railway (CPR) **111**
Canadian Union of Public Employees (CUPE) **218-219**
Cargnelli, Walter **212-214**

INDEX

Caribbean Soccer Club **50**
Carter, George **134-135**
Central Technical School **45**
Chinese medical students **215**
Churchill, Winston **24**
Chintoh, Jo Jo **181**
Clark, John **194, 203**
Committee for Due Process **201**
Commodore Business Machines **141**
Commodore Typewriter Company **141**
Communist Party **63**
Contrast newspaper **197, 206, 213**
Coombs, A.G.S. **18**
Cooperative Commonwealth Federation (CCF) **74**
Co-operators **143-144, 173, 174, 175, 177**
Council of Chinese Canadians in Ontario **215**
Craig, Ivan, B. **88**
Crittenden, Dorothea **194, 198**
Crown Colony Rule **15**
CTV **209, 219**

Daley, Charles **84, 86**
Davis, E.A. **38, 39, 101**
Davis, William, G. **216**
Dawson, J.T. **76**
Department of Citizenship and Immigration (DCI) **99, 116**
Deviney, David **231**
Devitt, Vince **216**
Dickenson, Dick **64-65**
Diefenbaker, John G. **90, 131-132, 146-147**
Donaldson, Gordon **83**
Donaldson, Lester **212, 231**

Downes, Chas. Arthur *n.11* **205**
Drabinsky, Garth **238**
Dresden, Ontario **81-90**
Drew, George **34-35**
Duncan, W. E. P. **107-108**

Edie, Francis **139, 143**
Eggleton, Art **190, 230**
Elgie, Robert **217, 221, 225**
Emerson, Matthew **86**
Evans, Buddy **195, 198, 199-203, 212**
Evans, Preston **195**

Fair Accommodation Practices Act **77, 84, 86, 148-149**
Fair Employment Practices Act **76, 80**
Fairclough, Ellen **135, 154**
Feinberg, Abraham **77, 82**
First Baptist Church **39, 71**
Flying Disco Tavern **195**
Fortier, Laval **114, 116, 135**
Frost, Leslie **77, 87, 148**
Fulton, David, E. **132**

Gairy, Sr., Harry **76, 101, 102**
Garvey, Marcus **17, 38, 93**
George, Gloria **199**
Ghandi, Mahatma **29, 72, 73, 173**
Glasspole, Florizel **22**
Gordon, William **14**
Gouzenko Spy Affair **63**
Gregg, Allen **107**
Grizzle, Gladys **83**
Grizzle, Norman **101, 111**
Grizzle, Stanley **111**
Grosch, H.E. **88-89**

INDEX

Gross, George **50**
Haidasz, Stanley **158**
Hamilton, Al **197, 198, 213-214**
Hargrove, Buzz **10, 232**
Harris, Mike **183, 241-242**

Harris, Walter **100, 105**
Hartman, Grace **218-219**
Hawkins, Freda **163**
Head, Wilson **163, 187, 220**
Hebb, Andrew **143**
Hill, Donna **11, 79, 83**
Hill, Jr., Daniel **83**
Hill, Sr., Daniel **11, 80, 188**
Himel, Irving **77**
Home Service Association **39, 102**
Hope, Jay **248**

Icelandia **76**
Inglis, William **212-214**
Islander newspaper **180-181, 189, 222**
Insurance Brokers of Canada **179**
Isaacs, Wills **180**

Jackson, Carl **180**
Jamaica Trade Union Congress **28**
Jamaica Workers and Tradesmen's Union **18**
Jamaican Canadian Association (JCA) **159-160, 161-162, 164-167, 180-181, 226, 232**
Jewish Labour Committee **87, 150**
Johnson, Albert **212-214**
Joint Labour Committee to Combat Racial Intolerance **78**
Joliffe, A.L. **97**
Jolly, Denham **197, 206, 213**

Kaplansky, Kalman **11, 87**
Keith, Russel **181**
King Jr., Martin Luther **29, 72, 173, 177**
King, George **102, 157**
King, William Lyon Mackenzie **95**
Kirkwood, Arthur *n.11* **204**

Lastman, Mel **190-191**
Laws, Dudley **213, 214-215**
Lewis, David **157, 158**
Lyons, Eric and Ethel **182**
Life Together **194**
Lor, Ruth **84, 87**
Macmillan, Harold **150-151**
Magnus, Mavis **159**
Mandela, Nelson **29, 228-230**
Manley, Michael **129**
Manley, Norman **18, 19, 25, *n.6* 31, 115, 155**
Mapp, R.G. **113**
Mascoll, Beverly **247**
Massop, Beatrice **108**
Matthews, "Big Jim" **48**
Mawande, Naison **194-195, 210**
Mboya, Tom **138**
McDermott, Dennis **59, 64, 65, 78, 84, 107, 108, 216, 232, 240**
McDonald, Donald **74, 111**
McKay, Morley **85, 86, 88, 100**
McMurtry, Roy **8, 198, 200, 201**
Meech Lake **229**
Mercury Athletic Club **78, 79, 80, 84**
Metropolitan Toronto Police Force **166, 195, 229, 231**
Michaels, Samuel **41**

253

INDEX

Moore (Don), Donald **93, 100, 108, 109, 126, 156, 229**
Morant Bay Rebellion **130**
Mulrony, Brian **228**
Myrdall, Gunnar **75**

Nakamura, Mark **188, 190, 197**
National Association for the Advancement of Coloured People (NAACP) **75**
National Association of Canadians of origins in India **210**
National Black Coalition of Canada (NBCC) **220, 233**
National Council of Jamaicans and Supportive Organizations in Canada **233**
National Unity Association **82, 83**
National Workers Union **129**
Negro Citizenship Association (NCC) **116, 156**
Negro Citizenship Committee (NCA) **102, 103**
Noseworthy, Joe **105**

Ontario Federation of Labour (OFL) **77, 130, 157**
Ontario Human Rights Commission **74, 77, 80, 149, 185, 190, 210-211, 215**
Ontario Labour Relations Board (OLRB) **216-219, 233, 242**
Ontario Multicultural Advisory Council **183, 185**
Ontario Racial Discrimination Act **77**
Order-in-council P.C. 2856, **97-98, 104**

P.C. 2743 **97-98**
Park, Eamon **148**

Peters, William **50,** n.5 **52,**
Peterson, David **192, 241**
Phillips, Gerry **192**
Pickersgill, J.W. **112**
Pickwood, Arthur **113**
Pinkofsky, Jack **201-202**
Pitt, B.J. Spencer **39, 41, 233**
Plaut, Gunther, W. **190-191,** n.9 **204, 239**
Porter, John **174**

Randolph, Phillip, A. **72**
Raynard, Malcolm **59**
Ricketts, Esmond **41, 156, 159**
Roach, Charlie **181, 213**
Robarts, John **150**
Robb, W.T. **79**
Robinson, H. Basil **152**
Roebuck, Arthur **102**
Rogers Majestics Soccer Club **49**
Rosemary, Vibert **201**
Ross, Anthony **201**
Royal Canadian Mounted Police (RCMP) **63**
Royal Commission on Bilingual and Biculturalism **182**
Royal Ontario Museum (ROM) **230**

Salmon, Bev **187**
Salsberg, Joe **76**
Schwenger, William, F. **86**
Share newspaper **206**
Sharpeville Massacre **151**
Show Boat **238-239**
Sister Fidelis **25-26**
Smith, Eva **124**
Smith, R.G.C. **132**

254

INDEX

Smith. C.E.S. **112, 113**
Social Planning Council of Metropolitan Toronto **162, 187, 188**
St. Laurent, Louis **109, 113**
Sterling, Ken **129**
Stewart, Cecil **39-41**

Tallawa **9, 177**
Thirdworld Books and Crafts **206**
Toronto District Soccer League **50**
Toronto Joint Labour Committee for Human Rights **73**
Toronto Maple Leafs **194**
Toronto Trades and District Labour Council **67**
Toronto United Negro Association (TUNA) **38, 64, 94, 154, 156**
Toronto United Negro Credit Union **38, 94, 156**
Tramiel, Jack **139, 141**
Trudeau, Pierre, Elliot **130-131, 172, 183**
Tyndall Nursing Home **206**

Ubale, Bhausaheb **189, 190**
Undergroung Railroad Restaurant **206**
United Nations International Declaration of Human Rights (1948) **72, 107, 147**
Universal Negro Improvement Association (UNIA) **37-38, 41-42, 156**
Urban Alliance on Race Relations **188**
Weiner, Gerry **237-238**
West Indian Domestic Scheme **113-117, 123**
White Nationalist Society **189**
White, Bill **42**
White, Bob **11**
Wholesale Typewriters **139-140**
Williams, G. **148**
Williams, Roy **158, 159, 161-162**
Williams, Sydney **133-136, 159**
Wilson, Gord **10, 232**
Wilson, Trevor **191**

BROMLEY ARMSTRONG